Earnie Larsen & Carol Hegarty

BELIEVING
IN MYSELF

*Daily Meditations for Healing
and Building Self-Esteem*

A FIRESIDE BOOK
Published by Simon & Schuster

FIRESIDE
Simon & Schuster Inc.
Rockefeller Center
1230 Avenue of the Americas
New York, NY 10020

Copyright © 1991 by Earnie Larsen and Carol Hegarty

FIRESIDE and colophon are
registered trademarks of Simon & Schuster Inc.

Manufactured in the United States of America

35 37 39 40 38 36

Library of Congress Cataloging-in-Publication Data
Larsen, Earnest.
Believing in myself / by Earnie Larsen & Carol Hegarty
p.   cm.
1. Self-respect. 2. Meditations. I. Title.
BP697.5.546L.37 1991
158'.1-dc20   90-46789
CIP

ISBN-13: 978-0-671-76616-0

ISBN-10:   0-671-76616-3

This book is dedicated to Dorothy Larsen, our mother and great good fortune, and to Father Jim Mifsud, torchbearer of hope on life's darkest streets.

Acknowledgments

Special thanks for the thoughtful contributions of Cathie C. Danielsen, Linda Santwire, and Ron Palmer

Even though time be real, to realize the unimportance of time is the gate of wisdom.
—Bertrand Russell

Most of us measure the realities of life by time. Without our even being aware of it, the context of time directs, defines, channels, and limits most of our thought patterns. Concepts like past, present, and future divide our lives as neatly as three acts divide a play: One begins where the other ends, until the play is finished. That is the outer world.

But clock ticks and calendar pages don't control the action in the inner world. As we develop the inner awareness that develops self-esteem, we get in touch with a different reality. In the kingdom of our own minds and hearts we discover a self that is neither old nor young, neither beginning nor ending, but just *being*. In this world there is no such thing as before or after, on time or late. There is only the peace and serenity of *now*—the now that was, is, and will be.

The healthiest people have dual citizenship: They live in both worlds. When they are saddened that some prized and precious time is passing by, they are also comforted by knowing that the richness of human experience is timeless. All that was good lives on in the inner world—not lost, not wasted, not past. In the soul there is only the eternal present.

Soul making has nothing to do with time as the world measures it.

January 2

Many fears are born of fatigue and loneliness.
—"The Desiderata"

Self-esteem is not static. Within boundaries, depending on the ebb and flow of the tide of our lives, our sense of well-being naturally fluctuates. Many of our low points, however, have not so much to do with a particular problem as they do with the state of mind we bring to that problem.

We may not always have control over certain fears. If we were once badly burned, for example, we may always have a residual overreaction to fire—and there are, of course, many kinds of fire. But we do have control over the fatigue and loneliness that set us up for fear attacks. Of all the efforts we may make to bolster self-esteem, avoiding such fatigue and loneliness may be the most important.

Is it always necessary to work as hard as we do? Can we never take a break or a little nap? When was the last time we took a vacation? And how often do we set aside time for a good long conversation with a friend? Sometimes "alone" is not a healthy place to be. Especially if we're also tired. Those are times when our fears find us most vulnerable.

I will avoid getting too tired to feel good about myself.

Comparisons are odious.
—Sir John Fortescue

Talk about a setup! What are we really doing when we compare ourselves with others? Are we simply gathering information—or are we actually gathering evidence of our own inadequacy? If that's our game, we're sure to win by losing every time.

Maybe we first learned to make unfavorable comparisons as a form of self-protection. Perhaps our tactic was to put ourselves down quickly—before "they" could do it for us. As children, we may have used self-effacement to deflect even worse verbal abuse. But we're not children now. And those bullies who lurked in the bushes aren't there anymore—unless we've internalized and generalized them into everybody who isn't us.

Do most of the people we know seem better, smarter, handsomer, more interesting than we are? If so, that's a sign that we're still playing out the same old self-defeating pattern. Out of fear, we're volunteering to be "worse" so that those who are "better" won't want to hurt us. After years of practice, self-effacement has become our habit.

But we can form a new habit if we want to. We can begin by refusing to idealize people who are in fact the same mixed bag of strengths and weaknesses that we are. We can stop making comparisons to put ourselves down and start taking a look at the worthy people we really are.

Today, I don't need to vandalize my self-image by making unfavorable comparisons.

January 4

The truth, the whole truth, and nothing but the truth.
                                        —Legal Oath

Some truths are harder to face than others. Yes. I eat too much and lose my temper with the kids. Yes, I tend to be selfish sometimes and manipulative, too. But no, I don't remember much about my childhood. I guess it was as happy as most people's.

Sound familiar? Many people working to improve their self-esteem identify themselves as Adult Children. To their great credit, they've joined forces for mutual comfort and support. But many Adult Children still spend a lot of energy fending off the past instead of accepting it. Understandably, they have more trouble than most in coming to grips with yesterday. Their yesterdays were a nightmare.

Perhaps their parents were practicing alcoholics or religious zealots or simply unavailable emotionally. Perhaps there was constant fighting, or demeaning remarks were made. Who wouldn't want to forget such misery? Yet that misery really happened; it is an important part of the Adult Child's personal truth.

Only by acknowledging and accepting that truth can Adult Children be done with it and get on with the task of making today everything it can be. Only then can healing and restoration of a positive self-image begin.

Denial ties me to the past.

Each is given a bag of tools,
A shapeless mass and a book of rules;
And each must make, ere life is flown,
A stumblingblock or a steppingstone.
                              —R. L. Sharpe

Who would try to nail boards together without a hammer or change a flat tire without a jack? To deny our need for tools would be ridiculous, wouldn't it? Yet many of us have trouble accepting that we need tools to repair our damaged self-esteem.

Sheer force of will won't lift a car so that a bad tire can be replaced—and it won't lift a heavy burden from our spirits either. Insight and knowledge of carpentry can't pound a nail—nor can insight and knowledge, without the help of tools, pound the dents out of our battered psyches.

It isn't weak or shameful to admit that a human finger isn't a screwdriver and a human eye isn't a microscope. Why do we resist the idea that spiritual work, like physical work, has its own set of tools? Reading, sharing, praying, attending our support group's meetings—these are the tools that help us do the job. They aren't optional niceties or crutches. If we need to lay a new foundation, we need to dig a big hole. And if we need to dig a hole, we'd better be willing to use a shovel.

My willingness to use the tools determines the outcome of the job.

January 6

No one may abuse the truth with impunity.
—R. Duane Joseph

A person's integrity is his or her own truth. To live honorably is to abide with the truth we claim as our own. Self-esteem is the sister of integrity; it's the natural result, the by-product, of honorable living. That's why both integrity and self-esteem are affected when we wander from the honorable path.

When we have affairs, go back on our word, tell half-truths, exaggerate to get approval, we chip away at our integrity. And any chipping away at our integrity undermines our self-esteem. This is the reason that even the smallest dishonorable behaviors are so destructive—no matter how we justify them.

If we're involved in any activity that violates our moral code, that runs contrary to our own value system, then we're in self-esteem trouble. All the psychological maneuvering in the world cannot and will not restore serenity to the soul if this involvement continues.

Is there a basic decision, a letting go, that must take place? Although it may take heroic effort, that turn-around decision will give wings to our self-esteem.

Peace with self is a treasure beyond measure.

We live in a fantasy world, a world of illusion.
The great task in life is to find reality.
—Iris Murdoch

Taking on impossible missions is the best of all possible ways to lose status with ourselves. Yet there are those of us who are powerfully attracted to the Superman cape, no matter how many times it failed to flutter before. Something in us keeps forgetting how short a trip it was from the roof to the sidewalk.

For the sake of our self-esteem, we need to remember how hard the sidewalk is the next time we're tempted to take on a task that can't be done. If we're trying to think for other people, resolve their self-made messes, or rescue them from their own willfulness, we're guaranteeing ourselves another hard fall. And the pity isn't that our attempts keep failing; the pity is that we hurt ourselves trying to do what no one on this side of heaven is allowed to do—save other people.

The purest, most noble intentions in the world won't make the Superman cape billow. No matter how loyal or devoted, we are still and only human. Steadfast love and encouragement are the best we have to offer our troubled loved ones. If we want to salvage our self-esteem, we need to accept ourselves and our loved ones, limitations and all. And we need to hang up the Superman cape.

Even in a good cause, my grandiosity is self-defeating.

January 8

Procrastination means paying twice the price when you eventually must act.

—T. A. McAloon

The relationship between procrastination and self-esteem is not coincidental. The reason is that self-esteem slips whenever integrity is sacrificed, and procrastinating always demands the offering up of a tiny piece of our integrity. Heavy-duty procrastination is also a first sign of depression in many people.

Suffering people say that when they are depressed they feel overwhelmed, overburdened with so much to do there's no hope of ever getting it done, of feeling powerless in the face of insurmountable odds.

Whatever the specific cause of a depression, however, procrastination often helps to set it up. Many of us have procrastinated until there really *is* an unmanageable logjam of undoable tasks. Or we allow terrible pressure to build up around a decision that we've put off time and time again. In these ways, procrastination invites depression just as honey invites ants.

Conquering my procrastination may eliminate the need to conquer depression.

In thy face I see
The map of honor, truth,
and loyalty.
　　—William Shakespeare

What higher honor can we give but to say a person is "true blue," or "faithful to the end"? Loyalty is one of the most endearing and noble of all human qualities. How terribly sad when we place this priceless gift in the wrong hands!

Many people suffering from low self-esteem have developed faulty boundaries around who is trustworthy and who is not. Of course it isn't *trusting* itself that threatens self-esteem, but trusting untrustworthy people is always devastating. While everyone makes an honest misjudgment now and then, some of us go on making the same mistake with the same person over and over and over again. Such foolhardiness goes beyond the limits of loyalty.

Misplaced loyalty, especially if repeated, is evidence of willfulness rather than love. Because self-esteem cannot long endure the battering of betrayal, we need to get honest about what we're doing when we offer ourselves up to people who have let us down. To fail to learn from our past mistakes is to take a hand in our own injury.

My integrity is always lost when I set myself up to be hurt.

January 10

Let not thy Will roar, when thy Power can but whisper. —Thomas Fuller

Surrender, as taught and understood in Twelve Step programs, is anything but shameful. It means that we call off the war we've been waging against life as it is. It means giving up the losing battle we've been leading with our popguns of delusion and denial. In recovery, surrender is not a sign of weakness but of courage and strength.

Surrender is critical because delusion and denial prevent any meaningful move forward. The stinking thinking they produce tells us that black is white—that getting our own sick way is winning, that the enemy is out there rather than in here. The longer and bloodier the battle, the more confused we become.

To get on with our lives, to have any chance of victory, means that we give up what doesn't work. We stop playing "general." In the face of our well-demonstrated powerlessness, continuing the charade now seems insane—even to us. Our surrender doesn't signify defeat, but the fact that we are sick and tired of defeat.

The surrender of willfulness is often my first victory.

All deep, earnest thinking is but the intrepid effort of the soul to keep the open independence of her sea, while the wildest winds of heaven and earth conspire to cast her on the treacherous, slavish shore.
—Herman Melville

Building self-esteem takes introspection. But some of us get nervous when we start thinking about ourselves. Somehow it seems wrong to spend so much time digging around in the basements and attics of our personalities. We're afraid we're becoming self-centered, and we feel guilty about it. Haven't we always been taught to avoid selfishness?

But the search for self-esteem is more like a rescue mission than it is an ego trip. It isn't selfish to try to know and understand ourselves. And taking credit where credit is due shouldn't make us feel guilty any more than taking a paycheck at the end of a hard week. We deserve what we've earned. And all of us have earned more healthy self-regard than we've dared to claim.

We don't have to worry. Self-centeredness is no more like self-esteem than a flood is like a summer shower. One causes devastation and the other causes growth. If growth is our intention, examining our lives is not only allowable—it's an absolute necessity. And if introspection makes us uneasy, it's because we're not used to it, not because it's wrong.

Squeamishness about self-scrutiny may spring from my false pride instead of my true humility.

January 12

A successful marriage is an edifice that must be rebuilt every day. —André Maurois

Without doubt a successful marriage can be a marvelous springboard for our self-esteem. When we are loved we live in the presence of a constantly reflecting mirror that tells us, regardless of all our faults and warts, that we are plenty okay people. What could be better than to have someone who loves you be there to scratch your back in the middle of the night?

But marriage, like self-esteem, requires daily effort. The bread can be no better than the grain that goes into it. To listen when we would rather not, to compromise when we feel like digging in our heels, to confront problems rather than let them slide on by, guaranteeing a more difficult time later—all of these are kneading the dough.

It's a lot easier to dream about the wonderfulness of a finished product than it is to roll up your sleeves every day and do what is necessary to ensure that finished product will be there at day's end.

My precious relationships are worth the extra effort.

Pessimist—one who, when he has the choice of two evils, chooses both.   —Oscar Wilde

The only sensible way to live our lives is with optimism—and a lot of it. It just isn't reasonable always to expect the worst to happen; it doesn't. Nor is it logical to paint all circumstances black; they aren't.

Although society has its fun teasing cockeyed optimists, cynical pessimism has far worse results. We have all known—and avoided—dismal people who long ago lost the heart to be happy and the nerve to be hopeful. Perhaps they chose gloom and doom because they were afraid the sun would never shine for them. Or perhaps their negative, peevish attitude toward life came from trying to be suave and sophisticated. But in any case, their negativity doesn't attract much company.

Optimism is healthy. Merry, upbeat people who look for the good *attract* the good, just as flowers attract butterflies. It is just as easy, and just as reasonable, to look up as it is down.

Habitual melancholy can be rejected as well as accepted.

January 14

Parentage is a very important profession; but no test of fitness for it is ever imposed in the interest of the children. —George Bernard Shaw

We are all born with a hunger for love. Our spirits crave acceptance and appreciation just as our lungs crave fresh air. We don't just wish or hope for love; we *need* it to thrive. Denied, we start to lose our grip on life and become frantic. That's why every one of us reached out early in life for that sense of belonging.

What happened when we reached out to people who didn't feel good about *themselves?* Understanding that they couldn't give what they didn't have can go a long way toward understanding where our self-esteem went. This is a sad realization for many, but it's a realization with an up side.

Understanding enables us to choose. And choice can free us from endlessly repeating lose-lose patterns. If the primary caretaker in our lives lived in a veritable haunted house of ghosts and demons, we must not go on looking to that person for protection from bogeymen. If they haven't been able to chase away their own spooks, it isn't likely they can help us with ours. Perhaps we need to spend some time grieving—for them as well as for us. But mostly we need to reach out to healthier people. Now that we're grown, we get to choose for ourselves.

The reason I can't get blood from a stone is not that the stone is unwilling to give it; stones don't have blood to give.

*Who ever is adequate? We all create situations
each other can't live up to, then break our hearts
at them because they don't.*

—Elizabeth Bowen

Things are not always just as we would like them.
Often we would in some way re-create ourselves if we
could. Some wish they were taller, others would like to
have been the other sex, many are born with physical
defects, some are just plain homely. But the most foolish thing in the world is to brood about our handicaps.
We need to be more creative in working with what we
have.

The great poet Lord Byron was one who did. He was
born with a club foot, so he could not excel as a runner
or a mountain climber, as he wished. Instead he became a championship swimmer, winning many important swimming events and setting swimming records.
Perhaps his experience of inadequacy was behind his
great success in the literary world.

Some conditions must simply be accepted. But that
doesn't mean we need to define ourselves by our limitations. It means we should make the most of what we
have in spite of them. Self-esteem is the result of a
positive self-definition.

**I must accept and work around my limitations if
I am to have a happy life.**

January 16

Man is not the sum of what he has already, but rather the sum of what he does not yet have, of what he could have.   —Jean-Paul Sartre

At times the obstacle course between us and improved self-esteem is a lonely run. Often the effort leaves us frustrated and tired. Persisting in some new behavior we have committed to may make every mental and physical muscle scream for relief. Easy for us to ask, "Why me? Why do I have to work so hard at this?" We tend to tell ourselves that there must be something unusually, perhaps hopelessly, wrong with us if we have to work *this* hard.

But the fact is that we really aren't much different than anyone else. The level of our self-esteem and the depth of our wisdom can always be increased. We're further along than some and further back than others. But everyone is somewhere on the self-esteem gradient. We're not alone, we're not last, and we're not the only ones who get tired.

The *me* in "Why me?" is the same *me* that runs along with everyone else. Of course, everyone else is not involved in a focused effort to improve self-esteem, but those of us who are, are a mighty force indeed. The more appropriate response is probably not "Why me?" but "Thank the Lord I am on the way."

Weariness after work is a sign of a productive day.

Friendship is almost always the union of a part of one mind with a part of another: People are friends in spots. —George Santayana

Screaming hunger makes a person unreasonable. This happens to those who have lived too long without nurturing relationships. Many, especially those of us who identify ourselves as Adult Children, imagine that there are ideal others out there if we can only find them.

But like all unrealistic expectations, this fantasy can only result in frustration and further injury to our self-esteem. No question that the world will go right on starving us out if we don't find friends. Yet how can *any* partner or friend be perfect? When we imagine that there will never be spaces in our togetherness, that there will always be complete agreement and fidelity, we set ourselves up for disappointment. Even our friendship with God is limited by our own partial ability to be a friend.

People come in many varieties, but perfect isn't one of them. As we become aware that we may be asking too much, we can start thinking of our friends as a wonderful mixed bouquet, each flower contributing its own unique fragrance and beauty to the whole. Our disappointment with past relationships mustn't make us demand perfection where perfection cannot be found.

Unrealistic expectations are detrimental to my self-esteem.

January 18

*There is no more certain sign of a narrow mind,
and of arrogance than to stand aloof from those
who think differently from us.*
—Walter Savage Landor

Many of us find that our self-esteem is attacked when someone resists our reasoning. When our analysis or plan seems so sound and logical, it's hard for us to understand why anyone would disagree. Then, rather than showing some flexibility, we dig in our heels and go to war over the seeming stupidity or denseness of those who prefer their own ideas.

Overcoming this resistance may become a crusade. We see the others and their ideas as an obstacle to right thinking. Often we never consider that we may be just as irritating an obstacle to them as they are to us. It may never occur to us that they may be just as "right" as we are. Eventually, our spirits stumble under the weight of the negativity we attach to their motivation. And when our spirits stumble, our self-esteem stumbles.

Without sacrificing our integrity, we can become more honest people by becoming more flexible. Our truth, however true it is, is not necessarily the *only* truth. Our line of reasoning, which is so crystal clear to us, may be as valid as any, and yet not be the only possible path to a desired goal. We have every right to assertively present our ideas. But others have the right to theirs as well. There's nothing wrong with agreeing to disagree, and no reason to put our self-respect on the line every time we have an argument.

"My Way or No Way" is the motto of a bully.

Relationships are not answers to problems. They are rewards for getting your life in order.
—Horst S.

Many of us think that a loving, trusting relationship would be the answer to all our loneliness and self-doubt. We see a committed, one-to-one relationship as the answer to our most vexing problems; therefore, we put all our eggs in a "relationship basket." We wait rather than work.

Starting from such a position invites disappointment, however. A good relationship is much more a result than it is a cause. Often a relationship is our reward for dealing with life in such a way that low self-esteem, repressed anger, chronic evasiveness, and the inability to share feelings are no longer pressing issues. A relationship does not come along and cure our problems. Rather *we* cure our problems and thus become ready and able to have a relationship. The relationships come after the work.

Like happiness and self-esteem, successful relationships are not ends unto themselves. Rather they are the rewards and results of living a life capable of producing such treasures.

How can I enjoy a relationship unless I'm capable of enjoyment?

January 20

God does not die on the day we cease to believe in a personal deity. But we die on the day when our lives cease to be illuminated by the steady radiance, renewed daily, of a wonder, the source of which is beyond all reason.

—Dag Hammarskjöld

Believing is not our favor to God; it is God's favor to us to invite our belief. God is not sustained by our caring for him; *we* are sustained by God's fidelity to us. To call it off between ourselves and God does not decrease his light, but rather makes us even blinder than we are as we make our way through the shadows.

Somehow, in our egotism, we get our relationship with God all turned around. We forget which one of us is God and which isn't. We give God lists of things to do, we try to make deals with him and may even try to pull the wool over his eyes. We make him a scapegoat for our problems, blame him for our own mistakes—and then whine about injustice!

The incredible thing is that God loves us anyway. Why would he care about people who behave so unlovably? Why would he invite us, again and again, to seek the dignity of wholeness? Why provide so many lessons to such slow learners? Why keep on sending help to rescue us from the pits we dig ourselves? As the quote says, it's a wonder beyond all reason. Perhaps ours is not to understand, but to be grateful.

The God of my understanding can be my anchor in stormy seas.

Closure means dead.
—Jonathan Jarvis

What could be harder on one's self-esteem than to be continually drawn back into a toxic relationship, or any toxic situation? Many of us, desperately trying to break free from an addictive stranglehold, make heartfelt, heroic efforts to break out. But ultimately, failing to walk *all the way* away, we slip right back, inch by inch, into the hell from which we had almost escaped.

When a situation has been deemed lethal, when we come to understand that to stay is to sacrifice self-esteem, then closure, and only closure, can set us free. Closure does not mean *sort of* separating. It means getting out all the way. It means the relationship is over and there is no possibility of going back. It means that even if the other person calls or invites or begs or pleads or cries or crawls the answer is no. Out means out. Closure means canceled, kaput, the end.

Difficult? Yes, indeed. Necessary? In some situations it is the difference between life and death, physical as well as spiritual. Most of us need a lot of support from healthy friends to stick to our guns when we're trying to do away with a dangerous, but compelling, relationship.

Successful closure means being open to the new as well as closed to the old.

January 22

*If wrinkles must be written upon our brows, let
them not be written upon the heart. The spirit
should not grow old.* —James A. Garfield

Of all self-esteem issues, the comeuppance of aging
has to be the most universal. Beauty fades, joints
stiffen, and unproven upstarts threaten to overtake us
at every turn. The calendar is exacting; no one is ex-
empt.

Common sense tells us to face facts and reassess our
options. But this is no small task in a society that wor-
ships at the altar of dewy youth. At the very time we
need the confidence to keep on going and growing,
authority figures no older than our children may be
discounting us, humoring us, and treating us as has-
beens. And loss of stature hurts our self-esteem even
more than it hurts our feelings. If we don't work on it,
we can let them convince us that we're no better than
they say we are.

That's when our wisdom and experience come into
play. These are our unfailing flak jackets. Whose standards will we allow ourselves to be measured by?
Whose judgments do we respect? People with strong
self-esteem ask themselves those questions every
day—and make their own decisions. Haven't we finished a lot of races the young haven't even begun yet?
Haven't we put a lot of hard times behind us through
courage and determination? Aren't we calmer now,
and wiser, than we've ever been before? These are the
prizes our years have won for us. If we want them to
be honored, we must honor them ourselves.

**I am only as vulnerable to societal judgments as
I am fearful of them**

No doubt Jack the Ripper excused himself on the grounds that it was human nature.

—A. A. Milne

To plead "human nature" to our misdeeds is easy enough to do. "I couldn't help it!" we cry out. "That's just the way I am!" Yet it is exactly those very human, we hope dismissible, misdeeds that compromise character and thus self-esteem.

A case can certainly be made that many of our less-noble *tendencies* can be chalked up to human nature. Self-preservation, for example, may inspire selfishness and lying. But it's just as much human nature to strive against those tendencies as it is to give in to them. We are *human*, after all, not jungle animals.

There are many excuses but few good reasons for some of the things we do. The real reason is usually that we "*felt* like it." Many times in our lives we will "feel like" running away from responsibility, but that's no reason for running. Human nature can't be blamed. It's we who decide.

Ultimately I am what I choose to be; my self-esteem follows the same path.

January 24

Divorce is the psychological equivalent of a triple bypass. It takes years to amend all the habits and attitudes that led up to it.

—Mary Kay Blakely

Who among us would shout "Hurry up!" to someone on crutches, or tell a bleeding accident victim "Snap out of it!" No one could be that unrealistic or insensitive, right? Wrong. That's exactly what we do to ourselves when we expect instant recovery from major life traumas. As unrealistic expectations go, that's about as unrealistic as it can get.

People who have recently experienced divorce—or the loss of any once-loved reality in their lives—are especially vulnerable to this self-harassment. Somehow we think we can skip right over the rehabilitation period that *must* follow so serious an injury. After all, there is not only the loss itself to be dealt with, but all the habits, patterns, and systems that grew out of this relationship. How unreasonable to expect that all of this can be dismantled immediately!

Even if we're glad the relationship is over, divorce is loss. And loss requires grieving, reflection, and healing. We not only have the right to heal, we have a responsibility to take all the time we need. Common sense, as well as self-esteem, forbids us to order ourselves to hurry up what can't be hurried.

How long does it take to heal? It takes as long as it takes.

*Happiness arises in the first place from the en-
joyment of one's self; and, in the next, from the
friendship and conversations of a few select companions.*   —Joseph Addison

The dictionary defines happiness as a state of well-
being and contentment, joy and felicity, which leaves
us out if everything in our lives seems to be going
wrong. Without our fair share of material comforts and
pleasures, happiness seems beyond our reach. Perhaps
the best we can do, we say to ourselves, is to try to be
a good sport about not being happy.

Yet when we think about it, most of us have known
people who seem to wrest happiness out of the most
unhappy circumstances. How do they do it? It must be
that they have discovered a happiness beyond pleasure and a serenity that is a deeper form of well-being
than merriment. The great social reformer Jane Ad-
dams was one of these people. Her life was a life of
service, not gaiety or pleasure. Yet she found happiness in the depth of her spirituality.

Happiness is not the result of getting everything we
want, but of doing something worthwhile. So even if
we are beset by many misfortunes, the example of
other people's lives teaches us that we can be just as
happy as we are wise.

**I may need to redefine happiness, rather than
put it on hold.**

January 26

Marriage is our last, best chance to grow up.
—Joseph Barth

Marriage has many advantages like emotional security and financial partnership. Seldom, however, does anyone mention that marriage provides a great opportunity for us to grow up. Yet surely it does. And the growth of maturity is always a growth in self-esteem.

The single life can be a veritable playground for faults, foibles, character defects, and the general acting out of selfishness. When we're on our own, who is there to say, "Stop," "No," or "You can't do that around here"? Marriage provides a boundary within which wackiness of all kinds—which would otherwise skip merrily on its way—gets confronted. In respectful, well-balanced marital relationships, we can't get away with the self-centeredness we don't even notice when we're alone. We are forced to listen better, share more, compromise fairly.

If we are married, we have profited from the responsibilities that may also have irritated us. Marriage is good for most people—not *in spite* of all its difficulties and demands but *because* of them.

Committed relationships deepen my commitment to self.

The beginning is the most important part of the work. —Plato

For the sake of physical fitness, a tennis shoe commercial urges us to *just do it!* Whether it is swimming, jogging, tennis, or slam dunking, just do it.

For the sake of emotional fitness, that's not bad advice either. Building self-esteem is like building anything else; nothing happens until you get started. Just do it!

It's a mistake to think that only major achievements count. We don't have to make president of the company or run a marathon or graduate from college to significantly boost our self-esteem. In fact the opposite is true. How we see ourselves is established more by the thousand and one small, daily things we do than by our infrequent moments in the limelight.

Speak up at a meeting, if that is new for you. Write a long overdue letter, especially if you have something important to communicate and you've been procrastinating. If you're working on standing up for yourself, express an opinion. If you're trying to mind your own business, keep your opinion to yourself.

Today it is enough to do whatever I can. I will just do it!

January 28

Resistance to tyrants is obedience to God.
—Thomas Jefferson

Truly overbearing, domineering people are a scourge on the face of the earth. They are executioners of self-esteem. As children, many of us quaked and quivered under the rule of tyrant parents. As adults, some of us are regularly bullied and browbeaten by tyrant spouses or bosses. Now that we're working on our self-esteem, we find these people easy targets to shoot at—and hit—when we go gunning for the bad guys who hurt us.

Yesterday's tyranny is one thing. Of course, we need to admit that it happened. It often helps to work it out by discussing it with a trusted friend, a support group, or a counselor. But beyond acceptance and understanding, there is nothing we can do but bind up our wounds and go on.

But the tyranny we're enduring today is another matter. As adults, we must take responsibility for our role in a tyrannical relationship. God made us to be happy, joyous, and free—not cowering and cringing. Until we find the courage to stand up for ourselves, self-esteem will be impossible. If we need help, we must ask for it.

Resistance to oppression is my duty as a human being.

Listen to every prompting of honour.
—Ralph Waldo Emerson

How we would all love to be honored! *Then* we would feel good about ourselves. Honor implies getting a medal, riding in the head car in a parade, or being recognized for some grand achievement. In these ways, honor is often publicly expressed.

Yet, far more often, honor is expressed by the private exercise of moderation, courage, and love. And these virtues are almost always demonstrated by frequent, small sacrifices. To be aware of the promptings of honor, then, is first to be aware of the promptings of these sacrifices. To hold back the negative word when everyone else is throwing stones at another gives rise to honor, even more so when we dare to contradict the stone throwers with a positive remark. We demonstrate honor when we reject a second, or third, helping of food when we are already comfortably full, or when we exercise even when we don't feel like it. Such sacrifices earn us the kind of medals we wear on the *inside*, rather than the outside.

Honor is an old-fashioned concept these days, a dinosaur among modern values. Yet honor is the foundation of self-esteem. And it is most often gained by the willingness to sacrifice little things many times over.

The honors I bestow are nothing compared to the honor I earn.

January 30

There are offences given and offences not given but taken. —Izaak Walton

We bring on a lot of unnecessary suffering by being supersensitive. How often, for example, do we get our feelings hurt by what someone else has said? If this is a regular refrain in our lives, we may need to listen more closely to what is actually being *said*. Perhaps it's a whole lot less than what we are *hearing*.

If our basic posture in life is defensive, we find ulterior motives everywhere. Then there can be no such thing as a simple statement that simply means what it means. No! Then *what* is said is not nearly so important as *why* it is said. When we're listening for motives rather than messages, we hear what we expect to hear. If we expect to be personally attacked, that's the way we'll translate whatever is said to us. Most of the time the speaker intended no such thing and may not even be aware that we were hurt.

Supersensitivity is always a sign of low self-esteem. It's a symptom of a deeper disorder called chronic defensiveness. Except in wartime, it isn't necessary to look for aggressors behind every bush. It isn't appropriate to "hear" put-downs and insults when none were spoken. Until we deal with that defensiveness, we have to accept responsibility for our own hurt feelings.

As I grow in self-esteem, I become less vulnerable to imagined slights.

God is never late.
—Jo Sibet

Let's get the show on the road! Here we are, ready to roll with a handful of new insights and all the good intentions in the world. This time we're going to throw off our negative old habits and charge straight ahead toward a better life. We've got a plan now and we're going to stick to it. Nothing can stop us because we've finally learned to reach out for help. With prayer as a new part of our daily routine, we're on our way at last.

So when is lift-off? What's the delay? Why are we so disturbingly like our old selves so long after we launched off in another direction? There's no question that we're doing *our* part; when is all this prayer going to start paying off? *Where's God?*

Perhaps the better question is "How does God work?" After persisting long enough with "our part," we can usually see that God was powering us all the way. Concepts like *slow* and *late* are always relative to expectations. Can we be so sure that ours are the same as God's? Can we even be sure that we were as ready as we thought we were to get the message?

Farther down the road, we often discover that God had been pointing and pushing us at some door that we were too blind to see for months or even years. Then, when we finally get the picture, we turn to our patient, sweating God and say, "About time!"

My Higher Power is never indifferent, capricious, or on vacation.

February 1

Only in growth, reform, and change, paradoxi-cally enough, is true security to be found.
—Anne Morrow Lindbergh

Low self-esteem is often grounded in a sense of vul-nerability. When we feel threatened and defenseless, we hang onto our security as hard as we can for fear of losing something. Security is the assurance that noth-ing will be lost.

Of course everybody needs a reliable port in a storm. It's careless and foolish not to provide for hard times. But an overdependence on security can actually make hard times of good times. It can make us unwilling to think new thoughts, to dare new actions, or ever take a risk. In our fear of rocking the boat, we may never pull up anchor and leave the dock at all.

Wondering and questioning are dangerous activities for security-tethered people. Any new information could jeopardize the status quo. Yet challenging the status quo is what self-improvement is all about. With-out asking new questions, we can't get any new an-swers. Without venturing down new paths, we can't make any new discoveries. How are we going to feel good about ourselves if we don't do anything to feel good about?

Many wonderful "could be's" are possible for all of us—but only if we're willing to take a few chances.

If security is the assurance that I will lose noth-ing that I already have, it's also the assurance that I will gain nothing new.

My God, I have no idea where I am going. I do not see the road ahead of me, I cannot know for certain where it will end . . . but I will not fear, for you are ever with me.   —Thomas Merton

If self-esteem means confidence and confidence means being sure about what's going to happen, then we're all out of luck in the self-esteem department. None of us knows the answers to the biggest, most important questions in life. If that fact makes us terribly insecure, we're going to be in for a whole lot of fear, worry, and anxiety.

The truly confident person knows that life is much more of a process and a journey than a matter of answers and destinations. It is one thing not to know where the road leads—but quite another to be paralyzed because we don't know. If the open road makes us too frightened and insecure, we will probably miss all the lovely scenery along the way. And we won't learn the lessons of the journey.

Confidence arises from self, not circumstances. Just because the road is uncertain doesn't mean that *we* are. If we have a Higher Power walking just ahead of us, we have all the security we need.

Confidence in God turns my insecurity into trust.

February 3

There are no grades of vanity, there are only grades of ability in concealing it.

—Mark Twain

What do people say of us behind our backs? While the question itself is unsettling, most of us have wondered about it. Maybe they say we are bossy or perfectionistic, stubborn or uncommunicative—those things wouldn't be *too* bad. But we wouldn't want to be thought of as vain. That would be embarrassing.

Because we have learned to preen in privacy and boast discreetly, we like to believe that our conceits are invisible. But the fact is that human nature is riddled through and through with inflated pride. Our difficulty is that we are too vain to admit and accept our own vanity.

If you don't believe it, check it out. How many times do you mentally replay an embarrassing situation to come up with a clever comeback or rationalize a mistake? Do you overreact when someone gets a laugh at your expense? Does a small slight grind away at you for days or weeks? Do you let battles of will grow out of all sensible proportion? Most of us do all of those things to some degree or another. Some of us are even vain about our imagined lack of vanity! But there's no way around it. We are all vain people. Our challenge is to accept this truth about ourselves so we can actively bring it under control.

No one is superhuman. My healthy self-regard is based on acceptance of human nature.

Each handicap is like a hurdle in a steeplechase.
When you ride up to it, if you throw your heart
over, the horse will go along, too.
—Lawrence Bixby

Too old to get hired? Too short to make the team? Too shy to ask for a date? These are just conditions, not insurmountable obstacles. Not unless we let them be. If we have enough desire, we can get over, around, or through *any* limiting conditions and keep right on moving ahead. But it *does* take heart. If our heart doesn't get there first, the rest of us never will.

Self-esteem requires overcoming obstacles like fear and paralyzing hesitancy. If we want to earn our own respect and admiration, we must practice making a mighty leap with heart and mind, perhaps several times a day, before our muscles will follow.

Afraid of a social occasion? Visualize yourself as the belle of the ball before you ever put on your dancing shoes. Nervous about a job interview? Practice seeing yourself as relaxed, confident, and impressive. Wondering how a new project will come out? Get your heart and mind there ahead of time. *Know* that your project will be a smashing success and *fun*, too! The actuality will follow just as the feet move in the direction the body leans.

Overcoming obstacles is a matter of heart over hardship.

February 5

*Sympathy is a supporting atmosphere, and in it
we unfold easily and well.*
—Ralph Waldo Emerson

People who want to learn more about self-esteem probably fall into two major categories: those concerned for themselves and those whose energies are directed at the self-esteem of someone else. After all, low self-esteem is about as limiting a handicap as a person can have. To see a loved one suffering self-esteem trouble is to suffer yourself in no small way.

But what is the best way to help someone else? Some buy that person books, tapes, lists of affirmations. Or they send their loved ones to workshops and seminars. All of these may help, but by far the best thing we can offer is our own steady friendship. This means becoming a multifaceted mirror in which our loved ones can see themselves reflected in a more positive light.

A multifaceted mirror reflects different images at different times. Sometimes we reflect encouragement, sometimes challenge, sometimes tough love, and at other times simply a safe harbor where the other can rest a while. People make much more impact on each other than any inanimate teaching guide.

Just being there for someone else is often the best help.

We possess only the happiness we are able to understand. —Maurice Maeterlinck

We could all be happy if we didn't set so many conditions on it. We, with all our *ifs* and *whens,* are the ones who handicap our own pursuit. Unless we choose to, we don't have to work or even wait for happiness for another minute. If we drop our conditions, we can have it right now.

A wise person once said that happiness is learning to accept the impossible, do without the indispensable, and bear the intolerable. If that definition seems unlikely—think again. What bars us from happiness as much as our *interpretations* of what is indispensable, impossible, or intolerable? What would happen if we were wise and mature enough to reconsider what we can't accept or do without? Then what would stand between us and happiness?

None of us can bend the mysterious rules of the universe. Just claims will often be denied, gifts will be distributed randomly, tragedy will strike the innocent. This is the world as it is. When we can accept that, we can stop quarreling with fate and learn to love life for its own sake. Thus we accept the happiness that was available all along.

I don't have to approve of the world's ways to accept them; I don't have to have my own way to be happy.

February 7

Plans get you into things, but you got to work your way out. —Will Rogers

Self-esteem sags when the tasks we intend to do somehow never get done. This is especially frustrating for disciplined, hardworking people who are anything but lazy. How can we be so busy, so active, so tired at night, without crossing off key items on our things-to-do list? *We* are the ones who made the list, after all. We are the ones who wanted those tasks out of the way. What's going on here?

Overpreparation may be part of the problem. Unaware of our pattern of behavior, we may be getting ready at the expense of getting the job done. Do we *really* have to rehearse our lines a hundred times before we ask for a raise? Must the spare bedroom be *completely* redecorated before we invite our old school chum to visit? Should we not send a gift at all if it isn't a *perfect* gift?

Fear of finishing is one form of the fear of failure. Jobs that we string out with endless planning and preparation are often those with chancy, nervous-making outcomes. To finish them is to risk disappointment or perhaps to remove our last excuse for not going ahead with the next step. Usually it's not the undone task that's the real problem, but the fear behind the stalling.

Greater self-awareness gives me greater insights about my true motivations.

Inside myself is a place where I live all alone, and that is where I renew my springs that never dry up. —Pearl Buck

Good fortune sometimes gives us a special person or place that we can run to when the going gets rough. Perhaps, for us, this refuge was a comforting, devoted aunt, a tender grandma who never saw anything but good in us, or an old schoolteacher or coach who helped us believe in ourselves. Perhaps it was a hiding place on the side of the garage beneath the lilacs or a dreaming place, like a tree house or shady back porch. When time and circumstances take these people and places from us, the world gets scarier.

As we grow up we need to find new sanctuaries. In addition to caring friends, perhaps we will find that a quiet library or a lakeside is a calming place to think through our problems and restore our souls. Most reliable of all, perhaps, as we grow to greater maturity, is our own inner space that is not under the direction of, or influenced by, any other person.

Our ability to heal ourselves, to maintain our self-esteem, depends on our familiarity with this inner retreat. When so many outside factors are beyond our control, the shelter inside ourselves can make all the difference.

There is a sanctuary in my own heart.

February 9

If you look at life one way, there is always cause for alarm.
—Elizabeth Bowen

Riding through life on bad attitudes is a lot like riding down the freeway on bad tires. It's bumpy, dangerous, and insecure. Any bump in the road can cause a blow-out and leave us stranded. Because the journey through life is bumpy at best, it only makes sense to check out our attitudes from time to time. How safely are we traveling? Can we look forward to miles of happy progress, or is an accident in the works?

Answering the following questions will give us a quick "attitude check."

- Do I see life as challenging and interesting, or do I see it as a painful struggle that must be endured?
- Do I actively take steps to promote my own well-being, or do I passively wait for someone else to solve my problems?
- Am I truly open to new ideas, or do I refuse to let go of old, familiar ways of thinking?
- Do I make my own decisions, or do I allow other people to direct the course of my life?
- Do I live comfortably in the present, or do I fear the future and bemoan the past?
- Do I accept the imperfections of myself and others, or am I often upset and irritated by human imperfection?

My self-esteem is best maintained by regular checkups.

*At times, although one is perfectly in the right,
one's legs tremble. At other times, although one
is completely in the wrong, birds sing in one's
soul.* —V. V. Rozanov

In many ways, human beings are perverse creatures.
Some good behaviors—like apologizing—may give us
bad feelings. Likewise some very bad behaviors—like
telling someone off—may make us feel very good indeed. That's why we can't allow our feelings to dictate
our behavior.

Of course it's important to identify our feelings. Feelings tell us a great many things. A big part of emotional
health is coming to understand and respect how we
feel. But too often feelings are blind guides to what is
right or wrong.

Because feelings are habits, they wind around old
behaviors like iron filings around a magnet. *Anything*
we do often enough we will come to feel comfortable
doing. The worrier is comfortable worrying; the work-
aholic, working; and the liar, lying. But no matter how
comfortable we feel, it doesn't necessarily follow that
these behaviors will lead to a full spiritual life based on
positive self-esteem. It's important to know how we
feel. But it's even more important to know that our
feelings have memory but no conscience.

**As I practice healthy behaviors, my feelings will
follow along.**

February 11

Too long a sacrifice can make a stone of the heart.
—William Butler Yeats

Healthy people don't go out looking for pain, frustration, and failure. Some of us who have low self-esteem, however, are seduced, validated, and comforted by these downbeat experiences. We are the good, hardworking, long-suffering people that other people call martyrs.

Like everyone else, our self-esteem is based on our self-image. But unlike everyone else, our self-image is practically nonexistent; when we look in a mirror, we see others. Somehow, somewhere, we came to believe that our needs weren't important or that normal self-interest was a sin. So we learned to justify our existence by rendering service. Because "they" came first, we took second best or nothing at all, gave beyond our limits, and exhausted ourselves. Perhaps we told ourselves that it was "God's will" that we serve and suffer, suffer and serve until we drop.

But now we are becoming wiser. We realize that our wants and needs are as legitimate as everyone else's. We know that the good God who gave us intelligence and free will didn't intend for us to return these gifts, to trade them in for slavery. We're learning to claim what was ours all along.

As martyrs slowly abandon themselves, the first thing they leave behind is their self-esteem.

If everyone contemplated the infinite rather than fixed the drains, many of us would die of cholera.
—John Rich

Decent unpretentiousness is always admired. But *extreme* modesty is a terrible handicap to self-esteem. The tendency, for example, to aggrandize other people's talents and abilities, to glamorize their professions and their personal lives, can only demean our own talents and jobs and personal lifestyles. Because "they" have or do so much, it only follows that whatever we have or do is little, small, and insignificant.

Oftentimes, extreme modesty is an attitudinal hiding place. "Important people *should* have better self-esteem than I do," we may say to ourselves. Or, "Lowly as I am, it would be ridiculous to think of myself as an equal of somebody really gifted."

Yet everyone who makes a contribution is important. The person who changes the bulbs in streetlights provides protection to everyone. The trash hauler's work prevents epidemics of disease. The person who cooks dinner for a child is making no less a contribution than the famous chef who cooks dinner for a roomful of strangers. All of us are entitled to be proud of who we are and what we do. And we are obliged to honor our own contribution if we want to feel good about ourselves.

Excessive modesty robs me of my self-respect.

February 13

Words, as is well known, are the great foes of reality.
—Joseph Conrad

Double-talk is the sly and slippery language we use to slither away from the truth. Like all other conning behavior, double-talk usually hurts us more than those we are trying to fool. What happens is that we ourselves get taken in, confused, and misled by words that say one thing but mean something else. With enough practice, we get so bad at it, we're good—or good at it, we're bad. See? That's how double-talk works.

Most double-talk is designed to turn attention away from our real motives for doing or not doing something. "I didn't have time," for example, very often means "That wasn't important to me." "I forgot" also says the same thing. "I don't need it" may mean "I don't want to put out the effort," and "That's dumb" often means "That's scary."

Double-talk is one of the self-defeating habits that keeps our self-esteem tethered close to the ground. If we're hiding laziness and self-centeredness behind slick words, we're weighing ourselves down. Integrity will not be ours if we insist that black is white—or even dark gray.

Self-esteem is built on truth.

Love is not easy. Love costs.
—Carl Sandburg

Sometimes we forget the difference between symbols and substance when Valentine's Day rolls around. Spurred on by all the hearts, cupids, and lacy cards we see in the stores, we may unconsciously stake our self-esteem on whether or not we're remembered with a box of chocolates or a pretty bouquet. *Of course* we want to be and have a sweetheart on this official feast day of love! Who wouldn't?

But that doesn't mean that those of us who aren't romantically involved are either unloved or unlovable. Romantic tokens are flattering and fun—but tokens aren't love itself. Many of the valentine tokens being given today are inspired by a sense of obligation—because old Hubert or Billy or Sam knows what's good for him! Some are even given to reduce guilt or to show off. Love itself costs a lot more than long-stemmed roses or even diamonds.

Real love is measured out in steadiness, commitment, and unselfishness over the long haul. It has to do with willingness and forgiveness and just plain fortitude. It means being consistently mindful of someone else's welfare. If we are engaged in such relationships, we are fortunate indeed, whether or not we have someone on hand today to tell us how wonderful we are. It's love itself that's wonderful, not the tokens.

Happy Valentine's Day!

February 15

"It's the sin of pride," said the homely woman to her confessor. "Every time I pass a mirror, I'm overcome by my own beauty."
"I wouldn't worry about it, my dear," answered the priest. "That's no sin, that's just a mistake."
—Father Ralph Pfau

It's a fact. More than a few of our pomposities have as little basis in fact as the homely woman's supposed beauty. The problem that we're willing to admit may be wholly different from the problem behind the masks we wear.

"I'm too generous," some of us might say in trying to explain away our inability to say no. "I'm too honest," we may say of our tendency to be insensitive and blunt. "I'm too trusting," we say of our chronic victimhood. But these are mistakes rather than admissions.

All faults described as an excess of virtue are really backhanded compliments to ourselves. They are old lies, not new truths. It isn't possible to be too generous, honest, or trusting. The problem is not excess, but what we *lack*. Generosity without prudence is foolhardiness; honesty without compassion is ruthlessness; trust without discernment is masochism. We need to peel off the masks and work on our real problems if we're going to make real progress.

Self-flattery is a poor substitute for honest self-appreciation.

Bacchus hath drowned more men than Neptune.
—Thomas Fuller

Statistics say that there are about 12 million alcoholics in this country; that's a lot of sick people! Experts have further estimated that every alcoholic's sickness has a major effect on the lives of at least 10 other people, including family, friends, and coworkers. Thus the "body count" of the afflicted and the affected goes up to 120 million—ten times as many people as live in New York or Los Angeles.

Few of us reading these pages, or any pages, have been untouched by our own or someone else's problem drinking. As the epidemic rages on, it is well for us to remember that recovery is a personal decision. As much as we hope and pray for the drinking to stop, we can't force anyone else to change. We can refuse sick alcoholics our money and our company—we often have to do this for our own survival—but the decision to change must originate with them, not us.

The most powerful tool we have is the example of our own lives. The only force we can bring to bear is the moral force of our own health, serenity, and compassion. We can turn on the light and put out the welcome mat, but mostly we have to get on with our own lives.

My self-esteem hinges on my own battles, not someone else's.

February 17

As far as the stars are from the earth, and as different as fire is from water, so much do self-interest and integrity differ. —Lucan

Self-preservation is the strongest instinct of humankind. When push comes to shove, all our noble resolutions go out the window when we feel too threatened or at the end of our endurance. The fact is that we do what we have to do to survive. Or what we *think* we have to do. Fostering self-esteem often means reinterpreting what we "have to do" to protect ourselves.

The self-talk we use to filter and process outside reality is a good index of our survival mentality. What do we say to ourselves when we're busy, but someone has a legitimate claim on our time? When we're tired, but someone asks our help? When a community crisis calls for talents and energies much like our own? Our response depends on our view of the world and of ourselves. Is the world a garden that needs our tending or a jungle that's too dangerous to enter? Our self-talk gives us clues.

"It won't do any good," "Why should I?" "It's none of my business," "I can't," and "I don't have time," are defensive phrases banged out on jungle drums. "Maybe I can help," "Why shouldn't I?" "At least I can show up and give it a shot," are the responses of confident, growing people who have broadened and deepened their definition of self-interest.

My concern for others mirrors my growing self-respect.

*Anxiety is the essential condition of intellectual
and artistic creation.* —Charles Frankel

Too much stress can wear down our resistance to assaults on self-esteem as well as to physical disease. At one time or another, we've all had trouble holding on simply because we were too tired to fight back. We gave in to fatigue. But we mustn't draw the conclusion that stress is always as harmful as fatigue is.

Fatigue is a matter of energy management—making sure we get enough recreation and sleep. Because exhaustion saps any program of growth, it's absolutely necessary that we rearrange our lives to make room for adequate rest. But productive stress is also necessary if we're going to experience success. Any "up and doing" creates anxiety, and anxiety creates the stress. Whenever we stretch to be more tomorrow than we were yesterday there is going to be stress—so we'd better rest up for it!

If we're translating the stress in our lives into positive experiences, we're elevating our self-esteem. Many of the new behaviors that become the building blocks of self-esteem are wretchedly uncomfortable at first. Even thinking about them may make us break out in a cold sweat. Of course, there will be stress—but it's the kind of stress that creates.

If self-esteem were bread, stress would be the yeast in the recipe.

February 19

Adapt or perish, now as ever, is Nature's inex-
orable imperative. —H. G. Wells

Some of us have pretty firm, even rigid, ideas about the way things "ought" to be. We want people and places to stay the same as they always were. Sometimes our unhappiness with change is simply nostalgia; part of our youth disappears when the corner drugstore gives way to a parking lot. But sometimes our resistance to change is more serious—as if the battles we've already fought took such a toll that all we can think of is digging in right where we are.

Yet all growth requires change and all change is a matter of adjustment. Perhaps we need to move forward or backward, lighten up or tighten up, let go of something old and reach out for something new. Perhaps we need to reconsider a negative attitude or be willing to do something we've never done before.

The circumstances and characteristics that bolstered our youthful self-esteem are sure to change as the years go by. As reality changes, so must our perspective change if we are to stay fully alive for all of our days. Adaptation is not only necessary—it's natural.

The survival of my self-esteem requires adaptation.

You only become real when . . . your fur has been rubbed off. —Margery Williams

Self-esteem is the reward for peeling away our fakery, looking squarely at our character defects, and building on our strengths. Whether we're trying to recover from disaster or simply trying to get more out of life, all of us are engaged in the process of becoming real.

The author of *The Velveteen Rabbit* makes the point that we become real when we are loved a great deal. And love always means being used. Not put on a shelf, not safely out of harm's way. Love is not, and never has been, safe.

We get real when we become involved and thus get our "fur rubbed off." Maybe we throw ourselves into a cause that seems doomed but is too important to ignore. Maybe we spend time with a troubled child who is too distressed right now to respect us, let alone thank us. Any conflict or discomfort we take on for the sake of some greater good is worth it because it's real. Never do we feel so alive as when we're trading off a little fur for a lot of love.

What's real in life is gloves-off, go-for-broke involvement.

February 21

*He that can't endure the bad will not live to see
the good.*   —Jewish Proverb

Many once-jolly travelers on the road to recovering
self-esteem have turned into wary travelers indeed.
Maybe we've started out on this journey many times
before and run into so many problems we had to turn
back. Perhaps we used unreliable maps or timetables
or our traveling companions proved untrustworthy. So
now we're guarded; we're afraid to expect too much.

Yet the pursuit of any treasure requires risk. Little
progress will be made if our first concern is to avoid
disappointments. In spite of our discouraging past experiences, we need to try again. Perhaps we need to
get going again with our affirmations, even if they
didn't prove magical last time. Maybe a new group
would help or even a different, more-realistic attitude
on our own part.

Might we be disappointed again? Yes indeed. The
affirmations may stick in our throats, some meetings
may turn out to be boring, the friends we choose may
be far more flawed than we expected. But partial as
they are, all of these efforts combine to *get us there.*
Standing on guard won't do it.

**Perseverance is my passage to improved self-
esteem.**

Procrastination is the thief of time.
—Edward Young

There are hundreds of pages in this book concerning self-esteem. Some encourage thinking, others acting, others understanding. Yet all that thinking, questioning, and understanding will be useless to some people; useless because they're facing a major decision that's blocking their progress. Until they're willing to take action, all the insight in the world isn't going to help.

Any work on self-esteem while we're acting out an addiction or an affair or staying involved in some on-going dishonesty like a dead relationship will bear little fruit.

Preparing to make drastic decisions can, of course, take time. And any effort made to get to the frame of mind where the decision can be made is valid. But let there be no confusion as to why we don't feel better about ourselves. The problem is us and our unwilling-ness to act.

Postponing my decisions often postpones my relief.

February 23

*Many a man has fallen in love with a girl in light
so dim he would not have chosen a suit by it.*
                                        —Maurice Chevalier

Sexual chemistry is a curious thing indeed. Who can explain the sudden, overwhelming attraction of one to another—perhaps a very unlikely other? Burned as we may have been, once the sparks start to fly we climb right back on that emotional roller coaster. And once on that wild ride, we're hell bent to take every dip and curve.

Yet emotional thrill rides are rarely worth the price of the ticket. As high as the highs may be, the lows come all too hard and soon. By sacrificing cool rationality to hot emotion, we trade off too much self-respect. By heedlessly becoming involved in relationships that are doomed from the start, we demean ourselves. In effect, we play with our self-esteem when we knowingly play with unwise relationships.

The fact is that we can't afford it. It is one thing to *feel* attraction, but quite another to follow it. While the temptation may be great, let us see whether any new relationship can stand before the tribunal of reason before we skip off to the roller coaster again. Reason should be the companion, not the enemy, of emotion.

Foolish love affairs can cost more than the time wasted on them.

Neither a wise man nor a brave man lies down on the tracks of history to wait for the train of the future to run over him.

—Dwight D. Eisenhower

Many of our employers promote concepts like "team spirit" and "company loyalty." In a world increasingly ruled by competitive specialization, cooperative effort is a must, of course. If we want to keep our jobs we also want our companies to stay in business, to make a profit. We give in order to get; we're willing to do what's necessary and good.

But there's a dark side to being defined as a "team member." We can abandon common sense and lose creative self-reliance if we let ourselves be completely swallowed up by any team or company. Sharon's company, for example, thinks in terms of "units," not people. Like many others, this company feels free, and is free, to pull up stakes and move entire operations from one end of the country to another. The disruption of human lives is never considered. Rumors of such a move sent Sharon to a counselor who told her to take matters into her own hands by making an A-B-C list of job opportunities she could pursue if the pullout actually happened. It all sounded good until the end of the session when Sharon said, "Yes, but when are they going to tell us what our A-B-C choices are? When are they going to come and tell us what to do?"

They aren't. The choices are ours, and the responsibility is as well.

Passive passengers often get driven where they don't want to go.

February 25

Bravery is being the only one who knows you are
afraid.   —Franklin P. Jones

Heroes, we think, are basically better people than we
are. Surely they have great self-esteem. That's why
they can do such extraordinary things. They don't
seem to feel fear. That's why they can charge a
machine-gun nest or rescue someone from a fire or
fearlessly respond to any life-threatening emergency.
But, in fact, our assumptions about heroes may not be
true at all. These people may have been terribly afraid,
but they went forward anyway. Perhaps that is the
essence of heroism—to go forward anyway, afraid
or not.

What seems routine to others may be terribly frightening to us. For some it may be a genuine act of heroism to apply for a job if there is a great fear of rejection.
It make take great courage to speak up to a browbeater
after a long life of passivity. To express our honest
feelings may make us break out in a cold sweat.

Difficult though they are, these nonnewsworthy acts
may be just what it takes to crack the self-esteem barrier. The point is not whether we are afraid, but
whether we do what needs to be done. That's the
hero's way.

**Any time I defy fear, I perform an act of
heroism.**

*Unresolved anger is often the hidden source of
low self-esteem.* —Bill Bartlow

What we don't see. we can't understand. What we
don't understand, we can't influence. And when that
blind spot relates to the source of our self-esteem, the
results can be devastating.

Hurt that has been denied, mislabeled, or unrecog-
nized still exists, no matter how long ago we were
wounded. In fact, such hurt—that is the hard core of
all anger—is all the more potent for not being recognized or for being called something else. The trouble
with burying something alive is that it will devour us
from the inside. Buried does not necessarily mean
dead.

At the core of much low self-esteem is just such a
hard knot of anger. Anger over the way we were
treated as children, rights that were denied, kindnesses
that should have been there for us but were not. Love,
encouragement, support, perhaps even the basic safety
that everyone has a right to—none of these were to be
had. Buried, that collection of hurts turned into anger
and seeped out sideways. Sometimes the seeping turns
into a flood. Often it becomes simply a prevailing state
of being—we are just always angry, always hostile,
always operating with a short fuse. That doesn't make
us very attractive people. To say the least, we're not
fun to be with. And so the anger over our long-ago
hurt generates loneliness and rejection even today.
Lest our tomorrows be affected as well, let us own up
to our buried anger.

**Hidden anger can kill me. I must recognize it
and address it.**

February 27

Whoever thinks a faultless piece to see,
Thinks what ne'er was, nor is, nor shall be.
—Alexander Pope

Perfectionism is complex and subtle. Out loud, few of us would say, "Perfection is my only acceptable standard," but in the privacy of our own minds, many of us talk out of the other side of our mouths: "I must *always* give 110 percent." "I must *never* fail a friend." "For winners, there's really only first place and no place."

Setting a high standard and holding yourself to it is certainly admirable behavior. No one who shoots too low accomplishes very much. But there is a big difference between striving for a high standard and expecting yourself to achieve it every time out. No one can "always" put out a 110 percent effort; there are days when we only have 80 percent to give. No one "never" drops the ball or bungles an opportunity; even world-class performers have their off days. And first place is only as sweet as it is because it's *not* a permanent position—not for anyone. In life, there is no such thing as a perfect score.

Impossible demands on self make self-esteem impossible, too. If our approval is only won by superhuman feats, we won't have much to cheer about. How much healthier and happier we will be when we eliminate words like *always* and *never* from our inner code of conduct. We need to hear more applause.

My opinion of myself must not rest on words like *always* and *never*.

Pride is the mask of one's own faults.
—Hebrew Proverb

Fear has many disguises. Sometimes it puts on sexy clothes and talks in the voice of lust. Sometimes it wears the mask of anger or greed or envy. And sometimes fear pretends to be pride. "I'm smart and strong," we say to ourselves. "I don't need help. Whatever I have to do, I can do alone." These are the kinds of things we say when we refuse to join a group or put off asking someone to be our sponsor or even confide in a friend.

But is it pride or fear talking? Pride takes the illogical stand that in spite of the pain we've lived with for so long we really are better than others. Fear, on the other hand, whisperingly suggests that others may be better than we are, so we'd be safer to hold back so they'll never know. Reaching out for any kind of help would make us vulnerable.

But no one grows as well without support. Strength and pride aside, we need other people's input, insights, and encouragement. We need people we can trust to hold us accountable. We need to hear about their struggles and successes. When we insist on going it alone, it's usually not because we're more independent and self-sufficient than other people. It's because we're afraid.

I need a community of peers for support.

February 29

*To admit I have been in the wrong is but saying
that I am wiser today than I was yesterday.*
—Allan Picket

Is your self-esteem based on always being right? It may
be if every error or misjudgment makes you terribly
embarrassed or angry. If this is the case, a little attitude
alteration may be just what you need to get back on
track.

Depending on our attitude, being in the wrong may
be seen as a chance to learn—an invitation to wisdom.
Everyone makes mistakes. The question isn't whether
or not we do, but how we handle it. If we use every
mistake as a chance to get down on ourselves, our
mistakes can teach us nothing. And every mistake
thereafter will not serve as an opportunity to learn,
either.

Think how different it would feel to simply acknowledge the error, pull up our socks, and forgive ourselves! Then, in the absence of all that disproportionate
emotion, we could learn from the mistake. Perhaps in
spite of the momentary embarrassment, we would find
it was well worth the tumble.

**When I exchange my mistakes for wisdom, I'm
making a good trade.**

When money speaks, the truth keeps silent.
—Russian Proverb

Money talks to all of us. Whether we admit it or not, a lot of our self-esteem is based on the amount of money we're able to earn, hoard, or spend. How could it be otherwise? The siren song of success calls out to us daily from advertisements, television shows, and newspapers: "You must have more or you are a failure." Because we hear the message loud and clear and because we don't want to be failures, it's hard not to buy into the idea.

But self has to do with being, not with having. These are totally different realities. Self-esteem is an art in itself, not a work of art that can be bought or sold. To have self-esteem is to know how much is enough. It is to value friendship over things and to have the ability to relax more, worry less, and find plenty to laugh about.

Certainly everybody needs enough money to live on. Poverty can kill a spirit as quickly as riches can. But even great wealth can't buy what isn't for sale. Truly happy people know that their real riches reside within.

I will avoid the trap of outward trappings.

March 2

Everything that irritates us about others can lead us to an understanding of ourselves.

—Carl Jung

The search for self-esteem is a search for truth. It involves trying to see ourselves as truly as we can—and learning to appreciate what we see. As we move along, the mirrors that reflect back our true selves often pop up in the most unlikely places!

Irritating people can be such mirrors. All of us know people we'd just as soon avoid. Somehow they just get under our skin and make us crazy. Yet if we are willing to figure out exactly *what* bothers us about them, we may find great insight into our own hearts.

The person who talks too much may irritate us because we miss the chance to monopolize the conversation with our own stories. The braggart may irritate us because we feel we should have accomplished more. The person who is always upbeat may make us jealous that we're not happier ourselves. Some insights are less flattering than others but no less valuable for that.

My own flaws and frailties are usually at the bottom of my trouble with other people.

When a man sells eleven ounces for twelve, he makes a compact with the devil, and sells himself for the value of an ounce.

—Henry Ward Beecher

People who worry a lot about being cheated often feel perfectly justified in taking advantage of someone else. Unlike safecracking, chiseling is more a pervasive pettiness of spirit than it is an outright crime. Yet both are dishonest. Most chiselers, as a matter of fact, don't even know they're chiselers. They think of themselves as shrewd, clever, and artful. Unaware of their own shabby reputation, these small-time wheeler-dealers may have no idea why other people don't respect and admire them. Obviously, self-esteem is shaken when appreciation is denied.

Pettiness of all kinds bespeaks old grudges. Because we feel we've been hoodwinked, brushed off, or in some other way shortchanged in life, we may subconsciously get even by giving "them" back the same kind of treatment they gave us. To be sure we're not giving too much away, we always hold back a little something extra for ourselves.

Chiseling is a way of thinking—a defensive, fearful betrayal of our own insecurity. It belittles us instead of protecting us. If we find ourselves counting out our gains in ill-gotten time or money, we're chiseling ourselves out of our own integrity.

My growing integrity forbids every form of pettiness.

March 4

Servitude debases people to the point where they
end up liking it. —Vauvenargues

Talk about guilty pleasures! What a joy it is to learn that building self-esteem doesn't require us to please anybody but ourselves. Can it really be? There must be a catch somewhere. It sounds too good to be true, or at least true for *us*.

Many of us have spent most of our lives in the service of other people. In our growing up years, we learned that that was our ticket for love and approval. Want to be loved? Make someone else happy. Want a pat on the head? Do their work for them. That's how we learned to look outside ourselves for our self-esteem. That's what made us virtual slaves to the wishes and needs of others.

Now that we're adults, old knee-jerk reactions will still tempt us to reach out for that brass ring. But now that we know better, we're going to be much less comfortable about giving away all that power. As we take it back little by little, so do we take custody of our self-esteem.

My self-approval no longer depends on other people's responses.

Any life is an unfinished story.
—Ron Palmer

Some of the most popular movies and television shows have the most predictable story lines. Maybe that's why we like them so well. Right from the start we can see the powerful forces of evil taking on the even more powerful forces of good. The plot is so familiar we can sit back, relax, watch for the thrilling close calls, and let the story unfold. No sweat.

Writing our own life stories as we do is a different proposition. For one thing, there's plenty of sweat involved. And for another, the ending is anything but predictable. A life story in process is full of unexpected twists and turns. New characters can enter—and leave. Heroics may or may not be called for. Mistakes may be corrected immediately or just in the nick of time. Tragedy may give way to comedy. But as long as we're alive, the story isn't over.

In whatever predicament we find ourselves today, tomorrow can be different. The possibilities are up to us; we can write anything we want to on the new pages coming up. What will happen next? That's entirely up to us. We are writing our own stories, and they will come out as we decide.

It's never too late to change my own story line.

March 6

Friendly counsel cuts off many foes.
—William Shakespeare

Contrary as many of us are, we crave attention but often run from it when we get it. If anyone comments on our behavior, whether they're giving us credit or blame, we tend to squirm like a fish on a hook. Our old, unrecovering selves are too tender, too touchy, too exquisitely self-conscious for their own good. Our new, recovering selves, however, are made of much sterner stuff.

Less vulnerable now than we used to be, we are learning to take both compliments and complaints without flinching. We know we need help and we're willing to take it when it's offered. If it's a pat on the back—wonderful! If it's a legitimate criticism—that's wonderful, too. We're not so frail anymore that we can't bear to hear a word to the wise.

Our new emotional sturdiness is a sign of maturity and self-confidence. For the first time in our lives, perhaps, we realize that our real self-worth is independent of what other people say of us, whether it's good or bad. We are who we are. Comments from others may hurt us a little or help us a little—but they don't change who we are.

When I am sure of who I am, other people's opinions will not matter so much.

Guilt always hurries toward its complement, punishment: only there does its satisfaction lie.
— Lawrence Durrell

The most useless phrase in the English language may be "If only I had . . ." What's done is done. Dwelling on past errors or missed opportunities is a terrible mistake. Some of our self-blame simply isn't justified: What happened wasn't our fault in the first place. And even when the failings were truly ours, the constant replay exaggerates and distorts what really happened way back then.

Guilt eats up a lot of energy that could be better used elsewhere. Most of us have already punished ourselves many times over. Isn't it time now to climb down off the rack, step away from the whipping post, and consider the debt settled? Enough is enough. We deserve a reprieve.

Self-esteem demands that we admit our mistakes and take responsibility for them. But it also demands that we accept and forgive what can't be relived. Endless self-recrimination has no place in recovery.

As my self-knowledge increases, my self-recrimination decreases.

March 8

Optimism enables a man to hold his head high, to claim the future for himself and not abandon it to his enemy. —Dietrich Bonhoeffer

The optimist and the pessimist find different implications and portents in everything they see. To an optimist, a stubbed toe may be a small price to pay for getting turned around in the right direction. The pessimist may see the same small injury as convincing evidence that all effort is dangerous and futile.

There are disadvantages at either extreme, of course. We optimists may not always recognize real and present dangers. But we who are pessimists may well miss out on many come-from-behind victories that could have been ours if we hadn't given up so early in the game.

A comfortable balance between the two extremes is what we want to achieve. If our nature or experience tilts us too far in either direction, we need to recognize that and begin to practice a healthier, more balanced viewpoint. Self-esteem hinges on realism—but realism and hopelessness are not the same thing.

Viewpoint is critical; I tend to get what I expect.

Loneliness expresses the pain of being alone and solitude expresses the glory of being alone.
—Paul Tillich

It may be said that the road between loneliness and solitude is the highway to self-esteem. As we begin our quest, most of us fear and flee loneliness. We make sure that we have plenty of company and continuous talk, lest in the silence we have to hear ourselves. When we're alone, we may keep a radio or television going to fill the airwaves. Or we talk on the telephone.

As we come to know and become more comfortable with ourselves, however, that "noise hunger" eases up. The disappointing, inadequate self that we always avoided starts to look more interesting—perhaps like someone we'd like to spend some time with, get to know better. When they're not interrupted, cued, or drowned out, our own thoughts become our most abiding source of challenge, comfort, encouragement, and self-respect.

The aloneness is the same whether we're suffering loneliness or enjoying solitude. The magical difference is in our attitude toward ourselves.

Getting comfortable with my own company is a sign of growth.

March 10

The remedy for wrongs is to forget them.
—Publilius Syrus

One of the very best ways to hang on to low self-esteem is to hang on to a resentment. Resentment is always about pain. It is about being cheated, being "done unto," being victimized. And victimization always makes its presence felt in negative definitions of ourselves—definitions like "I don't have any rights" or "You can't trust anyone" or "I will never be loved."

To foster a resentment fixates us at the point of our pain. Happiness, then, becomes like a butterfly transfixed with a pin. Because resentments and freedom are mutually exclusive, no one can have both. To insist on carrying around a resentment is to insist on retaining the source of our low self-esteem.

Often the hardest thing about giving up resentments is that we feel such a *right to them*. We may well have been cheated. We may well have been lied to and treated shabbily, perhaps even criminally. If that doesn't justify resentment what does! The truth is, however, that resentment is a self-defeating entitlement. We have a right to a stomachache too, but who wants it?

To harbor a resentment is to harbor an enemy.

Beware, as long as you live, of judging people by appearances. —Jean de la Fontaine

People who struggle with low self-esteem are quick to intimidate themselves. One way to do this is to make a snap judgment based on appearances. Some of the new people who come into our self-improvement programs, for example, may hardly seem to need improving. Some are so fit and healthy looking they could probably teach the exercise classes we're afraid to take. Some seem so intelligent they could probably find a cure for the common cold faster than we could find the mayo in the back of the refrigerator. How could *they* be in the same room with *us*? Surely they couldn't be having the same problems we're having!

But of course they could—and do. When we compare our insides to other people's outsides, the only picture we can come up with is wildly distorted and inaccurate. A snapshot is not the same thing as an X ray. When we only judge by what "shows," we misjudge—and miss the point—every time.

Despite appearances, the people we quickly rank above ourselves are just the same as we are on the inside. They have fears, worries, hopes, and dreams, just as we do. We deny them our compassion—and deny ourselves their fellowship—when we put them up to keep ourselves down.

I'm learning to compare myself with others for information rather than intimidation.

March 12

The only abnormality is the incapacity to love.
—Anaïs Nin

Sometimes, as we bravely but clumsily trudge the path of recovery, our priorities go out of whack. Heaven knows we are *trying* to touch all the bases and exercise every weak muscle. Perhaps we are trying to do too much at the same time. We may be busily learning to play, exercise, develop a prayer life, and assert ourselves with such passion and energy that we forget *why* we stirred up all that activity in the first place.

We need to remember that our final goal and first priority is to become healthy enough to participate in healthy relationships. All self-improvement efforts march in that direction. Each one builds and maintains the self-esteem that makes that final goal possible. In themselves, they are less—much less—than what they add up to.

We may never be able to play as freely as we'd like to, or pray with the concentration of the saints. Our thunder thighs may not submit to the exercise machines nor our timidity ever be completely overcome. But when we are able to share in loving relationships, no matter how the rest of our projects work out, we have found the key to the golden door.

All recovery roads lead to the ability to love and be loved.

*A sound mind in a sound body is a short but full
description of a happy state in this world.*
—John Locke

Health is a required subject in all school districts. Who
doesn't remember grade-school classes in hygiene?
That's where we learned all about the importance of
toothbrushing, fingernail cleaning, and face washing.
Usually, a little first aid was taught in those classes,
too. We learned what to do about common injuries like
cuts and bruises and burns.

Isn't it odd that no one ever taught us about mental
hygiene? But good mental and emotional health habits
were never mentioned, let alone explained. And there
were no first aid lessons to show us how to take care of
common emotional injuries. Surely punctured pride is
more common than a nail hole in the hand. And
bruised feelings must outnumber black eyes a million
to one!

Thankfully, it's never too late to learn. Here are five
simple prescriptions for the maintenance of mental and
emotional health:

• Assert yourself: No one can respond to what you
  don't say.
• Be teachable: The ignorance you won't admit will
  catch up with you.
• Find confidants: Friends double your joys and divide
  your sorrows.
• Contribute something: Takers end up empty-handed.
• Live today: Anyone can be strong for twenty-four
  hours.

**Simple daily disciplines can protect the wealth
of mental health.**

March 14

He too serves a purpose who only stands and cheers. —Henry Adams

As we think about all the different roles we have played in our lives, the tendency is to remember the times when we were up front, in the spotlight, delivering all the important lines. We're likely to pass over or even forget the many more numerous occasions when we had supporting roles—when it was our job to keep the action moving, motivate the main characters, or even cook everybody's lunch.

But there's nothing insignificant or second-rate about the supporting roles we play. As the saying in the movie industry goes, there are no small parts, only small actors. It's vain and self-defeating to make little of our opportunities to help and even enable other people to do their best work. We can't make other people shine without shining ourselves.

Baby-sitters, den mothers, and Little League coaches, if they play their roles to the full, can make life-changing contributions to their young charges. Just as our friends, fans, and mentors can enhance our adult lives by their encouragement and appreciation, we need to lose no chance to stand up and cheer each other on.

Supporting roles are often the most rich and rewarding.

Praise shames me, for I secretly beg for it.
—Rabindranath Tagore

Praise can be wonderful encouragement. Self-esteem blossoms when our brave attempts, as well as our actual successes, receive an adequate amount of notice and comment. Bravery deserves acknowledgment.

There's another side to that equation, however. Every move we make isn't going to make people stand up and cheer. Nor should it. Some of us actually become praise junkies who measure our self-worth by compliments and pats on the back. Then if that attention is withdrawn or withheld, we feel mistreated. In our hunger for appreciation, we've given other people the authority to validate our worth.

Robert is only four. His father, a taciturn mountain man, cuts and delivers firewood for a living. Robert works alongside his father. The father carries the larger logs from truck to wood bin. Robert carries the logs that are Robert's size. When they are working, neither one talks. Robert neither expects nor gets a flood of compliments for doing his part. He simply does his work because it *is* his work, not a remarkable feat that deserves a medal. Like Robert, we mustn't look for applause for simply doing what we're supposed to do.

Self-respect depends more on self-acknowledgment than the acknowledgment of others.

March 16

Much compliance, much craft.
—Thomas Fuller

Are some people "born to be boss"? Whether that's true or not, some of us would jump at the chance to manage the world. Taking charge comes naturally and decision-making is automatic. Nothing makes us feel better than leading the pack. On the flip side, nothing so rattles our self-esteem or makes us so uncomfortable as being the rank beginner at the rear of the pack. And that's just where we are when we born bosses first come in to any self-help program.

Struggling with unfamiliar principles and deferring to group wisdom are a baptism of fire for those who usually write the rules. It hurts to be the slow student rather than the respected teacher. It's hard to have so many more questions than answers. But a turn at being the new kid on the block can be the best thing that ever happened to us. There are things privates learn in the trenches that the generals in the map room never know.

Compliance, or going along with the program, opens our minds to new approaches to old problems, to new sources of strength. And the fellowship of equal, striving souls is a magnificent trade-off for the loneliness that goes along with leadership. Wise is the leader who knows when to follow

Another paradox of life: I can only take charge when I stop taking charge.

The only gift is a portion of thyself.
—Ralph Waldo Emerson

Some gifts only *we* can give to certain people. There is no other smile like ours, nobody's touch is just the same, no one else has our thought patterns or perceptions. There are hurts in others that only we can heal, spirits that only we can lift, words that only we can say.

Self-esteem that has been chipped and weathered away by hard times robs others as well as ourselves. And always those others are the ones we love most, the very people we would least like to hurt. One of the sad implications of low self-esteem is that in devaluing who and what we are we also devalue what we have to give. So we don't give it, and our loved ones lose out.

Putting up with low self-esteem is sad all right, but in a very real sense it's also selfish. It isn't honest to say "I'm only hurting myself," when we consciously refuse to lift ourselves up out of some gutter of hopeless self-pity. If there's even one person in the world who cares for us, who has a stake in our well-being, we are cheating that person by denying them our healthy company. Bruised and bleeding as we may be, if someone is watching for us at a window, praying for us every night, we have more on our conscience than just the crime we're committing against ourselves.

Unchallenged personal deterioration hurts the people who love me.

March 18

Beneath all depression lurks the demon anger.
—Andrew Carliss

Myra is as lovely as she is depressed. In spite of her many merits, she suffers from low self-esteem. With all of her heart, she's trying to do what it takes to pull herself up. Yet a powerful, inner anchor is holding her down. The invisible but very real anchor that weighs Myra down is the anger she will not own. And because she doesn't own *it*, it owns her.

Myra suffered through a painful divorce several years ago. Her husband left her for a much younger woman. Her hurt—and eventually, rage—knew no bounds. Then, like a volcano, it slowly stopped erupting. Myra decided to "put it out of her mind." Yet it never went out. Not completely.

Today Myra is dating a wonderful man who loves her. Everything looks promising—except for that invisible anchor. Myra is often down, uneasy, and fearful, even though her new relationship is going well. The new man in her life doesn't understand it, and neither does she. Yet it's really no mystery. Depression, and the anger beneath it, simply can't be dismissed. It must be faced and reckoned with if self-esteem is ever to rise.

I'm no longer willing to let yesterday's anger ruin today.

It takes twenty years to become an overnight success.
—Eddie Cantor

There are many kinds of success, of course—career, financial, relational, spiritual. Each brings its own reward. One kind of success gives us prestige, another intimacy, another money. What they have in common is that all are sweet and none are accidents.

Enjoying a positive self-esteem is surely one of life's greatest successes. How could it be otherwise? The quality of our lives is dictated by the quality of our self-esteem. To succeed in this arena means that we pay the same price that is paid for any other kind of success: We must work at it.

We musn't make quick judgments about how easy it was for others to overcome fear, doubt, complacency, and laziness. Whenever we see people who are serene and confident, we may be sure that we are looking at people who have paid their dues. Our success, as theirs was, will be won by taking each day as it comes and doing the best we can with it.

Self-esteem is worth the work of building it.

March 20

Avoiding danger is no safer in the long run than outright exposure. The fearful are caught as often as the bold.
                                                    —Helen Keller

Low self-esteem and timidity are often Siamese twins. Many of us have a long history of holding back and fading into the wallpaper. We never felt it was "our place" to get the ball rolling or to take charge in anyway. Yet building self-esteem takes boldness, at least to the extent of trying new actions that go against the grain. There is an overwhelming tendency to call passivity "patience," and to crown inaction with virtuous justifications like "letting go" or "turning it over."

The magic of building a healthier self-esteem is like the magic of building the great pyramid of Egypt or the medieval cathedrals of Europe. It isn't magic at all. These wonders were created by millions of hours of work and sweat on the part of hundreds of thousands of people. Beauty came to be because the effort was made.

You don't have to be a genius to know what it takes to build self-esteem. Most of us know darn well what it takes: enough boldness to challenge our limitations and do what it takes to get the job done.

I am entitled to take my own life into my own hands.

Stupidity is the deliberate cultivation of igno-rance. —William Gaddis

Innocence and naïveté are charming and touching in the young. But there is nothing charming about adults who refuse to read the writing on the wall. This kind of blankness is called willed ignorance because it's done on purpose, deliberately. With enough practice, willed ignorance can be indistinguishable from stupidity.

On the surface, this condition seems absurd. Who would will themselves to be ignorant? But there are many reasons for this sad tactic. If we have learned to be terribly afraid of conflict or anger, we may also have learned to ignore the red flags that signal danger. If we have learned to avoid vulnerability at all costs, we may also have learned to throw a wrench in the works if a growing relationship calls out for commitment.

If we don't see what's going on, don't know what's happening, we won't have to deal with it. So we choose not to know. But the price of willed ignorance is always loss. When intellectual integrity goes out the window, self-esteem goes right after it.

Facing the truth is not as difficult as ignoring it.

March 22

Trust men and they will be true to you; treat them greatly and they will show themselves great.
—Ralph Waldo Emerson

Most of us learn early on that a good offense is the best defense. In many areas of life, this is undeniably true. If we don't keep our wits about us in this risky world, we're sure to step in a bobby trap of one kind or another. All day long we may have to make judgments about which situations are dangerous and which are not. It becomes a habit.

But we need to be careful about making those same kind of defensive judgments about people. Especially if our judgments tend to be negative and frequent. Because people usually give us what we give them, our own suspicious, self-protecting ways are likely to come boomeranging right back at us—to the detriment of our self-esteem.

Suspecting the worst of others, not giving them the benefit of the doubt—these behaviors are usually bad habits rather than conscious decisions. If we want to, we can suspend judgment by being the first to give compliments, encouragement, and upbeat feedback. What a positive response we'll get! And it won't be because the other people in the world all shaped up at once.

Whatever I give out comes back to help me or hurt me.

Ride on over all obstacles, and win the race.
—Charles Dickens

While life's obstacles are irritating and frustrating, they need not defeat us. Bad luck is part of *everyone's* life, after all. But some people just roll with the punches and keep on going. Their secret is that they see their own power as greater than the power of any stumbling block.

Here is a true story of someone who made the best of a bad break. A brilliant violinist had the misfortune, while he was giving a concert before a packed audience, of having the A string snap in the middle of a beautiful sonata. Everyone would have understood if he had apologized and walked off the stage. But he didn't. Instead, he quickly transposed the selection and finished on three strings.

Wit and the will to win are invincible in overcoming any adverse circumstance. No matter what stands between us and success, we can get over, under, or through it if we have the determination.

Healthy self-esteem demands I make the least of my unlucky circumstances and the most of my ability to overcome them.

March 24

No one holds a good opinion of a man who has a low opinion of himself. —Anthony Trollope

Most people would say, "Of course I like myself!" But many of those people betray the opposite in a variety of ways. Slovenly dress and grooming habits betray passive hostility to self and others. Poor health care betrays a basic lack of self-respect. Cutting, self-effacing "jokes" about ourselves are really insults that we'd rather initiate than receive.

Obviously, any form of self-hatred is poisonous to self-esteem. No matter how subtle, every attitude and behavior that diminishes self-worth must be turned around. The person who says he doesn't care about clothes needs to buy a new shirt anyway. The person who feels she doesn't deserve to spend money on a new hairstyle needs to get to the beauty shop *now*. The moment we become aware of any form of self-neglect is the very moment we need to counterattack with an act of self-love.

Without exception, the roots of self-hatred are deeply buried in the past. If today we are trying to do what is good and right, we have every reason to hold a high opinion of ourselves. One day at a time, we can learn to focus on what we are becoming rather than who we were or what we did way back then.

Today is the only day I have; if I'm doing okay today, I'm doing okay.

Grown up, and that is a terribly hard thing to do.
It is much easier to skip it and go from one child-
hood to another.   —F. Scott Fitzgerald

Most young children in the first few years of school struggle with self-control. Without thinking, they push and shove, squirm and wiggle. But with a little social modeling and natural maturation, most all of them develop physical control. Emotional and mental control is another matter entirely.

Many of us know some babies, bullies, show-offs, hotheads, clowns, and fawning teacher's pets who haven't seen a schoolroom for twenty, thirty, or forty years. Maybe *we* are developmentally stalled types ourselves. It's not at all unusual for grown men and women still to be operating on the same emotional level as they did when they were twelve.

The pursuit of self-knowledge, of course, requires that we own up to our juvenile soft spots if those spots are there. If we still find ourselves striking back whenever we're offended, laughing at people's mistakes, or currying favor with more popular people, we're indulging in some pretty childish behavior. It isn't possible to be a mature adult and a tattletale at the same time. If self-esteem is our goal, we need to bring our childish ways under control.

I will practice self-control.

March 26

Why, since we are always complaining of our ills, are we constantly employed in redoubling them?   —Voltaire

"Know your enemy" has always been sound military advice, and it's not a bad way to safeguard self-esteem, either. All of us have enemy tendencies built right in, waiting to catch us off guard and pull us down.

To know where these pitfalls are is half the battle in staying clear of them. To understand our own personal and particular brand of self-defeating thought patterns is to be forewarned. Die-hard sentimentalists who are striving for practicality, for example, shouldn't "entertain" themselves by watching sad movies or listening to the blues. And vacationing workaholics need to read the comics, not the stock reports. As ripped up as we've been—why feed the tiger?

One doom-and-gloom sort of man admitted to his group that he always listened to police calls while he was falling asleep at night. As hard as he was working to develop a positive perspective, at the same time he was tuning in to crime and violence as the day's final lullaby! When the group laughed, he laughed, too. Then, with the sly look of someone who has just discovered a secret, he said, "I guess that's not such a good idea."

Avoiding my personal pitfalls takes common sense, not brilliance.

We find it hard to believe that other people's thoughts are as silly as our own, but they probably are. —James Harvey Robinson

What a boost our self-confidence would get if we could listen in on other people's thoughts! Particularly those people we imagine are so much wiser, more sophisticated, or more accomplished than we. How surprised we would be—not to mention amused—to find their mental ramblings so ordinary, random, and trivial. So much like our own!

Humanity is a common bond. Both kings and servants have stomachs that get hungry, backs that sometimes itch, and minds that wander a good bit of the time. As children of God, we all have dignity and limitless potential for spiritual growth, but our feet are rooted in clay. No matter how high or low we rank on any social scale, our human foibles and frailties make us a lot more alike than different.

The wonderful Wizard of Oz, if we remember, turned out to be a nervous little man shouting through a megaphone. He wasn't braver than the Lion or smarter than the Scarecrow or more loving than the Tin Man. He was just like them; his wizardry was all illusion. Much of the superiority we accord to others is illusion, too.

I share common characteristics with every person who walks the earth.

March 28

Our costliest expenditure is time.
—Theaphrastus

It seems that everyone is running at full tilt these days. We're so busy there's hardly time for the necessities, let alone time for play or reflection. Recovery and personal growth may well fall under the heading "If I get the time . . ."

But time doesn't wait for our schedules to clear. Postponed recreation or quiet time can easily be delayed for months or even years. By waiting for the time instead of taking the time, *later* can become *never* in spite of our best intentions to the contrary.

Yet what could be more crucial or immediate or deserving of attention than well-developed self-esteem? Our appreciation of ourselves enhances or detracts from everything we do; it colors and shapes the quality of our lives. In the big picture, how much does it really matter if the house gets painted this year or if we take the vacation of our dreams? If we're consistently too busy to take a walk, to comfortably relax away from a ringing telephone, to think our thoughts without interruption—then we're just plain too busy. What are our priorities? If we can't quickly say, then the chances are that we're spending most of our time on items that shouldn't be at the top of the list.

If I want to make the most of my life, I need to start now.

Rashness succeeds often, still more often fails.
—Napoléon I

Snap judgments can get us into trouble. We don't always know what we think we know—or even see what we think we see. If rashness is a character defect we must honestly claim, what better time than now to take a closer look at how this tendency can hurt us?

- A mother was *sure* she put change for the parking meter on the corner of the table. When it was gone she rashly accused her young son of taking it. Later, when she found the coins still in her purse, she apologized. But now, years later, the son still remembers his hurt.
- A man sees his fiancée having an intimate lunch with another man. After an afternoon of miserable anxiety, he confronts and accuses her with his eyewitness account. The fiancée's luncheon companion turns out to be a fellow worker whose mother had recently died.

The tendency to race to negative conclusions betrays a weakness in our self-confidence. Besides causing *us* unnecessary pain and embarrassment, it can hurt the people we love best. We do our self-esteem a favor when we learn to back off, take a second look, and think again before we jump to conclusions.

If I'm quick to take offense, I will always have plenty to be offended about.

March 30

Push a coincidence back far enough and it becomes inevitable. —Carl Jung

Some of us who didn't get a lot of help growing up take all the credit—or all the blame—for who and where we are now. But there's no such thing as a self-made man or woman, proud boasts to the contrary. Whoever we are today is the product of much coaching, conditioning, and example. Many cooks had a stir at the soup; many sculptors had a turn at the clay.

From teacher after teacher, we have learned who we are, what we deserve, what to expect from life, others, and ourselves. Thousands and thousands of learning events—verbal and nonverbal, behavioral and emotional—have gone into making us who we are. Perhaps we can't remember what we learned when and from whom, but remembered or not, our life lessons are still at work, creating the reality we call "normal." We didn't get to be who we are by random coincidence.

If our self-esteem tells us that all is well, we are fortunate indeed. But if it needs improvement, we have every reason to take heart: If one set of definitions and expectations can be learned, then so can another. We've already proved that we're good students. And this time we can choose our own teachers.

New experiences create new realities.

I shall stay the way I am
Because I do not give a damn.
—Dorothy Parker

Some self-improvement projects are doomed before they begin. One kind is the half-hearted little effort we may make to stop other people's nagging and get them off our backs. How could improvement come from that? Another losing venture is the search for a free lunch. In this case we try to fool ourselves that the *trappings* of healthy behavior can actually substitute for the behavior itself.

Let's get serious. There's no law that says we must improve ourselves if we don't want to. We have every right to stay just the way we are, or even to slip backward. But there are natural laws that will ultimately come to bear. One is that pseudopromises to ourselves and others erode our self-respect. Another is that a zero investment earns a zero return.

Obviously, self-improvement must be initiated by self or it's not going to work. There's no dignity in lying, and no one is fooled for long. And there's not much to admire about the expensively equipped golfer or tennis player who spends all his time in the athletic club bar. Until we actually decide to "give a damn," we can at least salvage some integrity by being honest.

Pretended self-improvement mocks my own integrity.

April 1

*Don't let life discourage you; everyone who got
where he is had to begin where he was.*
—Richard L. Evans

It's hard to run a race if you start off standing in a hole.
Yet that's just the handicap many people face when
they begin their quest for self-esteem. For them, because of early disadvantages, just crawling out of the
hole to get *to* the starting line is an exhausting effort. It
doesn't seem fair, and it isn't. But the fact is that we
can only take off from where we are.

We who have heard "You can't," "You'll lose," "You
don't deserve to win," all our lives have to shake off
those muddy messages before we can run free. All the
resentment and self-pity in the world, understandable
though it may be, won't turn what is into what ought
to have been. The mud is there. Until we commit ourselves to cleaning it off and throwing it out, our running shoes will be heavy. So what if others were better
prepared than we? So what if our would-be trainers
and coaches let us down? That's their responsibility,
not ours, and that all happened yesterday, not today.

Those of us who start out with handicaps, who today are standing in a hole dug by others yesterday,
need to give ourselves credit for *standing* at all. We
need to stop resenting where we are and start loving
ourselves for the daily courage it takes to suit up and
show up. We deserve a new start and we can have it if
we stop looking backward.

**Underdogs who start winning are no longer un-
derdogs.**

If we let things terrify us, life will not be worth living.   —Seneca

Are we prepared to do what it takes to win our own approval? Often that means being willing to wage war on our emotions. Old feelings of guilt, fear, rage, or impotence may well be circling our camp, threatening to stop our journey forward. These familiar enemies must be faced and dealt with if we mean to keep on going. It's not a campaign for sissies.

One thing that helps is to stop being surprised every time we see those feelings looming on the horizon. Haven't we learned by now that they're a persistent lot? Did we really imagine they were gone for good when we drove them away last time? If we did, we were kidding ourselves. Those feelings are as real as we are and they may very well be hot on our tracks as long as we're alive.

There's a reason for our feelings. That reason may be so hidden in the past that we'll never discover it—but a reason exists. That's why we can never take one last and final stand against negative emotions. Victory over marauding feelings is a matter of endurance and acceptance. The trick is to go on *anyway*, to gain as much ground as we can before they catch up with us the next time and to remember all the battles we've won before.

"Oh, it's you again" is the appropriate greeting when a negative emotion forces its way into my mind.

April 3

Work and love—these are the basics. Without them there is neurosis. —Theodor Reik

Cloud watchers and dandelion blowers may argue that work and love are not *all* there is to life, but without them we don't have the essential ingredients for a life worth esteeming.

Work is good for people. It is in work that we create ourselves by expressing our spirits in muscle. In order to be, we need to *do*, to make, to create. And it is in loving and being loved that what we are and what we are becoming is affirmed and celebrated. Who could appreciate a life without love?

Many things can go wrong in our lives. Many losses will be experienced—yet never, in one way or another, must we ever give up being creative or loving. As long as they exist, we continue. As long as we are working on something and loving somebody, we'll be a whole lot healthier than we are sick.

Good work and good companions are the building blocks of self-esteem.

The crime is not to avoid failure.
The crime is not to give triumph a chance.
                                    —Huw Wheldon

Tom still talks about not going out for the basketball team when he was fifteen. "I really wanted to play," he remembers thirty years later. "But I was afraid I wouldn't be good enough. It would have hurt a lot if I didn't make the team. I couldn't take the rejection, you know." So Tom never learned to play basketball.

Many of us have similar stories. Because we wouldn't risk failure, we didn't dare to try. And because we didn't try, we never did do what we dreamed of doing So now we still can't dance or sing or play the trumpet. And it's too late to try out for the basketball team.

Now that we're adults, we realize that we gave up too much to avoid the chance of failure. So these days we're making more mature decisions. If we're the least-limber members of our aerobics class, so what? If our kids laugh at our beginning ceramics projects, we can laugh along with them. We know that regret is too costly when we hear Tom say, "Every once in a while, in my head, I can see myself playing on that team. If I only had the chance to do it all over . . ."

Fear of failure clips my wings; if I want to fly I have to try.

April 5

*The trouble with most people is that they think
with their hopes or fears or wishes rather than
with their minds.* —Will Durant

Self-esteem demands a steady diet of success. It may
not always have to be the accomplishment of some
great external goal, it might be the successful simplification of one's life—which is no mean feat. Whatever
form the success takes, however, it must be a regular
experience if our self-acceptance and self-appreciation
are going to grow.

Most accomplishments of either the inner or the
outer variety require clear thinking. To move along a
desired and clearly chosen path means that we know
where we're headed and have some idea of how to get
there. If we haven't thoroughly thought that through,
especially if we've substituted emotions for thoughts,
we're not likely to make much progress.

It is not what we hope or fear or wish that makes us
winners—it's what we *decide*. To experience success,
we need to make good solid decisions based on good
solid thinking.

**Success requires that I push my surface emo-
tions out of the driver's seat.**

April 6

Who has deceived thee so oft' as thyself?
—Benjamin Franklin

How annoyed we are when we discover that someone has lied to us! We're hurt that they didn't trust us with the truth—and angry that they took us in. We feel resentful, betrayed, and righteously indignant. The longer we mull it over, the more they become disgraceful infidels and we become staunch defenders of honesty and truth.

We're a lot more lenient with our own lies, of course. Because most of us tell ourselves a hundred lies for every lie that is told to us, we've had a lot more practice forgiving ourselves. Why does a lie seem so much worse when we're on the receiving end? Is the lie itself so offensive? Or is it the fact that *we* were lied to? What was really violated—our moral standards or our pride?

Few people indeed belong on a pedestal of righteousness. Such lofty perches are always dangerous to self-esteem. If the cure for dishonesty begins at home, a first step may be to climb down from the pedestal. And a second may be to call a spade a spade. A lie is a lie is a lie, whether it's our own or someone else's. Whether we choose to forgive it or not depends on how badly our ego was bruised—not the fact that we were lied to. Hurt feelings don't entitle us to moral outrage.

It isn't fair to hold other people more accountable than I hold myself.

April 7

Let go and let God.
—Twelve Step Program Slogan

Like any other Twelve Step slogan, "Let go and let God" can be twisted to justify and support just about any wrong turn we decide to take. Indeed, to abuse the truth of a slogan is very much like turning an arrow so that it points away, not toward, a town. If we follow in that direction, we won't get where we were trying to go.

Basically, all this slogan means is that we should not take responsibility for outcomes over which we have no control. As so many have shared over so many years, we have either to "be" God or "let" God; we have to stop trying to force results.

But that doesn't mean we don't have *any* responsibility. We are still obliged to do everything we can to make the positive outcomes possible. It is not enough when we come to a roadblock to sit down, "turn it over," and wait for God's removal crew to come along and take care of the problem. The effort and the footwork are still on our own job ticket. It's only the *outcome* we have to let go.

Letting go means taking care of my own business, not abandoning it.

As he thinketh in his heart, so is he.
—Proverbs 28:7

"Read the Bible," said the country preacher to his little flock, "there are some mighty good things in that book." One of them is the quote above. The message is as clear and direct as it appears to be: Our thoughts define not only ourselves, but all expectations of what will become of our efforts and dreams.

Positive self-esteem is largely a matter of being grounded in positive thought. Many of us are only dimly aware of the constant dialogue going on in our heads. And even if we *hear* it, we often don't *listen* to it. Yet our habitual patterns of thinking are the very basis of our reality. Our thoughts dictate the quality of our lives.

One walks in the rain; another just gets wet. One prays; another just says prayers. One makes love; another takes hostages. The outward appearance of each behavior is the same, but the reality experienced within is totally different. The thinking behind the deed is what decides the matter. Are we shrinking back or pressing forward? Counting our losses or building our gains? Onlookers can't see the difference. Doing isn't being. Only the voice of the heart can tell us what's *really* going on behind the dancing mask of daily activity.

Positive thoughts translate into positive actions. How positive is the thinking that shapes my behavior?

April 9

If you keep your mind sufficiently open, people will throw a lot of rubbish into it.
—William A. Orton

There's a lot of difference between a mind that's willing to consider new ideas and a mind that claims *no* ideas as its own. But there are many who pride themselves, even base their self-esteem, on being open-minded when in fact they may lack the courage to take a stand. Whoever said that a mind should be open on both ends?

We aren't being flexible when we bend or suspend our own beliefs in favor of every new idea that blows by. We aren't being sophisticated when we listen without comment to ugly racist or sexist remarks. Judgment is a function of intelligence, and intelligence rejects as well as accepts.

Healthy openness means being willing to bounce new information off the body of information we've already tried and tested. No thinking adult is a blank slate. It's entirely appropriate to set up sensible boundaries around our own values and beliefs. "Who says so?" and "How does this fit?" are good questions to ask when testing new input. As always, integrity is defended by making wise choices.

The object of open-mindedness is *not* to let the wind whistle between my ears.

A person who is master of himself can end a sorrow as easily as he can invent a pleasure.
—Oscar Wilde

Words like *control*, *master*, and *take charge* appear again and again in literature that promotes self-esteem or any positive growth. These terms usually advise saddling some troubling emotion or putting a bit in the mouth of fear. When some impulse is running wild, we're taught to rein it in.

But restraint is not the only purpose of inner control. Taking charge has more upbeat consequences as well. If we can subdue fear, then so can we conjure up pleasure. If this control can diminish the power others have over us, can it not stoke up the power we have over ourselves? Once we can direct our own inner dialogue, we also get to decide how much fun we will have and which adventures we will choose. When we choose what shall stay and what shall go, a whole new world opens up to us.

To be a "master" of anything seems like heavy work leading to heavy responsibility. And it is. But mastery is also rewarding. What could be better than designing our own delights?

Anyone who can be a dungeon master can also be a circus master.

April 11

Nostalgia is a seductive liar.
—George Ball

Oh, for the good old days! In those long lost, golden times our self-esteem was sky high, life was sweet, and problems were few. If only we could return to the splendid days that were! Our lives would be just as happy and trouble-free as they used to be!

Hogwash. When we catch ourselves enshrining our yesterdays, we need to put on our glasses and take a clearer look backward. For all its remembered goodness, we will see that it was not all *that* good. We've forgotten all the hard knocks that won us the wisdom we have today. Forgotten, too, are the fears, jealousies, failures, and disappointments strewn among the glorious flowers of memory.

The days we have now are also good days. Flowers are growing. Music is playing. It's a wonderful thing to have happy memories. But we live in today and it is today that awaits our pleasure.

Self-esteem must be remade afresh each day, in the here and now.

One must not always think that feeling is everything.
—Gustave Flaubert

When self-esteem is the topic, feelings usually are the gauge. That is, most of us are only aware of positive self-esteem when our feelings tell us we have it. Most often, we let how we feel control our sense of who we are and how we are.

It can be most helpful to remember that feelings only face backward; they can only reflect what *was*. As important as it is to be in touch with our feelings, we must not let our feelings get us in a stranglehold. It is equally important to keep our feelings from making decisions that need to be made by our heads.

Self-esteem, of course, is made up of many things, only one of which is how we feel. Suppose we are trying hard to stick up for ourselves, to talk straight, to get started in a self-help group, open a savings account, or begin a weight-control program. But suppose we don't feel comfortable with the new behavior or don't feel like we are making enough progress. We *know* it's good but it doesn't *feel* good. The only thing to do at such a time is to keep right on moving the muscles. If self-esteem is to be a fact, it has to be more than just a feeling.

Feelings give me information, but rational thought must do the processing.

April 13

*Togetherness is a substitute sense of community,
a counterfeit communion.*

—Gabriel Vahanian

Some of us seek—no, demand—a suffocating degree of togetherness with the people we love best. Although we're far too mannerly to open a door without knocking, we think nothing of barging in on the lives of our grown children, for example. Although we'd never snoop in someone's purse, it never occurs to us that we're invading our friends' privacy when we insist that they "tell us everything."

Those of us who like to talk about how "close" or "inseparable" we are with others need to check out our motives. Does the togetherness we insist on meet the needs of the others, or just our own? Are we binding them to us out of love—which is liberating—or expectation and obligation—which is enslaving? Do we hold them so close because we love them so much, or because we feel so insecure and incomplete in ourselves?

Although we usually mean well, our trespassing on other people's personal space may be causing them discomfort and grief. Let's be very sure, before we latch on to others in a viselike grip of closeness, that their idea of loving behavior is the same as ours.

Even the "closest" people need spaces in their togetherness.

Those who know the least of others think the highest of themselves. —Charles Caleb Colton

Those of us who aren't vulnerable to chemical addictions often secretly feel superior to those of us who are. Although we're reluctant to admit it, we wrinkle our noses, raise our eyebrows, and shiver in genteel disgust at the addict's blatant loss of control. "Thank God it isn't me," we say in our heart of hearts as we tiptoe around the drunk slumped on the street, "I've got my problems, but at least they aren't *that* bad!"

Yet are we really so different? But for chemical invulnerability—an unmerited gift of fate—are we really better people? Are we as free as we think we are of ugliness and self-degradation? Do some of our toxic thoughts and behaviors not have a poisonous effect on ourselves and the people around us? Is sick in private so different from sick in public?

What of the vicious gossip? The remorseless liar? The selfishly indifferent parent? What of our compulsive eating or shopping or faultfinding? The fact is that chemical addiction is only *one* way to erode integrity; there are many others and most of us are familiar with them. There are more similarities than differences between us and our chemically addicted brothers and sisters.

Among the halt and the lame, there is little rationale for a sense of superiority.

April 15

Forewarned is forearmed.
—Benjamin Franklin

Many victims of depression, when searching for clues and patterns, find that their ailment is cyclical. For whatever reasons, at certain times of year, their spirits plummet to the ground like downed birds. Perhaps it's the anniversary of a parent's death, a business failure, or another sad time. Or perhaps it's related to the amount of sunlight available, or biorhythms, or brain chemistry.

Recognizing a predictable pattern can make a real difference. The ability to anticipate anything always puts a few more cards in our hand. It may not prevent the depression, but at least we won't be caught off guard.

If we know what's coming up, appropriate steps may be taken. Important appointments may be made for a later date, significant decisions may be worked out ahead of time or put off, perhaps something as simple as hiring more baby-sitting so we can have more free time may assist us in feeling better during a bad time.

When I fight *against* depression, I fight *for* self-esteem.

Becoming ill is the price you pay for driving your-self too hard.   —Gail Grenier Sweet

Low self-esteem doesn't always show itself as cringing passivity. Many overachievers are hounded by the need, rooted in low self-esteem, to push themselves beyond any reasonable effort. Even in recovery, such people may nearly drive themselves to ruin by relent-lessly practicing slowing down, taking it easy, and learning to enjoy. They work so hard at finding some enjoyment they get too tired to have any fun at all!

How can we learn to honor a self we're already abus-ing? If we were racehorse owners, we wouldn't dream of pushing our valuable animals so hard. "How much did you get accomplished?" is the wrong question for us. Instead, we should ask ourselves if we have hugged a friend, taken a walk, read a novel, or told a joke.

There is neither virtue nor valor in driving ourselves until we are ill. Utter exhaustion is the enemy of health and of self-esteem as well. We need to give ourselves at least as much consideration and care as we'd give a horse.

I deserve to relax and have fun.

April 17

The essence of being human is that one does not seek perfection. —George Orwell

The search for greater self-knowledge is much like an archaeological dig. The farther down we go, the more surprises we're likely to find. Some are more fun than others. Often, one of our less-pleasing discoveries is our skill in using acceptable words to name our unacceptable character flaws.

The quality we used to call perseverance, for example, may turn out to be plain old stubbornness once we clean it off and take a good look. Our compassion and generosity may look an awful lot like codependent enabling and our straightforwardness, like crass insensitivity. Of course, we realized we had flaws, but who guessed they would be so serious—or that so many of them would be the so-called "virtues" that we were proud of!

But we shouldn't be too discouraged by our character flaws. They're not evidence of our depravity, but of our humanity. Even the spiritual giants of this world are not perfect. Flawlessness is not a condition that applies to human beings. To identify a character flaw is like naming a disease after the lab results come in. The lab report doesn't *cause* the disease. It simply tells what it *is*, so a remedy can be prescribed.

I have to know what's hurting me if I want to fix it.

Reject your sense of injury and the injury itself disappears. —Marcus Aurelius Antonius

The old saying "Once burned, twice shy" doesn't tell the half of it. Some of us burn victims resolve that we'll never go near another fire for the rest of our lives. Rather than risk another scorching, we turn our backs on the warmth, the light, and the merry companionship offered by a blazing campfire on a chilly night.

We are victims of love gone wrong. Unlike others who wipe away their tears and go back to the party, we weren't just disappointed, but *devastated*, not just wounded, but *mortally* wounded. Our blood, when we were pierced by rejection, ran redder than anyone else's blood, our pain was more painful. So how could we be expected to take another chance, to try again?

Yet the fear of hurt can hurt us more than anything. And if we avoid injury by sitting on the bench, we miss out on the game. If a relationship crumbled in spite of our best efforts, then that relationship wasn't meant to be. A better possibility is out there waiting for us. But we'll only have the chance of finding it if we take off our bandages and get back in the game.

I am a lot more resilient than I think I am.

April 19

Be careful not to test the water with both feet.
—Charles Larsen

To put yourself in a lose-lose situation is to lose for sure. And when you lose often enough, self-esteem erodes. In striving for self-confidence, it is as important to know what *not* to do as what to do.

Many situations that look good on the surface may not really be good at all. Learning to test cautiously a situation, relationship, or new venture so as to minimize risk is a critical part of building self-esteem. Just because a proposition or a person *looks* good or *sounds* good does not mean he/she/it is genuine. We need to test it out without totally exposing ourselves before making a commitment. There's no insult in that to the other; sincerity is always subject to proof.

If mere words were facts, thousands of broke hustlers would be millionaires. Many are those who can make any deal sound too good to pass up. But the rosy picture can look quite different beneath the surface. It's just good sense to take your time, get references, check track records, before investing more than you can afford to lose.

A toe in the water before the headlong plunge will help me achieve and maintain my self-esteem.

*We are alive, and that is the only place we need
to be to start.* —J. Leeds

Our needs are much simpler than our wants. We may
want perfect flying weather and a detailed flight plan,
but insistence on ideal conditions may make the difference between staying or going. All we really *need* to
take off is to be alive.

No one is too beaten down, too old, or too anything
else to begin a self-improvement program. Willingness,
and willingness alone, is the total price of the ticket.
The next thing to do is to get rid of excess baggage—
like the notion that this or that condition must be met
before we begin. Once we take responsibility for where
we are and who we are, the only thing left is *here we
are!* Where else do we need to be?

Change is about process, and the improvement process has much more to do with our direction than our
starting place. If we're starting at 10 and going for 100,
or if we're starting at 1,000 and shooting for the strato-
sphere, we're still in process. It is the same infinite
journey for all of us. On this side of the grave, there
never will be a time when the journey toward completion is over. And that's not because we're so broken—
it's because the possibilities are so great.

Starting is all there is, so here I go!

April 21

*Nobody expects to find comfort and companion-
ability in reformers.* —Heywood Broun

When we can't find a perfect mate, some of us try to
make one. The recipe is simple, isn't it? All you need is
a diamond in the rough and a lot of elbow grease. Then
it's just a matter of polish, polish, polish! When we first
start out on such a project it seems so sensible, so
doable, and well—so *good* of us to go to so much trouble for somebody else!

But another person can't be a "project" any more
than he or she can be a pet. No healthy relationship
ever starts out as a salvage operation. We may say, "I
just want what's best for you," yet when we try to
re-create someone in our own image of perfection,
we're violating that person's integrity—and our own as
well. Eventually, although they may go along with our
meddling at first, our human projects get tired of our
one-upsmanship; they end up feeling resentful and we
end up feeling unappreciated.

Healthy self-esteem demands that we accept ourselves and other people for what they are. We don't
have the right to bully people into changing their habits and styles. To do so in the name of love demeans
them, us, and the concept of love itself.

**I'm not God and other people aren't lumps of
clay that need shaping up.**

Perpetual devotion to what a man calls his business is only to be sustained by perpetual neglect of many other things.

—Robert Louis Stevenson

As much as we hear workaholism decried, we hear even more compelling voices telling us that the fast track is the only place to be if we've got the right stuff to make it to the top. No pain, no gain is the motto that drives us to work through lunch. Go all out! is the battle cry that pushes us to produce by moonlight. To secure our place on the winning team, we may become afraid even to take a day off.

But constant work is as abnormal as constant sleep. Whatever the lopsided benefit, we violate our physical and spiritual need for rhythm, for ebb and flow, when we use up all our energy in one area of our lives. We deny human nature when we deny ourselves the rest and recreation we need to replenish our resources. And natural consequences occur when we deny human nature.

Exhaustion and emptiness are the inevitable result of chronic overwork. Any version of success that requires such dues is a counterfeit of the real thing. Shiny and seductive as the payoff may seem, dedication shouldn't cost us every waking moment. If it does, we need to think again about what makes a successful life. We need to stop looking for gold down there in the salt mines.

Work is a means to an end, not an end in itself.

April 23

The avenues in my neighborhood are Pride, Covetousness, and Lust; the cross streets are Anger, Gluttony, Envy and Sloth. I live over on Sloth, and the style on our street is to avoid the other thoroughfares. —John Chancellor

What do you think? Some of us have created a lot of awful messes through the years. We've committed some big, juicy sins that fill us with remorse and regret. Others of us have stayed out of trouble and kept our noses clean. Our records aren't full of black spots, but then they're not very full of anything. We haven't done much wrong because we haven't done much. Which of us is better off?

Both of us have work to do if we want to get more out of the future than we did out of the past. If we've done damage, our obvious task is to make whatever repairs we can, forgive ourselves, and start walking a straighter path. If we've hidden out in passive inactivity, venturing little and gaining less, we need to get out of the stands and onto the field. There's no virtue or joy in being a spectator of the game of life.

We can ruin our lives by omission as well as commission. What we *don't* do can often cause us more regret, in the long run, than the mistakes we make. Better to risk a wrong turn than to sit out our lives.

If I hang back, I will lose out.

Upon deciding, be quick to act.
—Maximilien Robespierre

Some gaps in the road can seem too broad for leaping. But if we can't get across them, we're stuck. All forward motion comes to a halt, and the journey toward self-realization is over. One of these gaps is the cavern that stands between decision and action.

After making a decision, a person is different. Whether you have decided to stay or leave, start or stop, risk or conserve, you have opted for change. Mentally, you have already done it. To fail to act on a well-considered decision is to invite confusion, double messages, and emotional chaos. With the loss of will, integrity is also lost.

Sometimes, because we're afraid to act, we won't even admit that, deep down, we've already made a decision. Perhaps, for example, we've completely withdrawn our spirits from a hated job or a dead marriage. By denying that we've already pulled out, we deny our own truth. This denial not only devastates our self-esteem, but it widens the gap between where we are now and our next destination. Sooner or later we're going to have to take the leap. Why not sooner?

Once made, an important decision will cause me trouble until I act on it.

April 25

What I'm dealing with is bad enough. I can't deal with worse right now. —Mary P.

Sometimes rallying cries like "Now or never!" are worse than useless. This is so when the situation we're facing is already, in its present form, draining every bit of energy we have. At this point to say, "All or nothing!" is to guarantee nothing.

Even well-intentioned friends may push us into thinking that some terribly difficult action must be launched *right now*. They may insist that we launch a mighty initiative, ready for not, *for our own good*. But only we can judge our own readiness or our own good.

The woman quoted above was telling her group that she was doing the best she could—today—with her chemically dependent son. She knew there was a crisis coming, that she would have to tell her boy he couldn't continue to use drugs and live under her roof at the same time. But that crisis was a "worse" she couldn't handle today. Right now it was all she could do to get to her meetings, build up her strength, and pray. She was wise to know that it's better not to shout "Do or die!" before you're ready to do.

Getting ready may be half the battle.

Nobody ever went to his deathbed wishing he'd spent more time at the office.

—Michael Josephson

Writing your own epitaph is a thought-provoking exercise at some personal growth workshops. What should our tombstones say? How do we want to be remembered? What mattered most to us in life? What legitimate claim can we make of our contribution to the world?

Participants in this exercise often begin with uneasy laughter and then start coming up with ways they would *not* like to be remembered. "Here lies Carla," one woman said in a flash of amused self-awareness, "she meant well." After that icebreaker, several others chipped in their own revealing self-characterizations. "He never missed a day of work," one man said with nearly as much pride as gentle self-mockery. More than a few people nodded and smiled in self-recognition.

The balance between work and play is crucial to our well-being. If we want our full share of joy in life, if we mean to honor the balanced values we profess, we would do well to meditate now rather than later on the legends we live by.

What do I most want to do or be before I run out of days?

April 27

The past is smoke. When necessary, blow it away.
—Ralph B. Binyen

It has often been said that our perceptions are like glasses that, once in place, affect and color all we see. That vision, of course, becomes our reality, our truth. But it is important to realize that most of our perceptions were forged in a fire that is now history. A fire long grown cold. What happened, happened, it can never be undone. However, there is no need to drag it through each day of our present life.

Most obstacles to enjoying a positive, gentle self-image are due to the negative lessons we learned long ago. Those lessons reinforce perfectionism; passivity; fear of intimacy; or feelings of unworthiness, love, or happiness. These are lessons of the past. As such, they are smoke. Not real anymore unless we allow them to be real.

Many a brave soul, trudging toward a better tomorrow, has come to learn how to deal with a "shame attack." That means recognizing that it is a flashback that can either blow away like dandelion seeds or take root in the present. We are the ones who must decide whether the power of the past will grow or go.

I *can* allow the ugly past to blow away. All it takes is the desire and the effort to let it go.

Friendships, like marriage, are dependent on avoiding the unforgivable.
—John D. MacDonald

Everybody knows that an ounce of prevention is worth a pound of cure. But perhaps we don't stop to consider how important this homely bit of folk wisdom may be to our personal relationships. Some words simply must never be spoken; some situations must never be allowed to occur. Our treasured relationships are just too valuable to handle carelessly.

Nothing is worth the unforgivable insult or betrayal. Far better for us to appear the coward and walk out the door if a confrontation is going out of control. Far wiser to shoot ourselves in the foot rather than pierce a friend's soft underbelly with an unhealable wound.

Occasional strain and friction are inevitable in any relationship. But we need loving relationships with our friends to support our self-esteem. When there is conflict, we may need to withdraw to protect their self-esteem as well as our own. At a later time, when tempers and tensions have cooled, we will both be glad of the self-restraint.

Sometimes retreat is the only way to win.

April 29

To know one's self, one should assert one's self.
—Albert Camus

There are times when a feeling of insignificance assails us. Very often this is a false perception that needs to be quickly banished. The truth is that we are more important than we sometimes think we are.

There is no reason not to be proud of the constructive things we have done. It is a mistake to minimize the successful completion of a task, the learning of a new skill, a good habit strengthened or a bad habit eliminated. Most of us have many, many worthwhile accomplishments, great and small, to feel good about. We are more worthwhile and attractive than we sometimes realize.

It often helps to advertise our achievements a bit, instead of always being so frank about our failures. This can be done without boasting. An honest recital of an accomplishment or a mention of a skill shows healthy self-esteem. It is not being "modest" when we shy away from asserting ourselves. We can't expect other people to continually reassure us of our worth if we're not willing to speak up for ourselves.

There's nothing wrong with tooting my own horn once in a while.

*Two things are bad for the heart—running uphill
and running down people.*

—Bernard Gimbel

Trashing others as a "harmless" form of amusement is a nasty habit. But it's common enough to prop ourselves up by putting other people down. No doubt it's the major sport in most workplaces. Unfortunately, people bashing is a sport that injures the self-esteem of everyone who plays it.

This is so for a couple of reasons. The first is the psychological axiom that the mind always moves toward its dominant thought. To run down people, we must first stoke our minds with negative thoughts. Those thoughts are then translated into cutting words. But the very act of inviting and hosting negative thoughts cuts into ourselves *first*. Before we even say a word, we've done damage.

The second reason we are hurt when we run people down is that we weaken any possibility of forming a bond of community with them. Self-esteem is based on membership in a community of some sort. It's fostered by people who care. People we can count on. People whose smiles tell us they are glad to see us. Habitually running people down makes us poor, untrustworthy candidates for membership in such a community.

Far better for health, mental as well as spiritual, to grow from the exercise of lifting others up!

Healthy people don't make sport of other people's flaws.

May 1

There is no such thing as absolute value in this world. You can only estimate what a thing is worth to you. —Charles Dudley Warner

Self-esteem is not magic. It is not a mysterious cosmic phenomenon that may or may come to be. Self-esteem is a product. The steps it takes to build self-esteem are not so different from the steps it takes to build anything else—from model airplanes to spaceships. First you have to understand the basic anatomy of what you are trying to construct. Once you grasp that, the most important part of the project is already done.

If *esteem* is the value we place on something then *self*-esteem, in its simplest terms, is the value we place on ourselves. Who we think we are determines how much we think we're worth. So how do we define ourselves? We need to scrutinize our self-definitions if we want to build self-esteem. If we work off of plans for a model airplane, we're not going to end up with a spaceship.

Suppose we wear an apron at work instead of a pinstripe suit. Do we value costumes so much that we devalue respectable work? We are not our costumes. Suppose we have spent some time in jail. Must we forever define ourselves that way—or may we now think of ourselves as free citizens getting on with our lives? "Less than" definitions must be retranslated if we want to feel good about ourselves. Self-esteem is a product of positives.

Negative self-definitions lay a weak foundation for growth.

If an ass goes travelling, he'll not come back a horse.
—Thomas Fuller

People who've already worn out shoes on the recovery path have much to tell us tenderfoots about what lies ahead. "Keep on coming!" they might say. "The hills aren't too steep and you can wade across the river!" And some of their messages are warnings: "Forget about detours. They'll only waste your time and get you lost." They caution us against wandering off in the wrong direction.

One of the ways newly recovering people tend to wander off is by "taking a geographical." This means looking in a different place for what we are too blind to see in our own backyards. It means moving—not to *get* somewhere, but to *get away* from somewhere. When we seek a geographical cure, we forget that the patient comes right along with us. *Where* we are isn't going to transform who we are into something we're not. Self-esteem isn't out there waiting for us in another town or state.

To be sure, there are times when a big move is necessary. But in the early days of recovery when self-esteem is shaky, we're usually wise to stick to the territory we know. We need to avoid detours, side trips, and meandering of any kind. We have more important things to think about than whether the sky is sunnier someplace else.

Following the advice of proven leaders can save me many a wrong turn.

May 3

God respects me when I work, but he loves me when I sing. —Thai Proverb

What image does the word *God* conjure up? A child may think of a beneficent, white-bearded, grandfatherly being who helps find lost dogs and creates sunshine for picnics. A teenager may envision a stern judge of adolescent sexual adventures. Weary adults, if they think about God at all, may have an exacting "boss" figure in mind. More of an eagle-eye overseer than anything else.

As Ultimate Authority, the God that hovers in our subconscious may well be a composite of every authority figure we ever knew—school principal, policeman, father, job reviewer. Perhaps that's why so many of us pay homage to that demanding God with unending work. We step lively to stay ahead of that report card, that evaluation, that's sure to be coming down.

In the light of recovery, however, we come to see a different picture. As our own self-image improves, so does our image of God become more loving. The critical taskmaster we once needed to justify our workaholism goes off on a permanent vacation. As we learn to lighten up on ourselves, we find a new God who values serenity more than sweat.

Reconsidering God is an important part of recovery.

He was afraid, but he never quit.
—David R.

David was talking with his friends about the death of his dearly beloved son, who had died of cancer at age twenty-nine. David called his son a "courageous angel." Courageous, because even though the young man died a small piece at a time, he never quit in his search for God. And by finding God, he found serenity. "My son was afraid, so terribly afraid," David said, "but he never quit. And finally, shortly before he died, he found what he was looking for. When he died, his eyes were bathed in a peaceful light."

David said his son was an angel because angels tell us of God. The grieving father told of how, before his son was born, he was an insensitive, self-centered man who was furious at the thought of being inconvenienced by a child. Yet the arrival of that child melted, softened, restructured his whole personality. "Like all angels," David said tearfully, "he reflected the face of God. I have never been estranged from that face since."

Fortunately, most of us do not need to lose a loved one to find peace, serenity, and a deeper understanding of what's important in life. All through our lives there are opportunities for spiritual awareness and growth. Angels abound if we are but open to recognize them.

Love of others can introduce me to the love of God.

May 5

*We know that habits are in control, the question
is are they friend or foe?* —M. C. Grimmond

Many of us who don't suffer from clinical depression
trudge through life in a depressive fog. Everything
seems to take too much energy. Nothing seems exciting or interesting. Sunny days seem like nothing more
than a prelude to the next rainstorm. And of course our
self-esteem sinks as low as our spirits do.

Although a depressive attitude about life can have
deeper causes, often it is simply habit. Just another bad
habit like frowning or finger drumming. If we didn't
grow up around positive people, the chances are good
that we learned to describe the world and everything
in it in negative terms. We may have been taught to
automatically distrust people and their intentions,
which put a hard spin on all of our days.

Healing a habitually heavy heart can begin by simply
directing our attention to everything positive that is
going on around us, by counting our blessings, and by
learning to say "thank you" for all that is.

Cheerfulness is as habitual as gloominess.

The one means that wins the easiest victory over reason: terror and force.   —Adolf Hitler

Human beings are both wonderfully and awfully adaptable!

Over time, people who put up with bullying come to tolerate and then accept this sad situation. They become so accustomed to intimidation, they no longer even recognize it for what it is—a forfeit of their basic human rights. Obviously, people who live under these circumstances have only two chances for self-esteem: slim and none.

Those of us who live with people who brutalize us emotionally or physically must get honest with ourselves about what's going on before we do anything else. We need to admit, even to ourselves, that we live under spirit-crushing conditions. Facing the facts brings us one step closer to achieving some improvement.

People who are constantly taunted, teased, insulted, or threatened, let alone physically abused, have every right to reclaim the basic human right to happiness they somehow let slip away. There is hope and help available. There is every reason to count on better days ahead if today we begin to tell the truth. Our situation is only hopeless if we deny that it exists.

I am too valuable a person to bow down in submission.

May 7

Allow me to assure you that suspicion and jealousy never did help any man in any situation.
—Abraham Lincoln

Expecting the worst is second nature for some of us. That's why it's so easy for us to expect negative motives in others. But it's just as reasonable to expect that other people are as well intentioned as we are. Both mental outlooks are just habits born of practice.

Faith in human nature bolsters our faith in our own possibilities. A generalized suspicion and distrust of other people creates enemies where no enemies exist. Why give in to that kind of defensive thinking? Why not give others the benefit of the doubt?

Abraham Lincoln was asked why he tried to make friends with his enemies, when he should be trying to destroy them. Lincoln replied that he *was* destroying his enemies when he made them his friends. This is a truth well worth contemplating, as we learn to make friends with ourselves.

I must look for the good in others, if I want to find it in myself.

Children will not remember you for the material things you provided but for the feeling that you cherished them. —Gail Grenier Sweet

More than one person's self-esteem has been dampened because, in comparing ourselves with other providing parents, we come up short. In a consumer society, value and love are often equated with "how much," "how often," and "how expensive."

Yet the deeper truth is that material things rust and are soon put aside and forgotten. What abides are the memories of being loved. These precious recollections are the ones that we tuck away in the treasure box of our minds. We hang on to the times when we were made to feel special.

Consider your own memories. Which are the sweetest? Chances are they have little to do with *things* unless those things were genuine symbols of true caring. It's much more likely that they had to do with a special nickname, a shared secret, a time when a parent was truly there for you. Our favorite Christmas or birthday memories are rarely about the things we received, but the warmth of caring behind the giving.

Gifts from my heart are more valuable than gifts from my pocket.

May 9

The fox condemns the trap, not himself.
—William Blake

When the subject of rationalizations comes up, many of us say "Right, I know all about that." Superficially, we well may—but it isn't the superficial dimension that gets us into trouble. Take blaming, for example. On the face of it, blaming is just another obvious cop-out. But the real problem with blaming isn't the finger pointing itself, it's the pattern it sets up.

Blaming says, "It's not my fault. I had no choice. It was done to me." What happens when this is our habitual response to harmful situations? Are we not also saying, "Because I was the victim this time, there may well be a next time. And I won't be responsible for that, either."

Thus we set up an easy out for our tendency to stay in abusive situations, say yes, when we mean no; stay home "sick," when we are really just lazy. Most of the time we *do* contribute to situations that diminish our self-esteem. It might not be easy, but we *could* assert ourselves, turn things around, if we really want to. The problem with rationalizations is that they aren't honest, and over time they make us dishonest people.

Today I take responsibility for my own choices.

You can't shake hands with a closed fist.
—Indira Gandhi

Are you one who keeps a list? Many of us take very careful count of all that has been lost. With the scrupulous exactitude of resentment, we tally up every wrong that was done to us, every privilege or pleasure that we were denied, every hardship or obstacle that blocked our way. Because we make such an effort to record everything, our list grows and grows with each passing year. And the longer it gets, the better we like it. Justifying resentments can be mighty satisfying.

The problem is that list making keeps us fixated at the point of our losses. It nails us to the past, forever victimized, forever on the lookout for more of the same.

Resentment closes the hand to a fist. How can a fist reach out in friendship or reconciliation? How can a fist receive love or any other gift? A fist may be fine for clutching a grubby little pencil and slashing away at a yellowing old score card. But it closes off too many good things. Nobody ever *gave* anything to a fist.

Most of the items on our list may be factual. Some may even be criminal. But what real purpose is served—and what price paid—by compiling a catalog of misery? Wouldn't it be better to let that stuff go? Bad enough that those things happened at all; worse yet that we're still keeping them alive.

I can't hang on to the old and reach out for the new at the same time.

May 11

The greatest and most important problems of life are fundamentally insoluble. They can never be solved, but only outgrown. —Carl Jung

The only way to deal with certain problems is by leaving them alone. In these situations we have to live with "what is" for a while and just wait. Like it or not, our mental health may depend on it.

Every fiber of our being may resist this wisdom. Our can-do culture tells us there is always something that must be *done*, and done immediately! We must attack. Fix it. Beat it to death. Do something.

Naturally, we often bring this aggressive mentality to matters affecting self-esteem. Sometimes vigorous action is indeed called for. But with many problems, there is simply no way to force a solution. Learning when to push and when to hold back can save us many heartaches.

How many late bloomers are there among us who simply outgrew their wallflower tendencies? Time took care of it. Many times an irritating coworker is transferred to another office or a nasty neighbor moves away. In time, without help from our plots and schemes, the maddening problem solved itself. In other situations it is just time and the maturity that comes with time, that turns on the light, answers the riddle, or tames some wild impulse.

Waiting is not only a legitimate option but sometimes my only option.

*The maxim "Nothing avails but perfection," may
be spelled "Paralysis."* —Winston Churchill

People are more than just the sum of their parts. When
we think of ourselves or others as *just* a mind, *just* a
body, or *just* a bundle of emotions, we miss the whole
person. In truth, we can miss the forest for our close
examination of the trees.

Self-esteem is like that. We may *hate* our noses or our
hot tempers or our pessimism, but the bottom line is
how we feel about ourselves as *people*, not our dis-
sected parts. While each part affects the whole, it's the
big picture that counts. If we can't look beyond our
irritating shyness or our excessive weight, we're standing up too close to see what's going on.

By all means, take whatever action you can against a
troubling flaw. Many have lifted a sagging self-esteem
by getting their bodies in shape or getting counseling
to tame a negative emotional impulse. But it is always
a mistake to hinge our self-esteem on the few clumsy
brushstrokes in an otherwise lovely portrait.

**Self-criticism robs me of more joy than criticism
from others.**

May 13

The value of persistent prayer is not that He will hear us, but that we will finally hear Him.
—William McGill

Praying is our way of communicating with God, our way of keeping up our end of the relationship. Because words aren't the glue that holds any relationship together, praying isn't always the same thing as saying prayers. Praying is "being there." It isn't mostly talking—it's mostly listening.

Any belief in a loving Higher Power, a "God as you understand him," is a valuable asset to our self-esteem. Partly this is because, having no God, we must *become* God—the ultimate source of our own power. Whose self-image can rise to that? It doesn't take us long in life to find *many* things that are beyond our power even to nudge, let alone control.

Surely a loving God wants to lead us toward greater health and happiness. After all, this is what *we* want for the people we love; would God want less for us? But to be led we must listen. Blasting the airways with prayers may often be less appropriate than taking time out to relax and listen.

The teacher will appear when the student is ready.

Between saying and doing many a pair of shoes
are worn out.   —Italian Proverb

Vacillation throws a damp blanket on the fire of success and, therefore, on self-esteem. Should I or shouldn't I? Good idea or bad idea? Now or later? Thinking about our options is one thing, but it's quite possible to take so long deciding that some of our options run out! Sometimes that's just what we were hoping for; when the *either* is removed, we'll have to settle for the *or*. The decision will be made for us.

At other times, though, we know very well which way we should go. Our hearts, minds, insights, and instincts are powerfully pushing us in a certain direction. These are the times we must force our feet to move where the rest of us is leaning.

Is there an opportunity that should be pursued? A move that should be made? A word that needs to be spoken, a hand clasped? Sometimes we have to move the muscles whether we *feel* ready or not. If we hide in a corner for fear of taking action, our self-esteem will be crouching right down there with us.

As hard as it may be to get started, action brings relief.

May 15

Going as we do by faith and not by sight, we are full of confidence. —2 Cor. 5:7

No one has such perfect foresight always to see what lies ahead, let alone around the corner. In spite of all our evidence and experience, we simply don't know what outcomes will come to pass. Too much can happen between now and then; some of these twists and turns are beyond imagining. At times the path ahead is so murky we can only travel by the light of faith.

Who can know how a confrontation with a problematic family member will come out? Yet the good of all demands that confrontation. Will a bold new venture prove to be wise or foolhardy? But we've made a decision and it must be tried. Is there any guarantee that we'll quickly find a healthy new relationship if we end a bad marriage? No, but our self-worth demands that we take the leap.

If we always waited until we could see the path, many a life-enhancing journey would never have started. We'd still be hoping for the light to improve rather than actively improving our own lives. Sometimes we just have to strike out in the dark. If we believe what we are doing is right, that faith will give us all the light we need.

Faith is a beacon that nonbelievers must do without.

Forgiveness or regret are the only choices we have.
—Ron Palmer

Mention skills and we usually think of things like playing a musical instrument, dancing, or cooking. We seldom think of things like *attitudes* that, in sum, equal self-esteem. But attitudes are skills. Perhaps one of the least mentioned is the skill of forgiveness.

There are many unfairnesses to forgive in this unfair world. Life often is frustrating and full of disappointments. At times there are genuine insults and traumatic absurdities that befall us. All are capable of destroying our self-esteem if we don't learn to become peacemakers rather than grudge-holders.

The skill of forgiveness, like any skill, must be practiced daily. An attitude of acceptance, sailing along on the greased rails of habit, enables us to forgive life for not being what we wanted it to be. We spare ourselves much regret when we come to peaceful terms with our own personal histories. If we didn't live up to our fondest expectations, that isn't so bad. Even those who have done us legitimate harm can be forgiven once we realize that *not* forgiving only prolongs the injury.

Forgiveness unties the knot that binds me to resentment and regret.

May 17

*Our unconscious is like a vast subterranean fac-
tory with intricate machinery that is never idle,
where work goes on day and night from the time
we are born until the moment of our death.*
—James Harvey Robinson

Not only do we all talk to ourselves, but we do it all the
time. On a deeper level of consciousness than "Where
did I put my glasses?" we ask and answer questions,
weigh information, and test different opinions. Our
self-talk reinforces our reality to the extent that our
entire self-concept and the esteem, or lack thereof, that
flows from that concept is continuously re-created.

Affirmations are simply statements of positive truth.
When we "do" affirmations, we take charge of that
critical inner dialogue. By telling ourselves, "I am worthy even when I make a mistake," we legitimize that
valid opinion whether or not we "feel" worthy at that
moment. If we face ourselves in the mirror and say, "I
am a lovable, competent person " we might hear an
inner voice saying, "Who are you kidding?" But just
the verbal expression of the positive self-definition en-
ters an authoritative new voice into the inner dialogue.

Someone has said that affirmations are the quickest,
least-bloody form of "brain surgery" ever devised. Of
all the tools for self-rescue, what could be simpler or
easier to use than affirmations?

**I will use affirmations to reinforce realities that I
know but don't yet feel.**

All people like us are We,
And everyone else is They.
—Rudyard Kipling

Friends and family may not always be as supportive as we'd like them to be. Especially about group sharing. They may fear we're "talking about them" or "airing dirty laundry in public." The very idea that we identify ourselves as "recovering" people may well make them anxious, defensive, or critical.

Those who have not yet discovered the wonderful advantages of group support may see us, those who are involved in groups, as "crazy" or "in the hands of some cult." There are personal implications, after all, when a family member or close friend admits a need, a lack, or a failing. Fear can make them frantic that they may also have a problem or shortcoming that we, the groupies, would just love to get a hold of. So threatened, they may try to tease or harass us into staying away from our groups.

In such situations, we need to stand fast. It is not true that they can handle their own problems and we can't. They're not healthier or stronger than we are. The only difference between people in groups and people who aren't is that people in groups are doing something about their problems and the others aren't. The difference is not in who is sick and who is well, but in who is taking responsibility for their lives and who is not.

All human beings share the same living problems.

May 19

Wisdom: *sagacity, prudence, common sense.*
—*The American College Dictionary*

There is no virtue in being foolhardy. Calculated risk is one thing, but careless risk is something else entirely. All growth requires an element of risk, of course, because growth means going where we have not been before. When we venture into new territory, it is always risky.

Most of us know that building self-esteem requires doing new things, trying new ventures, striking out in new territory—in other words, taking risks. But let us beware of jumping into hopeless situations and calling those suicide leaps "risks." Suicides are not risks. They are certain death.

If we have learned time and time again that a certain person or situation leaves us spiritually deflated, we need to stay away. Why keep going back? How many times do we have to lose before we recognize a bad bet?

If the odds of winning are too low, a risk is not acceptable.

Everybody is ignorant, only on different subjects.
—Will Rogers

Our ignorance of various subjects is nothing to be ashamed of. Usually, an area of total ignorance has to do with lack of exposure and experience. Or it may simply have to do with lack of interest. But in any case it's a sign of immaturity when we try to hide our ignorance or pretend to know something that, in truth, we don't even *want* to know. After all, ignorance about something isn't stupidity; it's simply a lack of knowledge in a certain area.

We'd be a lot less embarrassed about our pockets of ignorance if we realized that everybody else is in the same boat. Why do we imagine that *we're* the only ones who can't program a VCR or assemble a bicycle? If there's something we *want* to learn, we can take a class or study at home. But we shouldn't be intimidated by our imaginings: Plenty of well-educated, sophisticated people couldn't change a tire or make lump-free gravy if their lives depended on it!

In building self-esteem, ignorance of a nonvital subject is only dangerous when it teams up with arrogance or pretense. This deadly duo—one that makes us angry and defensive lest our ignorance be exposed, the other that turns its back on truth—handicaps our better selves.

Few people are as well rounded as I imagine most people to be.

May 21

Dear friend, theory is all grey,
And the golden tree of life is green.
—Goethe

Marcus, a gifted psychologist, is also a full professor at a major state university. For twenty-five years he has studied, taught, and written about the workings of the human psyche. Few experts are as well grounded or up to date in their field as Marcus is.

Yet Marcus's own life is in conflict. His stomach tells him so. In spite of all his credentials and qualifications, he has long-term, gut-level issues that aren't relieved by research or study. For all his knowledge, he still stews in a cauldron of unresolved anger. Marcus knows enough to write a book *about* repressed anger and its effects, but *his* repressed anger continues to be a mysterious source of misery.

If life were a theory, Marcus's analytical skills could certainly be used to untie his own knots. But life isn't a theory, and principles aren't the same thing as practices. Until Marcus the man, not Marcus the professor, begins to *personally* apply what he knows in theory, his knowledge will do his students a lot more good than it will him. Knowing isn't doing, and it's doing that makes the difference.

I realize that healthy living has more to do with behavior than theory.

*It is easy to live for others. Everybody does. I call
on you to live for yourselves.*
—Ralph Waldo Emerson

Selfishness, of course, is not conducive to healthy self-esteem. The point is that unless we first take care of our own business we will have nothing of value to give anyone else.

Selflessness can be a superficial hiding place. It is easy to live for others, to get involved in their lives, to endlessly ruminate on what is wrong with them, and what they need to do to improve their lot. But always and endlessly dwelling on others doesn't leave us much time to "look to our own houses." If our energies are always visiting, who's minding the store at home?

All real advances in self-esteem are made when we dare to deal with ourselves. Other people's issues aren't our affair. The real question is, what are ours? What are our own personal black clouds that keep the sun of self-esteem from shining from our lives? What character defects are making us want to run away from ourselves? What are our fears, insecurities, jealousies? These weeds must be rooted out if our garden is to grow.

Other people's battles are not mine to fight.

May 23

*The world is full of trickery. But let this not blind
you to what virtue there is.*

—"The Desiderata"

Self-esteem is easily starved out by chronic suspiciousness. This sour-spirited attitude would have us see
only what is false and deceitful about the world. It
blinds the soul from any vision of beauty or perception
of virtue—whether within or without. Self-esteem cannot grow in such toxic surroundings.

While it is true that "the world is full of trickery," it
is equally true that virtue abounds. And virtue has a
powerful influence on our self-esteem if we aren't too
closed off to appreciate it.

To overly concentrate on the world's deceit has us
constantly imputing false, shoddy motives to everyone
we see or any activity we take notice of. All preachers
become thieves; altruism anywhere is only someone
working an angle; innocence is disguised guilt; giving
is for tax purposes only; love is an illusion. Such pathological distrust must be challenged if we are to make
any progress.

The world is only as dark as the glasses I wear.

*Facts are stubborn things; and whatever may be
our wishes, our inclinations, or the dictates of
our passions, they cannot alter the state of facts
and evidence.*   —John Adams

Those of us who have chemically addicted loved ones
are often devastated by unrealistic expectations. One
of the greatest of these is expecting sane, rational, trustworthy behavior from those who may well not have it
to give.

Drug addiction is a form of insanity—perhaps not
the commitable kind, but it is still a disease that ren-
ders the victim incapable of functioning within the
boundaries of what most would call normal. Until recovery begins, the addict is subject to a bewildering
assortment of delusions, denials, manipulations, and
subterfuges of every sort imaginable. In short, addicts
who are still drinking or using are incapable of functioning in responsible relationships.

All the wishing in the world won't change a thing
until the drug use stops. When we expect anything
more from a nonrecovering addict, we set ourselves up
for heartbreak. Lest our love become madness and our
faith become obstinacy, we should remember that illness is illness. Wishful thinking doesn't cure diabetes
or pneumonia either.

**I must look among the healthy for healthy rela-
tionships.**

May 25

Man is a slow, sloppy, and brilliant thinker; the machine is fast, accurate, and stupid.
—William M. Kelly

Speed is what we like. Breakfast in New York, lunch in Paris, dinner in London—pretty dazzling, isn't it? Today's lightning-quick computers are sure to be tomorrow's slowpokes. More must always be done and it must be done sooner. We have to hurry up and find answers to important questions about cancer, world hunger, and many other critical issues. Faster—always faster.

Speedy calculations have indeed solved many problems and no doubt will solve many more. How wonderful to save lives by saving time! How marvelous to summon a world of information by just touching a keyboard! Yet we have to be careful about our love affair with speed. Speed isn't sacred. In some areas of life, going too fast may be part of the problem.

Peace of mind is often found behind a long stretch of Slow and Stop signs. Accustomed as we are to acceleration, we have to give our hearts and spirits time to reflect, wonder, dream, grieve, rejoice. How can a reflection be rushed? We don't dream on a tight schedule or grieve if we have some extra time. Human processes go at their own time and pace. *We* are not our machines. If we want to be fully human, we have to give ourselves the privilege of taking our time.

Faster isn't always better.

Nobody loves life like an old man.
—Sophocles

We don't have to be elderly to know that we are growing older. Long before it seems believable, we begin to notice that we can't see as well, stay up as late at night, or eat the same rich foods. Just yesterday we had none of those problems! And now there seems to be an increase of memories; yesterday becomes more dear. All these changes can make us nervous and apprehensive.

Self-esteem is often a casualty in this process called aging. If we peg all value on the things of youth, then, when youth dissipates, our self-esteem will, too. But it need not be so. A retired nun recently said, "My retirement offers me a golden opportunity to enrich my life. It gives me time to treasure every moment. Now I can read and think and write letters as much as I like. I have the time I need to embrace infirmity as my body gradually diminishes."

Like our youth, the quality of our old age is largely up to us. If it provides the leisure to cultivate an ever-growing intimacy with God, ourselves, and others, it can hardly be all bad. If with the wear and tear of the years we also get wisdom, we needn't be so afraid to be old.

Every stage of my life offers new opportunities.

May 27

*Avoid loud and aggressive persons, they are vex-
ations to the spirit.* —"The Desiderata"

In striving to achieve any objective, knowing what *not*
to do is just as important as knowing what to do. Before we can learn to fly, for example, we must learn
how to keep the boulders out of our pockets. It would
be difficult to think of any endeavor this truth applies
to more than building or maintaining positive self-
esteem.

Perhaps we don't need to be told that it's hard to be
around "loud and aggressive persons." We already
find these people far worse than mere "vexations to
the spirit"—they are downright killers of the spirit.
Yet, because we're trying to be good sports, perhaps,
we don't actually do what it takes to keep these people
at a distance.

But some people and places are really poisonous. If
we choose to get close to them we can actually get sick.
These people and places leave us depressed and beat
up. When we rub up against them, we come away
dirtied. What we rub up against, rubs off. There is no
reason good enough to justify keeping such dangerous
company.

**I not only have the right, but the duty, to avoid
spirit killers.**

Prayer begins where our power ends.
—Rabbi Abraham Heschel

We need prayer. That is a constant. The reason, as experienced by millions of people, is that the hurdles and obstacles we must overcome are sometimes too great for us to deal with alone. It follows then that if the rock needs to be moved, and we can't move it by ourselves, there is only one thing to do. Get help.

Prayer is the act of reaching out for power that is greater than our own. Much like turning on a light switch, or jacking up a broken-down car, praying allows us to do our work better. So much of personal reconstruction, at least at the beginning, involves clearing old boulderlike thinking habits from the building site.

Fear of rejection or failure, difficulty in learning to feel or express feelings, undesirable habits that are as deeply etched as the lines on an elderly face—all must be confronted. A thousand times, they may have been looked at, acknowledged and then backed away from. Unmoved, they remain in place, blocking our path, waiting for us to ask the help of God as we understand him.

My power is not sufficient. I will not deny my need of help.

May 29

There is one quality more important than "know how." This is "know what" by which we determine not only how to accomplish our purposes, but what our purposes are to be.

—Norbert Wiener

Outstanding achievements, whether they be in science, art, education, or sports, fill us with awe and admiration. Before the breakthrough was made, we know there was a daring dream, mental dedication, and usually plenty of drudgery. Before the public acclaim, there was often private pain and discouragement. Achievers deserve their rewards.

But big-time, nationally televised achievement isn't the only game in town. And outside goals aren't the only targets worth shooting at. Chasing headlines, as a matter of fact, can be soul killing. Those kinds of pursuits are dogged by high-pressure problems and pitfalls that most of us will never have to worry about. Too many uncontrollable obstacles!

Character development, on the other hand, is an achievement that also takes daring and dedication. Unlike the pursuit of outside goals, however, this project is well within our control. And the reward of blossoming self-esteem is better and longer-lasting than any headline or new world record. The *how* of all achievement is the same; it's only the *what* that varies.

My inner victories have richer rewards than any outer victory.

Great God, I ask thee for no meaner pelf,
Than that I may not disappoint myself.
—Henry David Thoreau

Impulsive people act before they think, so they consequently have to "undo" a lot of what they've done. Counting to ten *beforehand* is still an excellent, if child-like, practice. We need to learn to pause a bit and think things through. If we always took that simple step before we spoke cruel words, raised our hand in anger, or made a rash decision, we'd have a lot less apologizing to do.

We could all come up with many instances when others have disappointed us. But how many times have we disappointed ourselves by impulsively, and inappropriately, lashing out? Most of us can think of many. We spanked a child, we were rude to a store clerk, we stomped out of the house over a silly point of pride. None of these overresponses was necessary or fruitful. We just didn't stop to think.

Improving our self-esteem requires that we work to control ourselves and monitor our actions. This involves avoiding impulsive mistakes that hurt others and consequently make us ashamed of ourselves. The more we practice the long pause, the better we'll get at it. As uncomfortable as it may feel at first, constantly apologizing is even worse!

My impulsiveness fades as I grow in serenity.

May 31

Most men are in a coma when at rest and mad when they act.   —Epicurus

In the remark above, this ancient Greek was counseling a kind of moderation that was apparently as rare in his time as it is in ours. Some things never change. Still today, nothing very good comes from excess in either direction.

So how do we keep rest from being "coma" and activity from being "mad"? How do we find and maintain a healthy balance? Only by consistently paying attention, reflecting, and thinking through some of the whys and wherefores of our lives. That's how we come up with sensible, valid reasons for deciding whether rest or action is appropriate in a given situation.

Many, seemingly mysterious questions about self-esteem have answers that can be understood. Questions like "Why does my self-esteem seem high at home but low at work?" "Why do some people have such a depressing effect on me?" "How do I get going again after I've had a setback?" aren't really all that difficult. Not unless we're dozing or running around in circles. If we can find the balance to sit quietly and think, most of our answers will come to us.

Good judgment is a result of calm deliberation, not frantic activity.

Wherever you go, there you are.
—Earnie Larsen

Oh, to just escape and get away from it all! Negative relationships, problems at work, unresolved issues at home, bantering self-talk, unmet challenges. And these are just a few of the demanding situations we live with day in and day out. No wonder we want to run away!

But before we change our name and start over again someplace else, we'd better think about the common denominator in all our problems. At least in part, most of those thorny situations have a lot more to do with us than they do with "them." Our unfair boss doesn't know our irritating neighbor, and neither of them knows our nagging mother-in-law. The only common element in all those relational problems seems to be *us.*

Resolving the issues that face us almost always means changing something in ourselves. Much of the hurt that stems from all of them is self-inflicted, whether actively or passively. Even if we ran from those situations, we would likely re-create them in a new setting. When even a part of the problem is us, the solution is ours as well. We can't run far enough to escape ourselves.

Who will I see in the mirror once I get "there"?

June 2

We find great things are made of little things
And little things go lessening till at last
Comes God behind them.

—Robert Browning

In this age of overhyped extravaganzas, we tend to undervalue anything small. "If it isn't spectacular," the popular culture tells us, "it must be insignificant." But real life is quite a different proposition from the slick imitations of life we see all around us. Don't be fooled.

Small gains count. When we can accept that, we give our self-image a dignity and a value it didn't have before. Rather than see ourselves as falling short of some theatrical ideal, we can see ourselves as steady climbers making real progress on a steep hill that was not created in Hollywood. Being real, most of our personal dramas are not big productions. They don't draw a crowd or put our pictures in the papers. But that doesn't mean they don't deserve notice.

We don't have to lose seventy-five pounds to give ourselves a hand; seven pounds is a worthy accomplishment. We don't have to run a marathon, let alone win it. If we got off the couch and walked around the block three evenings in a row, we're on our way to fitness. If we've made *any* progress in the right direction, something significant has happened and credit is due.

Public acclaim isn't necessary for private achievement.

No one has time; we have to make time.
—James Rhoen

If self-esteem can be considered a work of art, then, like all great works of art, the time it takes to create it is well worth it. The problem with many of us is that time is the last thing we seem to have to contribute to any enterprise.

Time, however, is far more a question of priorities than of amounts. If someone has "run out of time" and then finds that her child has been hurt—or that she has won a large cash prize if only she can get to a phone in time to call in and collect—all of a sudden time is "found." Time can always be found if the desire is great enough.

So it is with finding the time to do the things that add to our self-esteem. If the wish is strong enough, the time will appear. Time to take a daily walk, or to do daily reading; time to call a friend or write in a journal; time to attend a weekly meeting or do some important volunteer work.

Having the time may well not be the issue. Making the time to build my self-esteem may be.

June 4

*Nothing on earth consumes a man more quickly
than the passion of resentment.*
—Friedrich Nietzsche

Of all the emotions, unleashed anger and resentment
shout the loudest for attention. When either is bellow-
ing, any other thought or behavior quickly runs for
cover. That's why it's important to know what these
booming voices are saying. The answer is crucial in our
pursuit of positive self-esteem.

Like a raging fever, raging anger is a messenger telling us that something is wrong. The tendency, of
course, is to strike out or blow off steam in some other
way. To do anything that will provide relief *right now*.
But anger is really a red flag of warning that's meant to
make us turn around before we go too far in some
dangerous direction. Anger is a needed service, as is its
simmering sidekick, resentment.

When we learn to get the message, we can make
short work of raging and stewing and turn our energies on the unfinished business that is causing all that
misery. Serenity may well depend on using these con-
suming emotions as stepping-stones rather than roadblocks.

**Uninvestigated anger and resentment halt my
forward progress.**

Hope is a risk that we must run.
—George Bernanos

"Where there's life there's hope" is certainly true, but the reverse is an even more valuable truth: "Where there's hope, there's life."

Despair can seem the only realistic response to problems that are too deeply rooted or long-standing. When all our efforts have been mocked, all of our prayers seemingly unanswered, we may feel like fools to keep on clinging to the tattered little shred of hope we still have in our hearts. But as long as our hope is alive, so are we.

An attitude of hopelessness is more of a problem than any problem. Is the steadfast parent who hopes for an addicted child's recovery better or worse off than the parent who has given up? Is the indomitable cancer patient who hopes for a medical breakthrough stronger or weaker for refusing to give in? Hope doesn't guarantee that the child will recover or the cancer will be overcome, but it does guarantee that we will be active agents of positive change for ourselves and our loved ones. Who is to say that might not tip the balance?

Hope creates spiritual energy.

June 6

To smell the roses is not enough. They must be tended, also. —Anonymous

Remember Aesop's fable about the ant and the grasshopper? Unlike the busy ant, all the grasshopper did was smell the roses and enjoy life. When the winter came, he was out of luck. He would have starved if the ants hadn't been willing to share the food they had stored up. Such are the risks run by those who consume without contributing.

In building self-esteem, we often have to learn to appreciate all the good things that are around us. But we are as shortsighted as the grasshopper if we take those things too much for granted. Many of the beautiful things around us are not our due—they were put there and are being maintained by others.

Self-respect requires that we make a contribution. It's a wonderful thing to become aware of the many graces and benefits we receive in our daily lives. But it's even more wonderful—and much healthier—to become aware of the relationship between give and take. When we tend some roses so that others may smell them, we give back some of the blessings we have received.

A sense of purpose makes self-esteem bloom.

The best is yet to be.
—Robert Browning

"The best is yet to be" is a poetic sentiment. The *belief* that the best is yet to be is a way of life that can lead us to a constantly expanding awareness and appreciation of ourselves and others.

Low self-esteem, of course, pooh-poohs the possibility that anything can get better, let alone that some marvelous adventure may be just around the corner. Yet that belief is exactly the right prescription for negativity, cynicism, and all the other ailments that prevent our enjoyment of life.

Once we accept the dignity and the responsibility of choosing, how could we doubt that the best is still to come? If today's choice is good, and we have the power to choose the content of our tomorrows, there are sure to be better days ahead. Of course, they won't all be up days, but as long as we can choose the positive over the negative, the smile over the frown, we can be absolutely confident that we will not have dreamed and hoped and labored in vain. Goodness creates goodness multiplied, one day at a time, as far as we can see into the future and beyond.

Hope in the future creates a sense of joyful expectancy.

June 8

Be thine own palace, or the world's thy jail.
                                        —John Donne

By whose standards are we doing well or not so well? Every time we check ourselves out, we're positioning ourselves against one yardstick or another. Obviously, we need to be very choosy in our selection of yardsticks. It's a mistake to automatically accept any outside evaluation as gospel truth. We need to think for ourselves if we want to take charge of our self-esteem.

The tendency to people please is very powerful. It not only gets us approval but it lets us off the hook. But our *own* approval is even more important. When we find ourselves second-guessing other people's wishes, we need to think their counsel through before we swallow it whole. Advice from others can be helpful, but only as a guide. Only as input to inform our own decision making.

There's dignity in running our own lives according to our own standards. Only the decisions that *we* make will truly satisfy us. Satisfying others may be socially convenient, but it won't give us the self-respect we're striving for.

Growing self-confidence allows me to be my own decision maker.

Be yourself.
—"The Desiderata"

Great teachers have always counseled us to be ourselves. From the admonishment "Know thyself," inscribed over the ancient temple door at Delphi, to the above-quoted advice from "The Desiderata," wise people seem to have long known there is an amazing amount of power in simply being who we are. Self-esteem, of course, is the artwork that rests on the pedestal of self-knowledge.

It isn't possible to become comfortable and positive toward ourselves if we won't *be* ourselves. That can only happen if we accept who we are without putting on airs, wearing masks, or trying to be someone other than ourselves.

Even without makeup or props, we are wonderful people who have every right to feel good about ourselves. To constantly run in the rat race of competition, comparison, and jealousies is to exhaust ourselves for nothing. Other people are not our enemies or opponents or judges. We can be our own true selves without feeling pressured to change colors like a chameleon in a thousand different situations.

Self-knowledge sets me free from the judgment of others.

June 10

*What is our praise or pride
But to imagine excellence, and try to make it?*
—Richard Wilbur

Developing healthy self-esteem means growing ever more comfortable with who we are in and of ourselves—not how we stack up in comparison with others. The ancient Greeks' concept of excellence, which they called *arete*, had nothing to do with superiority over others, as it does in our culture. To the Greeks, excellence was achieved when people became all they could be. Accomplishing that meant finding as many balances in life as possible. Their ideal, unlike ours, was "moderation in all things."

Constantly comparing and competing can be ruinous, especially as far as self-esteem goes. There will always be greater and lesser persons than ourselves. And comparisons often lead to either arrogance or bitterness. Neither unholy glee in winning nor crushing disappointment in losing promotes a realistic, balanced self-concept.

What does it matter how much others do or have? If we are striving for excellence, we are winning our own race. Our only opponents are our own deficiencies.

To achieve excellence in my life is to achieve my own potential.

To see things as they are, the eyes must be open;
to see things as other than they are, they must be
open even wider. To see things as better than they
are, they must be open to the full.
—Antonio Machado y Ruiz

Our perceptions are like the knotholes in a fence through which we peek at life. Although the view we get is limited, what we see is the truth as much as we are able to see it. Low self-esteem is always built around a narrow, limited perception that we have mistaken for the big picture. In fact *most* of what we regard as real is nothing more than our *perception* of reality. Thus our perceptions create our reality.

Not surprisingly, our negative perceptions were almost always formed when we were too young to understand what we saw on the other side of the knothole. In our innocence and inexperience, we thought we saw the big picture, the *only* picture. That's why self-esteem issues are so often Adult Child issues. Both are matters of early imprinting. That imprinting may very well be interpreting reality for us today.

What are the facts of life as we see them? If we believe that nothing good will ever happen to us, or that we are responsible for anything bad that happens to others, we need to go back to the fence and take another look. The world is wider now than it seemed to us when we were children.

Different perceptions create different options.

June 12

Inward ho!
—Christopher Morley

Everyday life seems like dull stuff indeed compared to the dramatic exploits of fantasy. Oh, if we only had been born in a more exciting time and place! We could have been explorers or inventors or mountain climbers or astronauts. Too bad we didn't have the opportunity to take on a heroic challenge—something we could really sink our teeth into. How wonderful it would have been. If only we'd had the chance.

But the chance for adventure is always there, knocking at the door. Talk about challenge! If we want mountains to climb and new territories to explore, we need look no further than our own hearts and minds. Want to scale a treacherous peak? Choose your weakest social skill and try inching your way up to a respectable level of competence. Want to chart a wilderness? Work on a Fourth Step inventory or a family of origin investigation.

Our time and place is now and here—as is our opportunity to do all the pioneering we've ever dreamed of. As in all other times and places, courage and imagination are all that's needed to go where no one has ever gone before!

Self-discovery is a greater adventure than any other; inward ho!

Often the difference between a successful marriage and a mediocre one consists of leaving about three or four things a day unsaid.
—Harlan Miller

An unstoked fire doesn't take long to flicker and fizzle. You don't need a bucket of water to douse the flames, just the lack of attention will do. Relationships are like that, too. If they go too long ignored, they start to die.

It's terribly difficult to maintain positive self-esteem in the midst of a failing relationship. Because of what we do or don't do, our relationships, like all living things, grow stronger or weaker every day. How easy it is, in our superbusy world, simply not to notice that a beloved relationship is faltering. How easy it would also have been to add some wood before the flame died completely.

It's common sense as well as positive spirituality to make sure that we make good connections with our loved one on a daily basis. There is no substitute for paying attention to our partners, saying words that heal and encourage. And there is certainly no substitute for touch—a pat on the shoulder, a squeeze of the hand, a passing hug. What priority could be greater? When the "us" is lost, the world is cold indeed.

Self-esteem slips when my priorities slip.

June 14

We do not see things as they are,
we see things as we are.
                    —The Talmud

The same blossoming cherry tree looks like profit to the grower, a painting to the artist, a bookcase to the woodworker, and a feast to the birds. What we see is often different than the objective reality in front of our faces. Depending on our viewpoint, any event or circumstance may be wonderful or awful, opportune, or disappointing. Usually we see what we expect to see.

Building self-esteem means having our eyes checked. We need to know how much of *us* is creeping into the picture we see outside of us. We need to be aware that past experience can distort the present and that motives cause us to squint. To clearly envision a better world and a better us, we may have to throw out our old glasses.

Is a joke just a joke or is it a veiled insult? Are our children burdens or blessings? Does the future look rosy or gray? Our answers to questions like these reflect interior, not exterior, realities. The good news is that these are the only realities that we're in charge of. If we choose to, we can get out of our own light and let the sun shine on a golden road we've never seen before.

Beauty is in the eye of the beholder.

When I work, I work. But when I sit, I sit loose.
— Appalachian Saying

In this fast-paced world, so full of stress, learning how to relax is even more important than learning how to get ahead. It may be, as a matter of fact, that we will have better careers if we take better care of our "equipment." Our bodies and minds are wonderful machines, of course, but all machines have a breaking point. The sad fact is that many of us simply don't know when or how to turn off our motors. We haven't let down in so long we seem to have lost the ability.

Here are a few tips for lightening up a grinding workday:

- Sit loose; hum a tune; call a friend for a quick hello.
- Unclench your jaw; let it go limp.
- Walk up and down the stairs a couple of times a day.
- Stretch, touch your toes; raise your arms up over your head.
- Take deep breaths.

Learning a few relaxation techniques to use when we're under pressure can be a lifesaver. Not only do such physical and mental exercises relieve stiff necks and headaches, they also help us bring better energy back to the job.

Taking a few stress breaks every day helps me keep my perspective.

June 16

Anger is not evil. It is simply power waiting to be directed.
　　　　　　　　　　　　　　　　　—S. Dale Smith

How each of us handles anger is a matter of personal style. Some of us slam doors or throw things. Some of us mutter insults through clenched teeth or bellow in rage. Others go to bed with sick headaches, and still others simply deny that they are ever angry.

Incapacity for anger is just as unhealthy and dysfunctional as smashing dishes or screaming uncontrollably. Wild "acting out" is one kind of problem, but repressive "acting in" is a problem, too. Anger is a normal emotional response to perceived injustice. To be out of touch with our own anger against life's unfairnesses is to be out of touch with a major chunk of reality. It isn't normal never to feel outrage in this often outrageous world.

Better far to admit our anger and convert it into positive action. We are stronger, not weaker, when we channel legitimate anger and use it as a power source to solve the problems we're angry about. Confronting unfairness builds self-esteem because it makes us feel good about ourselves. Maybe directed anger is just the generator we've been looking for.

Anger isn't too hot to handle if I direct its energy.

June 17

The art of being wise is the art of knowing what to overlook. —William James

It's not unusual to panic when we recognize some of the mistakes we have made and the years of practice we have put into unwittingly handicapping our own self-esteem. But panic is the last thing we need when we sincerely want to turn our lives around.

Building self-esteem means unearthing the truth and getting to know our own history and the forces that have made us who we are. In the process of self-discovery, we inevitably come face to face with those mistakes and behavior patterns that cause our unhappiness. Sometimes these new insights make us feel even worse about ourselves than we did before. "How could I have been so stupid?" we may groan. "I must be the dumbest person on the planet. My life is wasted. It is too late."

But it's never too late and almost nothing is fatal. What was learned can be unlearned. Old habits can be overturned and replaced by new, positive habits. The only requirement is the courage to think and act in a new way—that and the willingness to reach out to other caring, growing people. With such new resources, we are in a position to write our own glorious history from here on out.

I can fly into the future if I leave the past behind.

June 18

A mob has many heads, but no brain.
—Shankara

Recent research has led brain specialists to understand that the human mind works less like a computer than a town meeting. Apparently there are many inputs offering different responses to the issues that confront us. And the brain cells that "speak" the loudest get heard and acted on.

Who calls the shots for us when self-esteem issues demand settlement? If one input says, "Face it; deal with it," and another input says "Hide till it blows over," which command drowns out the other? Does panic speak louder than patience? Is "Attack!" a roar and "Negotiate!" just a whisper?

Sorting out contradictory messages is a primary task of those who would foster their self-esteem. If we give all our "voices" equal time—or repeatedly back off from the bully in the crowd—our lives are subject to mob rule. But if we listen, think, and practice filtering out the negative messages, the noise of the rabble will die down. If we persist in our efforts, the calm voice of reason will get stronger and stronger. The mob that heckled us toward diminished life will be quieted by reason's gavel. Then decisions can be made as they are supposed to be made—at an orderly town council meeting where the best tactic is chosen from many.

Nature gives me inner contradictions; character gives me choice.

*It isn't that they can't see the solution. It is that
they can't see the problem.*

—G. K. Chesterton

Every man Mary dates turns out to be a cheat and a
liar. Jack has never had a boss who was reasonable or
fair. Kim gets a stomachache every time she goes on
vacation. Paul's relatives always get their hands on every penny he's got. What's going on here? Are these
the unluckiest people in the world, or what?

The dooming "what" in many of our lives isn't fate
or coincidence or bad luck. It's the role we play in a
drama we keep writing as we go along. For some
reason—and there *is* a reason if we could dig deep
enough to find it—we cast ourselves as losers. Then
scene after scene, act after act, we get victimized by the
bad-guy characters.

Because the problem is *us*, the solution, obviously, is
to rewrite the script. Soap operas kill off characters that
get tiresome and predictable; why can't we? Victimhood isn't compatible with growth. If we want a happier ending, we're going to have to stop walking onto
the same old sets and repeating the same old lines. We
deserve a chance at a new role.

**Once recognized, self-defeating patterns can be
crossed out and rewritten.**

June 20

Buffaloes are held by cords, man by his words.
—Malay Proverb

We can't work with what we haven't got. That's why we can't think of ourselves except in the terms we use to think about anyone else. To put it another way, the words we use for ourselves and others show how we think of ourselves and others.

We might claim that we rarely use *any* words to talk about ourselves, meaning that most of us reveal very little that's personal to others. But all of us talk about ourselves to ourselves! There is a constant flow of self-talk, an inner dialogue, going on within. People with low self-esteem have learned to live with words like *useless*, *stupid*, and *ugly*. These are the kind of words we use to describe how we succeed or fail, how we look, how we react to others, and what they must think of us. And we tend to give others the same kind of going over we give ourselves.

Consider this: What power we have when we consciously decide to use only positive, supportive words, first with ourselves and then with others. What wonders can happen if we start using a whole new vocabulary!

It's interesting and instructive to stop and listen to myself talking to myself.

He is a man whom it is impossible to please because he is never pleased with himself.

—Goethe

How much of our self-esteem depends on what other people think? Too much. How often do we withhold self-approval until approval from other sources tells us it's okay? Too often. Whether we're coming out of modesty or fear, we make a mistake when we assume that outside evaluations are more accurate than any inner reading we may have. Who knows us better than ourselves?

Other people's indifferent or negative reactions to us may have nothing to do with us and everything to do with them. Maybe the person we are trying to please can't be pleased. Perhaps there is no possibility that we, or anyone else, will ever get positive feedback from that negative source. Some people are so full of fear, resentment, and hurt, that their major effect on life is to make everyone as miserable as they are. Obviously, when we look to such people for validation, we look in vain. As we learn to be more honest with ourselves, we can more comfortably trust our own judgment.

I wouldn't give a bank robber my savings to hold. Why should I let negative people take charge of my self-esteem?

June 22

In the mind and nature of a man a secret is an
ugly thing, like a hidden physical defect.
—Isak Dinesen

A friend who confides a secret has every right to expect us to keep that information to ourselves. If we claim to be mature, trustworthy people, we must behave that way. Perhaps we, too, have the need of a trusted listener.

What lives in the dark, grows in the dark. Do we have deep, shame-inducing secrets that we keep locked away, terrified to tell anyone? Refusing to reveal such secrets can produce personal monsters—real fire-breathing, ferocious monsters that will intimidate us and control our lives if we don't bring them out in the light.

Unshared secrets tend to grow. In the darkness, the mouse becomes the lion; in the light of revelation, however, the lion becomes the harmless mouse. Even the most dreadful secrets lose their power to frighten us when we say their names out loud. And what we share with others is not what drives them away, but what binds us to them, deepening the trusted friendship. If we have been imprisoning our self-esteem behind some long held, festering secret, we can turn on the sunshine by simply telling someone about it.

Shared troubles are cut in half.

Practice makes imperfect.
—Mariette Hartley

This unusual twist on the saying we're accustomed to may seem off at first. But it depends on what we're practicing. What if we're spending time in the pursuit of some attitude or habit that diminishes the quality of our lives?

Subconsciously we may regularly practice avoiding conflict at all costs, stalling on decisions, always putting work before play, or play before work. If we practice hard enough, there is no limit to just how imperfect we may become! Eventually, we could be world-class perfectionists, controllers, manipulators, or workaholics.

All self-esteem is rooted in our attitudes, habits, and perceptions. Those that are already healthy translate into positive self-esteem. Those that are negative are the basis of our negative self-esteem. There's no question about the power of practice. What we need to check out is what it is that we are practicing.

Practicing some things can make me worse.

June 24

Most of what we want to be, we already are.
—Kevin K.

How easy it is to become anxious and upset over what we are not and who we are not. As if we were starting out from scratch to create worthy selves! What a disastrous impact this mistaken idea has on our self-esteem.

Just as the oak is in the acorn, we already are most of what we want to be. At least in germ, if not in full flower. The potential for development is, and has always been, with us. The task is not to become something totally different, but to develop what we already have, what is already there.

Are we not already capable of loving and being loved? Are we not, at the present time, able to see beauty and celebrate it? To at least some extent, are we not already actively involved in getting better and growing? Believing that we'll get there is a matter of patience and persistence.

An acorn isn't worthless because it's not yet an oak. Neither am I worthless because I'm not yet what I'm going to be.

No *can be a love word.*
—Ron Palmer

Much is said in self-esteem literature about the triumph of saying yes. *Yes* to life! to risk! to intimacy! to bold new adventures! Amen. But there is no universal, absolute goodness to either of the words *yes* or *no*. Because much of life is a balancing act, there are times when both words are conducive to positive self-worth, and other times when both are lethal.

No is a word of love and health when we consider lose-lose situations or risks that are not risks at all but traps. For many of us, learning to say "no" as a complete sentence is a great sign of growth. When we can turn down a bad idea or a dangerous invitation without justification or explanation, we are truly on our way to freedom.

Just as often as it is brave and good and hopeful to say yes it is appropriate and beneficial to say no.

Learning to say *no* will break my bonds of passivity.

June 26

It is often possible to get greater enjoyment from what we are already doing, rather than try to find something else. —L. Don Siebet

It is true enough that self-esteem comes from greater fulfillment, which translates to a happy life. In the pursuit of that happiness, many people do just that—passionately go after something, anything, that's *different*. But the fact may well be that the harder we run, the farther away we get. Newer pastures aren't necessarily greener.

There is, of course, nothing wrong with keeping our eyes open for new things we might do that are exciting, fun, or just plain different. But there is also something to be said about possessing or developing the wisdom to take more pleasure in what we are already doing. Perhaps our dissatisfaction is really more with *ourselves* than with our jobs, our friends, or our current activities.

If we enjoy a hobby, is that not marvelous in itself? If we find that looking at new houses or cars gives us a lift, it may be that we don't need to find something else that is "really" fun. Maybe we need to organize more activities with our friends rather than find new friends. Can that not be done right where we are? Maybe the job we already have would be more interesting if we threw more energy into it. Need we be in some other, more glamorous place than where we are? Greater self-esteem always generates greater happiness. Maybe we can have it right where we are now, and from what we're already doing.

Sometimes it's only my attitudes that need changing.

The guts carry the feet, not the feet the guts.
—Miguel de Cervantes

Mitch's boy is arrested for dealing drugs. Diane finds another lump in her breast. Lupe's husband is diagnosed with Alzheimer's disease. Art is fired three years before he's eligible for retirement. Every day in every city and town, thousands of people are confronted with paralyzing personal disasters. How do people survive, let alone cope with, such things?

Everyday gripes and irritations are put in their place very quickly when catastrophe grabs us by the throat. Suddenly there is no time or energy to fuss about going bald or growing old. The urgency of the situation demands that we focus every strength we have, every resource, on just moving one step at a time. Thus is character forged on the white-hot anvil of necessity.

It takes raw courage to stand fast when every fiber of our being wants to hide under the covers, split, or retaliate in some self-destructive way. But like any business, tragic business is taken care of by walking through it, one foot ahead of the other, one day at a time. Plain old guts—the kind we didn't think we had in us—is what carries us through the cruelest challenges.

One step at a time is the way to bear unbearable sorrows.

June 28

Character consists of what you do on the third or fourth tries.
—James Michener

Most of us want to play the piano, not learn the piano; speak a foreign language, not study it; enjoy success, not earn it. We want our dreams to come true quickly and without too much effort. We don't want to accept the *becoming* that comes before *being*.

But character is built, not wished into being. Character is a prerequisite of self-esteem, the wind in the sails of success. And in spite of our daydreams, character is always earned the hard way—by getting up after failure and trying again. And again. And again.

So what if we promised ourselves to quit smoking by now? We can set ourselves a new deadline and try again. Have we failed a second time to make a dreaded phone call? Try a third. Has the ladder to success slipped out from under us *again*? Maybe it will take another three or four tries. Once we arrive, no one cares how long it took for us to get there.

Character building is a lifelong enterprise.

*How many of our daydreams would darken into
nightmares if there seemed any danger of their
coming true!* —Logan Pearsall Smith

Wishful thinking can actually prevent our dreams from
coming true. When we fantasize about perfect life circumstances, we're not out there on the playing field,
where life is lived. And it's only in the rough-and-
tumble where skill can be gained, points scored, and
the game won.

Self-esteem is built on the flesh-and-blood selves we
are in the real world—not in our daydreams. Rather
than wishing to be different kinds of people doing different kinds of work in different kinds of places, we
can change our daydreams. When it comes right down
to it, we *all* have the same wish—for happiness, freedom, peace of mind. The difference is in our imaginings of what it would take to make that dream come
true.

Singing *Madame Butterfly* or pitching for the Yankees
would be fun, all right, but it wouldn't make us more
trustworthy, kind, or courageous. It wouldn't erase the
sad events of the past; nothing can. Even if our glamorous dreams came true, we'd still be human beings
with problems, blind spots, and limitations. As far as
we know, the lives we have now are the only lives
we're going to get. Let's *live* our days, not dream them
away.

**The only "perfect" life for me is the one God
gave me.**

June 30

From the cowardice that dares not face new truths,
From the laziness that is content with half-truths,
From the arrogance that thinks it knows all truths,
Good Lord, deliver me. —Kenyan Prayer

Successful life management must be based on reality. Because, in turn, reality must be based on truth, we need to be very watchful for attitudes that would blind us to the truth.

In the quest for self-esteem, sometimes new truths must be faced:

• This really is a bad place for me, even if it is familiar.
• This repeated failure is partly my fault.
• It is time for me to act.

Sometimes half-truths must be jettisoned:

• Nothing good ever happens to me.
• I have no choice in this affair.
• The world really is evil.

Sometimes arrogance needs to be confronted:

• I know all of this already.
• Groups don't work, because "they" are all too sick.
• Reading is a waste of time.

Does any of this sound familiar? For each of us as individuals—what is the truth? What is the reality?

I must work to become aware of my underlying attitudes.

In nature there are neither rewards nor punishments—there are consequences
—Robert G. Ingersoll

Only the very young imagine that they can play with fire without getting burned. The rest of us, looking at the world under singed eyelashes, have learned to our regret that the bill for heedless behavior eventually comes due.

If we thought we could drink or smoke with impunity, the passing years showed us our mistake. If we told ourselves that charm would forever disguise lack of accomplishment, we discovered that "forever" has a short run. If we procrastinated, hid, and lied to avoid responsibility, we ran out of people who would take us seriously. In short, we had to face the consequences of our own behavior.

Most of us are crushed when the piper demands payment. We're embarrassed, ashamed, and disappointed in ourselves. Our self-esteem, already propped up on slender sticks of pretense, takes a nosedive. But there is a bright side to this gloomy picture. Indulgences that have hardened into habits give us clarity and focus. Instead of vaguely wishing that our lives were different, we can immediately hone in on our target habits. We may be mortified, but we're not confused about what needs to be done. The day of reckoning that we avoided so long may be the best day of our lives. Because from that day forward, we can divest ourselves of our miserable habits the same way we acquired them—one day at a time.

Daily effort to improve myself has consequences, too.

July 2

Trouble and perplexity drive us to prayer, and prayer drives away trouble and perplexity.
—P. Melanchthon

No one ever said that achieving and maintaining positive self-esteem was trouble free. Doable, certainly, but not without some setbacks. The fact is the course that leads to this worthy goal is pitted with trouble and perplexity.

Many have found that prayer, our conscious contact with God as we understand God to be, is an invaluable help in the effort. Partly because prayer helps us both to realize and experience that we do not have to carry the load alone.

When trouble and perplexity slow us down and trip us up, our tendency is often to pull back, push others away, and isolate. We withdraw into the mind-set that says, "I am alone with these awful burdens. I must carry them all by myself." Self-esteem is often demolished under this crushing weight. We simply cannot handle some problems without help. Many times prayer keeps us moving. We either have to reach for the stars or stop our journey.

The road is hard. Thank God I do not have to go it alone.

The property of power is to protect.
—Blaise Pascal

Just think of how wonderful it would be! When we read about powerful people, our imaginations take off. If only *we* were the ones in charge! At last we could have our day in the sun. We could *buy* anything we wanted, *do* anything we wanted, *make other people do* anything we wanted them to do. . . . And that's the trouble with power. Whether we're individuals or nations, we tend to confuse power with force. Somehow we want to use it to make other people submit.

The fact is that we can all be power brokers if we want to. If we use the kind of power we have, instead of the kind we don't have, we can empower other people to fly free, to unburden their loads, to throw off some crippling self-definition. This is power indeed.

We don't need high connections or advanced degrees to wield this power. All we need is the wisdom and the willingness to give a smile or a compliment to someone accustomed to put-downs, or an ego-building invitation to someone hiding in the shadows. These are the simple tools of the truly powerful.

To help others be all they can be is to "play God" in one of the few legitimate ways open to us. If this isn't big-time power, what is?

To promote another's freedom and growth is to guarantee my own.

July 4

Every person's feelings have a front-door and a side-door by which they may be entered.
—Oliver Wendell Holmes

A familiar song tells us to whistle a happy tune so no one will know we're afraid. Unlikely as it may seem, there's a lot of truth to that. Acting the way we would like to feel really does help us feel that way.

In a university experiment, psychological researchers asked student volunteers to make six different facial expressions. The six emotions to be expressed were fear, surprise, disgust, sadness, anger, and happiness. The findings were surprising. When the volunteers looked afraid, their bodies reacted as if they really were afraid; their heart rates speeded up and their skin temperatures dropped. For the most part, appropriate physical reactions also occurred when the other emotions were portrayed.

"Act as if . . ." is an important coping technique in many self-help programs. If you are fearful, act as if you are the bravest person you know. If you're having a down day, act as if it is your job to cheer everybody else up. The point, of course, is not to fool yourself about how you really feel. Pretending is just the technique; *practice* is the point.

When I "act as if," I can accelerate a positive result.

Time cools, time clarifies; no mood can be maintained quite unaltered through the course of hours.
—Thomas Mann

The search for serenity does not lead us to a state of full-time bliss. The idea that we should never have a bad day is another of our unrealistic expectations. No one, no matter how hard they're "working the program," has a good day every day. Who knows what the trigger is? Maybe it's gloomy weather or hormones or a skipped breakfast. But the fact is that we all feel down sometimes.

Emotional stability is an important component of self-esteem. Wild mood swings and chronic crankiness are symptoms of deeper disorders that need attention. Often, deeply buried anger is the wellspring of the attitudinal misery that is bubbling up. Work with a counselor or support group can usually relieve such unhappy, long-term conditions.

But for the ordinary ups and downs of life, good old-fashioned acceptance is the best remedy we've got. Even people with naturally cheerful dispositions and even tempers get up on the wrong side of the bed once in a while. While we strive for emotional balance, we need to remember that *stable* and *static* aren't the same thing; our goal is an acceptable, comfortable range.

The upside is that bad days are just as fleeting as good days.

July 6

This free will business is a bit terrifying anyway.
It's almost pleasanter to obey, and make the most
of it.   —Ugo Betti

Many of us bristle like porcupines if anyone dares to tell us what to do. We're insulted by the very idea that we need advice or guidance of any kind. Allow ourselves to be bossed around? Never! Thank you very much, but we'll make our own decisions.

Yet the vast majority of us are crowd followers at heart. Our dress, talk, tastes, and habits are almost always styled by the dictates of one community or another. In our need to fit in, we have formed and shaped ourselves very carefully to be "a part" rather than "apart." Business executives and college professors may criticize the peer pressure that has gang members wearing their distinctive colors. But what of all those pinstripes and wing tips marching in lockstep? What of all those rumpled tweed jackets and baggy wool sweaters? Is that not conformity?

Most of our waking hours are spent following guidelines that are not of our own making. We go along to get along, keeping pace with our fellows as best we can. The fact that we *do* conform is unquestionable. To ask ourselves why we so hotly proclaim otherwise is the real question in our search for greater self-awareness.

In matters of dress and style, crowd following is usually harmless; in matters of substance, less so.

*I never heard of anyone stumbling on anything
while sitting down.* —Charles Kettering

If we are to live full lives, we need to get clear about
what we want to accomplish, and pursue those goals
with energy and determination. Some say, "Oh, if I
had only gone to college!" If they are sincere, there is
no reason not to get started. They well might say, "But
it will take me ten years. I'll be too old." But how old
will they be ten years from now if they *don't* go to
college?

So many of us, probably most, never reach our potential. Mostly because we never get started. Whatever
we can do, or think we can—we need to begin it. Procrastination is so comfortable and inviting. Inertia can
so easily become a way of life. We need to resist,
though. We must take that first step, which is a struggle with our own limited self-image. Once we are on
our feet and moving the battle is half won.

If we just get started and keep on going, we'll immediately earn a better reputation with ourselves. Our
chances for success will improve as our self-image improves. It's never too late to get started.

I can do whatever I believe I can do.

July 8

We are astonished at thought, but sensation is equally wonderful.

—*Philosophical Dictionary*, 1764

We live in an age that crowns reason. "Smart" people are those who get good grades on tests. To "know the answer" is to come up with the facts and figures that match the teacher's question. Even when we ponder a subject so subjective as self-esteem, we may find ourselves looking for the "right" interpretation or approach or equation that will most quickly solve the problem of disappointment with self.

But rational intelligence isn't the only path to enlightenment. There are *many* ways to broaden and deepen wisdom. To "know" an apple, for example, is as much to have tasted its sweetness and felt its juice on your chin as it is to recite the chemical makeup of the fruit or its biological name. Thinking isn't the same as experiencing.

We know a lot more than statistics about the people we love. By looking at them, listening to them, holding their hands, we use our senses as much as anything else to touch them from the inside out. We learn to love ourselves in much the same way. The road to self-appreciation winds through our senses as well as our brains. Getting there is an experience to be savored, not a problem to be solved.

The senses are pathways to self-realization.

July 9

Every calling is great when greatly pursued.
—Oliver Wendell Holmes

Inez works at a big-city airport serving up candy, hot dogs, and soft drinks to hassled, tired people who are not always courteous or pleasant. She stands on her feet all day and sometimes has to wait an hour or more for someone to give her a break.

Few would call Inez's job a "calling," or volunteer to trade jobs with her. But Inez does her work with all the flair and energy of a true artisan. She turned her counter into an oasis the day she looked up to see a downcast man asking for a hot dog. Noticing how carefully he was counting his money and digging in his pockets for coins, she realized he didn't have enough for a soft drink to go along with his hot dog. So with a smile as bright as the sun, Inez said, "Can I get you a cup of water, sir?"

Who knows the hard road the man was traveling? But today, because of the sensitivity of a snack-counter waitress, his way was made a little easier, a little softer. No statues get erected for people like Inez. But that doesn't diminish her light one little bit. Wherever she goes, flowers grow.

Kind words and bright smiles light up the world.

July 10

Have the courage to live. Anyone can die.
                    —Robert Cody

Many a popular novel or movie has a touching death scene. Often, one of the principal characters *chooses* death as the only possible response to some unbearable melancholy or star-crossed love. "How romantic," we say. "He gave up his life for her. He *died* for love!" Yet in the real world, far more often the greater sacrifice is to *live* for love.

Self-esteem and the will to live go hand and hand. Many of us have come close to drowning in a swamp of bad luck, tragic family of origin events, betrayal, and sheer exhaustion. All could become reasons, easily justified, to die, either physically or spiritually. All we have to do is to give over our spirits to cynicism, negativity, or passivity. We die by simply defaulting on life.

Choosing life is what takes courage. Never are we more alive or loving than when we get up off the mat and try again, take another risk when the scars of past wounds still lie red and vivid on our souls. That is life. That is self-esteem. *Living* is the proof of love. Anyone can die.

For all its hardship, my life is precious to me.

Conquered unhappiness always lies in back of tranquility. —David Grayson

Some nuggets of wisdom are rarely recognized. One of these is the fact that a gift is hidden in any problem. Most of us, of course, would handle our problems with ten-foot tongs if we could. The quicker we can do something about our problems and forget about them, the better. We want to move on to more cheerful pursuits.

But unhappiness, which is caused by problems, has a value of its own. When we dash away from it too quickly, without considering its whys and wherefores, we can lose out on an enlightening truth: Traversing troubled water without drowning is no small thing. The fact that we've managed to do it at all proves that we're doing something right. And our bouts of unhappiness have even more specific lessons to teach.

Rebounding after betrayal teaches us to be prudent with our trust. Overcoming discouragement teaches us to make sure that our expectations are realistic. Besting the blues teaches us that the sun will come up in the morning. Such lessons learned are gifts that came to us wrapped up in problems.

Some lessons can only be learned on the battlefield.

July 12

Whining is a great deal of self-pity pushed through a small hole.   —Anonymous

Even whiners recoil from the sound of whining. But although it makes people cover their ears and leave the room, whining is more of a symptom than a cause. People whine because they sense they have no power, no choices, and consequently, no responsibility. Whining is the sound of victimhood.

People with adequate self-esteem don't whine. They might very well acknowledge a problem or pain—but then they take appropriate steps to remedy the situation. Whiners stop short of action. They just sit in their pain and make noise about it, like coyotes baying at the moon.

Heaven knows all of us have sadnesses to bay about. But we don't have enough time for griping and complaining once we take responsibility for our lives. We're too busy working on the attitudes and behaviors that set up our ill fortune in the first place. We're not sitting now, we're moving and doing. The last thing we want to hear is the sniveling sound made when self-pity is pushed through a small hole.

Most of my "bad luck" is directly attributable to conditions I allowed to develop.

*A smile goes beyond language; it is understood
by all persons.* —Joanie Roy

Some situations strike us speechless. Obviously *something* needs to be said, heartfelt joy or sorrow needs to be communicated, but the words fail to come. We stand there dumb.

Perhaps a friend has been killed in a car accident; how can we possibly express our grief to the family? Even worse, what can we say to a loved one who is dying? In our embarrassing loss for words we may even avoid seeing such a person until it's too late for talk. Happy situations can also strike us dumb. On the day of our daughter's wedding, there may be no words to express the happiness, pride, and pleasure we feel.

Often, when communication fails, we feel that *we* have failed—and our self-esteem plummets. But words are not the only way we have of communicating. Sometimes just a touch, a hug, or simply our presence, says far more than words ever will. Sometimes a smile, a nod, a thumbs-up sign, says it all.

Just *being there* for people delivers a comforting message.

July 14

Take time to deliberate; but when the time for action arrives, stop thinking and go in.
—Andrew Jackson

To be stalled in indecision is to be trapped in one of the worst hells there is. Most adults don't need anyone to tell them that straddling a fence is painful. They've done it before and they know how it feels. So why do they keep finding themselves in the same predicament?

Efficient decision making is a skill. And like all skills, it must be practiced before it is learned. Of course, some decisions are devilishly difficult. But even those that will clearly take us from a bad place to a good place can make us defensive and uncomfortable. After all, our shaky self-esteem is put on the line every time we make a judgment. When we declare ourselves, we risk disapproval and maybe even blame. It takes courage to be the one who makes the decision.

But "waiting for a better time" is rarely a valid tactic. When will a better time be? When will it be easier? When will they or we hurt less? No matter how much we dread what we have to do, what is to be gained by hesitating? Until we dare to decide, there's no way off the fence and out of the pain.

My self-esteem profits as my decision-making skills increase.

*Death, like life, is an affair of being more fright-
ened than hurt.* —Samuel Butler

Death is no doubt the most unmentionable of all unmentionable topics. Just the word itself makes us feel
nervous and fluttery inside. Bad enough if the idea of
dying crops up in our own minds—worse yet if it
comes up in conversation, which, to our great relief, it
rarely does. And even then, as if in a never-discussed
but commonly understood conspiracy, nearly all of us
have one or two glib remarks to make before we quickly
change the subject.

The truth is we'd rather not talk about death because
we'd rather not think about it. Yet death is a central
fact of life. If we're so afraid of death that we can't look
at it, wonder about it, or talk about it, how can we ever
come to the serenity of acceptance? We can't hide and
understand at the same time We can't prepare for
what we won't acknowledge.

Of all realities, the death of our loved ones and eventually ourselves is the most certain. How healthy and
wise it is to put all that fear and dread right out on the
table where we can can look at it in the light of our
beliefs, our experience, and our best thinking. What
growth to becoming willing to talk about death with a
trusted friend. What peace to discover that fear, not
death itself, has all along been the stumbling block.

**When I avoid the subject of death, I avoid
reality.**

July 16

A stumble may prevent a fall.
—Thomas Fuller

Everyone trips up once in a while. As skillful as we are, as carefully as we go, sooner or later a crack in the sidewalk is going to get us. Pratfalls aren't fun, of course, but they're not all that important, either. Occasionally, a good self-inflicted smack may be just what we need.

Say that we made a rash judgment. Or did something that, in hindsight, was undesirable or even shameful. If we stop to think about it, we can often figure out the whys and wherefores of our mistake. Maybe we were especially tired that day. Maybe we took out anger on an innocent person because we were afraid to confront the person who really made us angry. Self-respect can be salvaged if we use our slipups to help us become more aware.

Life is full of hazards. After we've taken a few falls, we can learn to catch ourselves before we go down. An occasional stumble may be a warning. If we learn from them, our blunders can be our blessings.

My self-esteem profits when I profit from my mistakes.

There is joy and comfort in a thick skin.
—Dr. James Bender

Hurt feelings—who needs them? Many of us do, in spite of the fact that they are painful and terribly destructive of our self-esteem. We can get a lot of mileage out of our misery.

"Feeling hurt" can be our way of controlling other people. Extremely thin-skinned people are good at using the most trifling incidents to create a grievance. By taking offense, they take power. Perhaps they demand apologies from a family member who forgot to mail a birthday card. Or maybe they're after sympathy for a difficult, but commonplace, life situation, or for ordinary, everyday hardships. In any event, they use their distress to claim other people's attention. In skillful hands, emotional frailty can be an effective club indeed.

It's our choice if we want to feel good by feeling bad. But it's really not fair to twist other people's arms for sympathy.

Sometimes I may need to toughen up a bit; I don't have to bleed to be loved.

July 18

Responsibility is proportionate to opportunity.
—Woodrow Wilson

Reaching out for more responsibility seems akin to giving yourself a hot foot or volunteering for a root canal. Who needs it? Yet in the realm of self-esteem, deliberately taking on responsibility makes all the sense in the world.

Self-esteem depends on a competent self-image. And competence only comes from repeated experience. Without sufficient experience of success, all of our claims to competence are just so much chest beating. Experience means *doing*, not waiting for a chance to do, but getting out there and mixing it up. Often that means proactively reaching out and making something happen.

Opportunities to prove that we are competent, capable people are everywhere—if we're willing to take the responsibility. Volunteer at a children's hospital or an old folks' home. Help out at the PTA or Little League. Whatever your choice, set a deadline and then share it with someone who will hold you accountable. The rewards will surprise you.

Initiative creates its own opportunities.

*Who would you see if you saw yourself walking
your way?* —Chester Davison

Recently a man was relating an amusing incident that
had a heavy impact on his self-esteem. While on a
Chicago business trip, he went out for an early morning walk. He began to notice that other pedestrians
were tending to avoid him. As soon as they caught
sight of him, they looked away. No amount of attempted eye contact worked. As he approached, people would cross the street or give him a wide berth.

Ugly, angry, negative thoughts started popping into
his mind. At first he condemned them. Then he began
to wonder what was wrong with him that he was being
treated this way. Stopping at a coffee shop to lick his
wounded self-confidence and to warm up, he caught
sight of himself in a large mirror. Then he understood!
As friendly as he knew himself to be on the inside, his
outside told a different story. He had forgotten to
shave, his hair was mussed, his eyes were heavy and
rather bloodshot as a result of a long, tedious meeting
the night before. *He* knew who he was inside, but now
he got a look at how others saw his outside!

His comment about who would you see if you saw
yourself walking your way made his listeners think.
Inside and outside don't always match. We need to
investigate further before we draw any hard and fast
conclusions—about ourselves *or* others.

Appearances are sometimes deceiving.

July 20

If you do not raise your eyes, you will think that you are the highest point. —Antonio Porchia

Too much concentration on self results in what some people call "belly-button gazing." Rather than healthy self-examination, that unattractive phrase describes self-absorption—a total focus inward. Hardly the balanced view necessary to help us find our place in the universe!

Raising our eyes shows us that we are part of a world much bigger than ourselves. When we look up and around at the glory that surrounds us, we can't help seeing our own concerns in a new perspective. Just watching and listening to the birds in the trees tends to modify situations that we may have taken too seriously. And when hopelessness holds us in a bear hug, an effective escape has always been to lie back and look at the clouds, realizing that all are moving, changing, and no two clouds are the same.

Raising our eyes also raises our hearts. The balanced view has breadth and height as well as depth, panoramic majesty as well as personal misery. A realistic sense of self depends on the balanced view.

I wear blinders when I concentrate too closely on myself.

Making terms with reality, with things as they are, is a full-time business for the child.
—Milton R. Sapirstein

As much as we'd like to, we can't give self-esteem to our children any more than we can give youth to the aged or health to the sick. Certainly we can and must do our best to protect them when they're small. And we should strive to model the self-respectful behavior we want them to imitate. But self-esteem is a prize that nobody else can win for you. Claiming it is an inside job.

Some child development experts of yesteryear made us believe otherwise. They suggested that any unhappiness in our children's lives would have long-term effects. Awful effects that would be our fault. So we stopped making unpopular decisions and started walking on eggshells around our kids. We neglected our own lives to lavish them with attention. We praised them whether they deserved it or not. In short, with all the best intentions, we led them to believe that this is not the real world at all, but Disneyland. And we gave them all the rides for free.

Now both parents and experts know better. They know that even young people have to struggle to be strong. The problem-solving skills that make us confident can only be learned by facing some problems. Frustration teaches inventiveness and patience. And in the long run that's just what self-esteem is based on—the proven ability to take care of ourselves.

I improve the odds for my children's self-esteem when I stop cushioning their every fall.

July 22

The voice is a second face.
—Gerard Bauer

Because none of us lives in a vacuum, most of our success in life depends on the success of our key relationships. Different people use different modes or styles to get through to one another. Some methods, as well as some messages, are more productive than others. It's a valuable exercise to think about how and what we usually communicate.

Some of us try to influence others with overpowering logic, others by talking so sweetly we can hardly be refused, and still others dominate by sheer volume. Sometimes we deliver threats as jokes and pleas as compliments. None of these manipulated communications do us or our relationships much good.

In the long run there is no message more worthy of delivery than simply saying it is safe to be with us. When we say straight out that we will do our best to be a port in the storm and a willing listener, that we will not mindlessly say the careless word or inflict the careless wrong, we are saying all that anyone wants to hear. The style doesn't matter if the substance is there.

Heartfelt communication tends to be plain rather than fancy.

Assumption is the mother of screw-up.
—Angelo Donghia

It may be truthfully said that assumption is not only a hotbed of error, but also the cause of much self-esteem bashing. Especially if we place our self-worth in other people's hands. And *most* especially if we don't tell them about it.

Martha's assumptions flattened her spirits every day. Unknown to Eric, her boss, Martha used him as a mirror to check out her self-worth. Every day she looked to him for approval—not just the normal, appropriate approval that a good employee deserves—but the kind of deep affirmation that children need from their fathers. Martha assumed that Eric's approval would make up for the love she missed. But she was wrong. Not only did Eric not know what she was looking for—he had no interest in being her father. So her assumptions set her up for disappointment time after time.

We can't assume something is true just because we *need* it to be true. When expectations are based on wishes rather than facts, our self-esteem is as fragile as a flower in a blizzard.

Examining my assumptions may help me light up some dark corners.

July 24

Women have felt the need to pretend to be happy in order to be feminine. —Gloria Steinem

Responsible people do what they have to do. Figuring out what we have to do, unfortunately, is a lot harder than it looks. How many "shoulds" should we listen to? How many are true? Should we really behave, think, and feel differently than we do? Who says so?

Those of us who are females with families have been held responsible for too many "shoulds." In our efforts to be everything to everybody, we've too often become nobody to ourselves—always standing at the end of the line when wants and needs are being addressed. Obviously this doesn't do a lot for our self-esteem. What's even worse is the popular culture's insistence that we should be happy about it.

But unrealistic ideals are not healthy. No one should be bullied into pretending happiness—or accepting responsibility for other people's happiness. Because the goal itself is false, pursuing that goal diminishes self-esteem.

In general, pretending is of little use in building a better, happier life. Pretending that is grounded in delusion and denial is not true femininity or true anything else that has any value.

I am free to choose my own goals and the means of achieving them.

It is easier to confess a defect than to claim a quality. —Max Beerbohm

Self-esteem can stumble when we so bravely and thoroughly confront our flaws that our flaws are all we think about. We can get *too* good at searching out imperfections—so good that we spend most of our time concentrating on what's wrong rather than what's right. What we must *not* do—whether it's bossing other people around or loading up on junk food—can become the focus of our lives.

Certainly it makes sense to identify and work against our personal pitfalls. But we are who we are and many of our deep-seated characteristics have an upside as well as a downside. If boldness is in our nature, we need to learn to control it and use it—not wipe it out. If we're control-crazy, we need to learn to lighten up—not let go completely. The major characteristics of our personalities are almost always double-edged swords that cut both ways. The trick is to use them *for* and not *against* our own best interests.

Self-knowledge includes awareness of our strengths as well as our weaknesses. When we can accept that both pluses and minuses often come wrapped up in the same package, we can stop being so hard on ourselves and start working with what we have.

A balanced self-image is the only true self-image.

July 26

I take care of me. I am the only one I've got.
—Groucho Marx

What makes us think we don't measure up? Why do we expect so little from ourselves? What kills our self-respect? The answers vary. Consider these:

- Are we looking too much for the approval of others?
- Are we perfectionists, expecting too much from ourselves?
- Are we intimidated by the lost battles and failures of the past?
- Are we overimpressed by the success of others?
- Are we trying to escape responsibility by claiming to be a failure?
- Are we lacking a sense of proportion? Do we tend to make mountains out of molehills?
- Is our sense of humor weak? Can we laugh at ourselves?

The best way to enhance our self-esteem is by direct action. Take on some responsibility that we have been dodging, enroll in a gym class to improve our appearance and health, practice ignoring small annoyances, or start looking for healthy friends.

We need not worry about overcompensating. It doesn't often happen, but when it does it can sometimes lead to greatness. As a child, Winston Churchill was a stutterer who also lisped. By working on his shortcomings, he became a world-class orator. So, too, working on our shortcomings is what will raise our self-esteem and bring us success.

Self-awareness is the springboard to successful living.

*All men should strive to learn before they die
what they are running from, and to, and why.*
—James Thurber

In our quest for a healthier self-image, some of us find it hard to accept that long-ago events are still holding us back. We figure that if we can't remember the past very well, or hardly ever think of it, it must have been erased somehow. Out of sight, out of mind. Out of mind, out of reality.

But what was doesn't disappear just because we turn away from it. Imagine a car that was in an accident twenty, thirty, or forty years ago. If this car had simply been parked, unrepaired, wouldn't it still be dented? Or would the years that passed somehow have made it whole? When we're talking about cars instead of people, we know very well that time alone doesn't pound out dents. Work pounds out dents.

If we were neglected or otherwise abused as children, the fact is that there was damage done—first and foremost to our self-esteem. The words and deeds that put us down, that shut us out, are the dents that underlie our negative self-definitions. If they haven't been looked at and worked on, they're still there. That long ago "lifewreck" might have been just a fender bender or it might have been a head-on collision—but the results will be with us until we stop denying what happened.

After a car accident, blaming the driver is not nearly as important as getting busy pounding out the dents.

July 28

We often give our enemies the means for our own destruction.
—Aesop

Of course, our self-esteem takes a whipping when others come at us with hurtful comments, criticisms, and put-downs. What makes it even worse is when these cutting remarks are justified.

Margaret is a wonderful young lady who has very little sense of how wonderful she really is. Her self-esteem is downright flimsy. One of her worst nightmares is that someone in her crowd will accuse her of being an "airhead." Yet Margaret has also slipped into a most unfortunate habit. When a situation comes up that might make her look dumb, she tries to fend it off by pretending that she wasn't paying attention. If she doesn't understand what is happening, she reasons, she can't be held responsible for making an off-base remark or a foolish decision.

But this strategy, of course, only makes her appear to be what she's trying *not* to be—an airhead. Her behavior gives friends and foes alike all the ammunition needed to shoot her down. Clearly, she set herself up for the name-calling she most dreaded. Until she learns to deal with the cause of the criticism, she's not likely to get a different result.

I will no longer hand out rocks for people to throw at me.

We never reflect how pleasant it is to ask for nothing. —Seneca

Few of us retain independent judgment as to what makes a successful life. Our "gotta have it" society actually induces need as it barrages us with images of the glorified selves we will be once we have "it"— whether it be a better body or a bigger car. The result is an abiding sense of ourselves as incomplete. And when self-completion always hinges on acquiring one more thing, self-esteem will always be left waiting in the wings.

Do we need—or even want—everything we think we do? Must we always be in the position of waiting for, saving for, wishing for . . . ? Is there any such thing as that "last thing" we must have to put us over the top? Or have we mindlessly bought into a false image of ourselves as lacking and hungry? Could it be that we already *have* what we really need?

Independent judgment enables us to make a distinction between necessities and add-ons. Are we able to think, to love, to laugh? Can we see and enjoy the beauty in the world? Are there people who care about us? If that isn't enough, there is no such thing as enough. How gratifying to stop putting happiness on hold!

Serenity is knowing that I already have what I need.

July 30

Anxiety is the space between "now" and "then."
—Richard Abell

Everybody hates to be anxious. The sweating palms, the thudding heart, the nagging little headache that wakes us up in the middle of the night. But occasional anxiety is not only unavoidable, it's necessary. Without unrest, why would we ever stir ourselves to move forward?

The growth of self-esteem is often fertilized by several good doses of anxiety. When we're feeling really uncomfortable, we tend to seek comfort. Frequently that comfort comes in the form of the relief we feel when we stop procrastinating. There may be anxiety in putting pen to paper, but even more anxiety in *not* writing that letter we need to write. And apologizing out loud *once* can't be more stressful than practicing that apology over and over again in our own minds.

Personal growth takes risk, energy, and dissatisfaction with the status quo. If that means an occasional bout of anxiety, then so be it. When we learn to accept the message that anxiety is trying to deliver—that we need to get up and going—we'll have a lot less to be anxious about.

I can channel my anxiety into creative energy.

When a child, my dreams rode on your wishes,
I was your son, high on your horse,
My mind a top whipped by the lashes
Of your rhetoric: windy, of course.
—Stephen Spender

There is a delicate balance—in the pursuit of personal growth, in general, and self-esteem, in particular—between loving and courting acceptance from our parents and being enslaved by the need for that acceptance.

It is helpful, as the poet tells us, to recognize that our 'dreams rode on your wishes," but also to know that those wishes and rhetoric may indeed have been "windy." When we consider our parents and the role they played in shaping our self-esteem, it is only fair to acknowledge that they were and are only human.

Just like us, our parents were shaped by their origins. They too, had their disappointments, their needs both met and unmet. They, too, had their share of good and bad life experiences—some of which, just like ours, were the result of nothing more than random luck. They, too, were subject to the windy rhetoric of others. Understanding, patience, and forgiveness are as good for us to give as to get. On either end, we profit.

I take a major leap when I allow my parents the same rights I allow myself.

August 1

Let us always be open to the miracle of the second chance.
                                        —Reverend David Stier

Nunc coepi is a Latin phrase often heard in seminaries of old. It means, "Now I begin." Novices were taught to say this each morning, signifying that what *was* is past, what *will be* is hidden in the future, and it is only *now*— this day, this moment—that counts. Not what I did yesterday or what I may do tomorrow. *Now* I begin. *Nunc coepi.*

Every day is another chance and a fresh start. It's important to remember that. Too many of us are hyperaware of all the yesterdays we wasted or the phantom tomorrows that could bring us down. Yet we're hardly aware at all of the day that's right here in our hands, shimmering with possibilities. Why do we do that? Why do we so habitually discount and brush off the wonder of the present moment?

One reason may be that we don't trust ourselves. Because of past mistakes, we're afraid to get very hopeful. In fear of failing again, we choose to downplay the possibilities and try to settle for what comes, rather than actively creating it. The bottom line may be that we really don't believe in second chances.

But each day *is* new whether we believe in it or not. We can begin fresh every morning if we decide to live our lives that way. The miracle isn't that the chance is there; it always has been there. The miracle is what happens when we reach out to embrace it.

As long as there is life, there is the chance to start over.

Man is not a creature of circumstances. Circumstances are the creatures of men.
—Benjamin Disraeli

Some of the tragedies and losses people encounter in life are almost too terrible to think about. Many of them are completely random and unpreventable. And along with calamity comes the temptation to give up hope, to abandon the will to continue, to fold up the tent of our self-esteem and just sink into the ground.

Yet there are those who would not give in or give up. These are our examples of the strength of the human spirit. To them, the tragic part of their lives was just that—a *part* of their lives, one circumstance among many.

Dorothy, at sixty-three, went back to school and got her college degree. This was shortly after her husband died. She learned to drive so she could put her degree to use in a professional job. Then she fell victim to a stroke—a blood clot in the brain. Surgery left her partially visually impaired and subject to a debilitating numbness on her entire right side. No longer able to drive or to keep her professional job, she responded, "Just because my body no longer works very well doesn't mean my mind quit." Now she is an author. Some folks just won't quit. Instead, they create new circumstances.

Persistence is the homely virtue that underlies all others.

August 3

Come forth into the light of things,
Let Nature be your teacher.
> —William Wordsworth

As a landscaper specializing in small spaces, Janet is often asked to create miniature gardens in the courtyards outside of offices. During the planning stage, she's often amused by her client's wish for a "sweeping vista" effect—on a fifteen-by-fifteen-foot plot! But she's less amused when they want her to rewrite Mother Nature's rules. "They wanted a shade tree, they got a shade tree," Janet said. "And now they're mad about it. Can you imagine people getting mad at a tree for dropping leaves?"

We do it all the time. Foolish as it is, we often get exasperated with people and things for being what they are. We get irritated to find that some of their charms have a most uncharming flipside. Like Janet's client, we only want the beautiful shade in the summer—not the messy cleanup in the fall.

In many ways, people—including us—simply are what they are. We are our height, our hairlines, our backgrounds. We are our coloring, our race, our sex. Much about us cannot and should not ever be changed. To take all of Nature's gifts and then bewail the downside is ungrateful as well as foolish.

Self-esteem must not be based on changing what is better accepted.

He was my North, my South, my East, my West,
My working week and Sunday rest,
My noon, my midnight, my talk, my song,
I thought that love would last forever—I was
*   wrong.*   —W. H. Auden

Falling head over heels in love is about the sweetest tumble there is to take. But like all falls, it can be dangerous. We can lose ourselves in our fascination with our newfound beloved. We can literally get carried away from our senses on a sea of love.

To allow another to be "everything" to us is not only injurious to the loved one, but a terrible disservice to ourselves. Being someone else's "noon and midnight" is a heavy responsibility. Is it really loving to create and hand over such a burden? Especially if we've already placed that person on a pedestal too high for comfort?

And what about ourselves? If the beloved is "our talk and our song," what will become of our own ideas, our own music? The bedazzlement of a new relationship doesn't last forever. Sooner or later our heads will clear and our perspective will be regained. In the meantime, we're wise to keep our feet as close to the ground as possible.

To make anyone my "all in all" is to damage my self-esteem.

August 5

Behold I do not give lectures or a little charity,
When I give, I give myself. —Walt Whitman

Self-esteem is certainly one of life's greatest treasures. That's why we'd dearly like to instill this trait in those we love. But how can we best accomplish this?

Self-esteem is often associated with performance This is so because the size of our self-esteem account depends on our repeated experiences of success or failure. Positive for success, negative for failure. Therefore, helping someone achieve positive self-esteem means helping them achieve. But again, how can we best do this?

Count the ways this has been tried: the carrot and stick routine, demanding, threatening, bribing, coaxing, pleading—all have been tried again and again. Yet nothing seems to make more difference than simply showing the others that we care—care about *them*, about *their* goals, about *their* dreams, and the problems *they* encounter. Which, of course, is far different than promoting our own version of what's in their self-interest.

I know that caring attention paid to other people's own goals is the greatest motivator of all.

*As far as we can discern, the sole purpose of
human existence is to kindle a light in the darkness of mere being.*
                                        —Carl Jung

A truly beautiful object, like a well-designed building
or a magnificent gem, can be appreciated from many
angles. From either side, top, bottom, close up or far-
away, a thing of beauty is still beautiful. Photos of
earth from space, for example, show the entire planet
as a breathtaking sight indeed. The microscopic view
of a single drop of water, by the same token, reveals
dazzling complexity.

Human life, in general, and self-esteem, in particular, are much like that as well. Through self-esteem we
can appreciate the close-up beauty of life as we deal in
specifics: Do the right thing, strive to make the hard
decisions, slow down, make love. There is plenty to
admire in the personal.

And beyond that there is the "more" that makes up
the long-range view. Every positive personal act lights
a candle in the great unknown of human possibility. If
we could stand back far enough, where individual actions merge into nonrecognition, we could see that a
single act of goodness, of heroism, may continue to
flicker long after we are gone. Together, we may well
be lighting the way for generations yet to come.

**Even the smallest act of courage or kindness con-
tributes to the whole.**

August 7

How many cares one loses when the decision is made not to be something, but someone.
—Coco Chanel

Toddlers want to do what "big kids" of six or seven can do. Ten year olds want to be like teenagers. Admiring, comparing, imitating, are all part of the developmental process. We want to be as big, pretty, strong, or just plain wonderful as "they," our models, are. As best we can, we make ourselves fit the mold. That's how children learn and grow.

But adults stop learning and growing when they try to be *what* someone else is rather than *who* they themselves are. We turn our backs on our own uniqueness when we ape another person's personality or mannerisms or style. We belittle our own potential when we fashion ourselves to be "just like" a person or group who, in their need for acceptability, tried to be "just like" someone else.

Self-realization is neither a spin-off nor a patchwork of imitated bits. Who we are and are capable of being as individuals is singular and unrepeatable. There is not only dignity but great adventure in doing what it takes to discover our true, inimitable selves, each of us a "one and only" with a unique presence to be established and a unique contribution to make.

Self-discovery is the first step toward self-appreciation.

It is trying to treat half-truths as whole truths that plays the devil.

—Alfred North Whitehead

With a little reflection, it's easy enough to see some of the ways we try to wiggle out of responsibility. Half-truths, for example, at least half-satisfy our tattered code of honor. We know there's a big difference between saying "I tried," and going on to admit, "but not very hard." But how much harm does a little fudging do? What's the big deal?

The problem is that playing with truth is like playing with fire. When partial honesty becomes a habit, we may not even notice that we're losing the good right along with the bad.

Here are examples of what we can lose out on if we get used to chopping off truths in the middle: "I make mistakes, but I'm better than my mistakes." "Life is full of tragedy, but great beauty as well." "I have many doubts, but I believe in my ability to resolve them." "The future looks uncertain, but I'll deal with that when I get there." The whole truth is really the only truth there is. Stopping short of that costs us more than it spares us.

As my self-esteem grows, I am able to speak the whole truth.

August 9

We can't win if we want to lose.
—J. W. Wheeler

Sometimes what we *think* we want is different from what we *really* want. Who would want to lose? When success means winning, who would ever choose to lose and thus reinforce low self-esteem? *We* would, if losing is what makes us feel comfortable.

Due to many powerful family-of-origin reasons, a great many of us are programmed to lose. These motivations are subconscious, of course. In spite of our best intentions, that programming, drumming in our heads—"You don't deserve much," "It can never turn out better than it is," "Who do you think you are even to try to succeed?"—is like a constant, mental heartbeat. If the tracks lead to last place and the train is on the tracks, where will the train go? There can be only one answer.

On the road to improved self-esteem, we often find ourselves getting sidetracked and stalled. We are perplexed when our best efforts meet with surprising resistance. The reason may well be that we are battling deeply ingrained mental attitudes rather than outside obstacles. Often what we need is reprogramming. A good start would be daily affirmations like, "I am just as worthy of success as anybody else" or "There are no limits to my personal growth."

Only when I can envision myself in the winner's circle can winning become a real possibility.

Love thy neighbor as thyself.
—Lev. 19:18

If everyone followed this command from Scripture, the world would be a much safer, more nurturing place to live. The systems that create devastating self-esteem in so many of us would cease to exist.

Yet this imperative rests on the assumption that most people *do* love themselves. By nature most people tend to look to their own survival first; we learn how to *protect* ourselves. But that doesn't mean that most people learn to actually love, respect, and honor who they are.

How well can we love our neighbors when we're not at all sure that *we* deserve to be loved? What if we feel we have no rights, that our feelings don't count? That we are only as good as our work, that everything we do must be perfect, or that we are just basically unworthy human beings? If such thoughts and convictions are our starting point, what kind of love can we offer our neighbors?

If I would truly love others, I must first learn to love myself.

August 11

Keep not ill company lest you increase the number.
　　　　　　　　　　　　　　—George Herbert

For our own good, sometimes we have to turn our backs on what is not so good. Often these are relationships that have a negative influence on us. When our healing depends on sticking to a new set of behaviors, we simply can't afford the risk that these people represent.

It may hurt to say good-bye to people who were important to us in the past. But going backward now would hurt even more. We can remember our old friends fondly without feeling guilty about moving on. Their lives will go on just as ours will. We can give them the right to make their own choices—just as we make ours—without blaming anybody. But we can't stay on the same path with them once we've turned the corner.

Growth means change and change means letting go of the old to make way for the new. A seed doesn't "betray" other seeds when it grows into a flower. As we head off in new directions, we will find new friends who are going the same way. By sharing new experiences, we'll form bonds that are just as strong as the bonds we now have to break with our traveling companions of the past.

Positive, supportive friends are essential to my program of growth.

*At first I thought I was in love. Then I discovered
I was just dependent.*   —Joan H.

Love and dependency are as different as night and day. Although at times they may look and even feel the same, understanding the difference may be the only way to preserve self-esteem.

Whenever we are dependent, we devalue ourselves. Addiction always results in the loss of freedom and dignity. To compulsively cling to any relationship is to forgo choice, which is a requisite of love. Rather than loving as an act of free will, we are simply acting out an addiction. When a relationship focuses only on the wishes and needs of the other, self-respect is impossible.

The person experiencing an addictive relationship suffers enormous stress at the thought of losing the relationship. Thus there is irrational willingness to do, say, or think whatever it takes to keep the relationship going. Self-esteem is always traded off in such situations. Whether we deny them or not, we do have our own needs. What we think matters, how we feel counts, and what we have to say must be listened to and taken seriously. Fear, not love, is what impels us to put any relationship before our own well-being.

Emotional independence is a must for my self-esteem as well as for my relationships.

August 13

*Faith is to believe what you do not see; the reward
for this faith is to see what you believe.*
—Saint Augustine

When stressful circumstances in our lives sadden or
frighten us, the Twelve Step slogan "act as if" can be a
powerful tool. That means that we get our behavior out
there *in front* of our emotions—not the other way
around. We whistle a happy tune, for example, in spite
of our unhappy circumstance. The point is that we
believe in progress enough to *anticipate* improvement.
In our certainty that the negative emotion will pass,
we, in effect, say "thank you" for the gift of serenity
because we know that gift is on its way.

Self-esteem seekers who pretend that there is no difficulty to be overcome are *not* "acting as if," but fooling
themselves. Like all program slogans, "act as if" can
cause us more trouble than good if we misinterpret its
meaning. The counsel is to put some management back
in our lives, not to deny that better management is
needed. Not to slack off on the new behaviors that are
slowly building up our self-confidence.

By courageously forging on, people who are "acting
as if" are asserting, in the face of life's very real downside, that there is *also* an upside. They are acknowledging both but making a conscious choice to match
their behavior with their belief.

**My behavior is dictated by my faith, not my emo-
tions.**

Deceive not thyself by overexpecting happiness in the married estate. Remember the nightingales which sing only some months in the spring, but commonly are silent when they have hatched their eggs.
—Thomas Fuller

Many people would say that marriage is a major factor in determining self-esteem. Those who are not married often feel that their state of singleness causes their unhappiness. Those who are married often blame their less-than-ideal marriages for their less-than-ideal lives. Both are mistaken.

Contented self-acceptance doesn't depend on being either married or single, but whether we are *happily* married or *happily* single. To place too much importance on marital status misses the point. Our self-esteem is contingent on our own ability to be happy, whether we live alone or have a partner. There are just too many single people with grand self-esteem and too many married people in desperate trouble (and vice versa) ever to doubt that this is so.

Single or not, married or not, we can be a whole lot happier if we take responsibility for our own fulfillment. A partner can only add or detract from what we already have. If we know how to be happy with ourselves, we *will* be happy. If we don't, then changing our marital status isn't going to help us.

My self-esteem depends more on me than it does on any partner.

August 15

Integrity: *firm adherence to a code of moral values.*
                                    —*Webster's Ninth*

What rules govern our daily lives? Besides stopping at red lights and waiting our turn in the supermarket—no one wants to make trouble in public—what standards of behavior do we use as a yardstick? It's important to know what they are because our internal "rules" define our integrity.

All of us have our own personal "code," whether we're aware of it or not. Most of it we got at home. If Mom yelled but didn't slap, we probably draw the same line. If Dad was generous on the street but stingy at home, we may see double standards as normal. And some of our rules were forged out of our own experience. Perhaps a long-ago humiliation in the schoolyard taught us to trust no one. Or maybe we have been harshly punished into believing that honesty is *not* the best policy—that honesty is for fools.

The rules we can quickly identify may be quite different from the hidden rules that direct our lives. Discovering them can take some digging, but we need to know what those rules are, where we got them, and whether or not they still make sense.

Following self-defeating rules is my sure path to self-defeat.

I am not now
That which I have been.
　　　—Lord Byron

Sometimes all of our efforts to move ahead seem like fruitless busywork. We try so hard and seem to change so little! In the last flickers of consciousness before sleep, we may hear our inner voices of doubt and despair asking, "Is change possible? Do people really change—or do they just make little changes? Is it really possible to heal a self-image that's riddled with bullet holes?"

When we feel that way, it might help to think about Mike. Sober eight years, Mike was sharing from his heart at a Friday night AA meeting. "I lived on the street for twelve years," he said. "When I first came into AA I had to hold onto my chair with both hands, I was shaking so bad. But my sponsor told me that every day I stayed sober would be Christmas, so I kept coming back. The day I began my sober life was December 23."

Many in the room knew of Mike's journey up from the alleys and dumpsters and flophouses. Some remembered him when he came in—more dead than alive spiritually and physically. But tonight they saw him brimming over with wisdom, warmth, and most of all gratitude.

"To remind myself of where I was, I've kept my little plastic Christmas tree up for all of these eight years. I plug in the lights every morning to remind me of what can be done, one day at a time."

I am not now what I was.

August 17

*In silence alone does a man's truth bind itself
together and take root.*
—Antoine de Saint-Exupery

Constant noise can slowly but surely condition us to a
constant inner cringe. Adaptive as we are, we may not
even notice that we're barraged with noise most of our
waking hours. But our bodies and spirits notice it, and
cry out for relief.

Our precious peace of mind knows that *something* is
hammering at it, assaulting and disturbing serenity.
Even our hearing is being affected, according to German
scientists who recently warned that before long
hearing aids will be as common as glasses. And police
statistics show that crime rates are higher in areas
where noise levels are consistently high. Noise is the
background music of tension, anxiety, and rage.

Regular periods of quiet time are absolutely essential
to emotional and spiritual growth. Unless we can put
three or four thoughts together without a bang or a
roar, we'll never be able to think very deeply. We can't
dream our dreams to the tune of thumps and buzzes.
If we want to get in touch with our spirits, we're going
to have to get away from noise in whatever way we
can—perhaps by using earplugs, or by spending noon
hours in the library. Only then will we be able to hear
what Wisdom may whisper to us in the hallowed halls
of silence.

**Creating noise-free time may help me more than
I realize.**

Whatever needs to be maintained through force is doomed. —Henry Miller

When someone we love is in trouble, we may try to control or at least curb the trouble-causing behavior. With the sincerest wish for their welfare, we throw out their liquor or hide the doughnuts when we see them coming. Our justification is that "we're only trying to help," and well might that be. But we enter a gray area when we try to manipulate reality on someone else's behalf.

Of course, we care about our loved ones and feel genuine concern when we see them heading for a fall. But caring and caretaking aren't the same thing. For our own emotional well-being, "hands off" other adults' lives is usually the best policy.

More often than not people are doing what they choose to do. We can influence, but they choose. Better than rearranging the environment, we can offer loving advice and then let the subject drop. Our loved ones will do what they want to do anyway. If their unwise choices finally bring them down, we can be there for them. At least we won't have ruined the relationship by nagging and manipulation.

The calisthenics for self-esteem do not include manipulation.

August 19

Laughter is as good as jogging for our heart, lungs, and brain. —Gail Grenier Sweet

Laughter is good for our self-esteem, too. Wise people throughout the ages have told us that laughter is the best folk medicine there is for whatever ails us. Some studies have even shown that laughter seems to alter our brain chemistry and, thus, our immune system. The well-known publisher Norman Cousins' laughter-powered recovery from devastating illness is a convincing case in point.

But scientific proof isn't even necessary. Just look around you. Don't the light-hearted, playful people you know seem to get more out of life than everybody else? Laughing is *fun*. And when we're having fun, it's hard to be down on ourselves, think negative thoughts, or in any other way sabotage our prospects for success.

Laughter lightens the soul, makes friends of enemies, and plugs us into the heart of God—who wants nothing so much for us as happiness. All of the above are marvelous for our self-esteem.

I have as much reason to laugh as I do to scowl.

I was successful because you believed in me.
—Ulysses S. Grant

Anyone who is fortunate enough to have a cheering section—even a one-man band—has a priceless advantage in the search for self-esteem. If we don't have someone to applaud our victories, we need to find someone. And if *we* aren't shouting encouragements at someone else's efforts, we're missing out on one of the finest connections that can be made between human beings.

The young boy playing in his first baseball game will do better if he can see his father sitting in the bleachers. The nervous friend going for an all-important job interview will gain confidence from our pep talk beforehand and the replay over coffee. Knowing that other people have faith in us strengthens our faith in ourselves. Knowing that someone is behind us makes us less fearful of falling backward.

Neighborhoods, offices, clubs, and churches are full of people who will support our efforts if we invite them to. These are the same people, by the way, who need to hear, "You can *do* it! Go get 'em!" just as much as we do. Mutual encouragement can prevent each of us from throwing in the towel.

Self-admiration is made possible by my sincere admiration of others.

August 21

Character cannot be developed in ease and quiet. Only through experience of trial and suffering can the soul be strengthened, vision cleared, ambition inspired, and success achieved.

—Helen Keller

Self-esteem is totally relative to integrity. When integrity is defended, self-esteem is enhanced. When integrity is compromised, character suffers, and self-esteem is the first casualty.

The dictionary tells us that integrity is unimpaired wholeness, or incorruptibility. What corrupts character? In a nutshell, it is always dishonesty, in one form or another. That makes the solution obvious, doesn't it? All we have to do is to get honest with ourselves.

The problem is that getting honest can be traumatic. Many of the thinking and behavior patterns that erode character are the selfsame patterns that have made us feel safe. They are the thoughts and deeds we thought we needed to survive. Perhaps all our lives we have used these dishonesties to get approval, acceptance, and what we imagined was our best shot at intimacy.

Many people are now struggling with self-esteem because they habitually agree when they want to object, smile when they want to cry, work when they want and need to play. These are dishonest behaviors. No matter what benefits they may have provided, we have to confront them now as the liabilities they have become.

Self-honesty is displayed in actions, not words.

*Flowers leave part of their fragrance in the hands
that bestow them.* —Chinese Proverb

It is a paradox that the more we give away the more we
have. Not in money, perhaps, but certainly in character and self-esteem. When we are thinking of others,
we are much less likely to be worrying about ourselves.
There's a double payoff.

True giving asks no return. There is no remember-
ing, no expectation, no greediness for gratitude. And
none of us is too poor to give love, respect, attention,
encouragement, time, caring, assistance, compassion.
These busy days perhaps the most precious gift we
have to offer our family and friends is the gift of listening. And we can never give the gift of attention
without being repaid in deeper understanding. What
we give comes back to us.

Scripture tells us to bear one another's burdens. Experience tells us that it is impossible for a generous
heart to give away more than it gets. To ease another's
pain is to ease our own.

**When I reach to help others, I cannot help feel-
ing better about myself.**

August 23

No one like you was ever born or ever will be.
—Constance Foster

We may laugh at the oddballs and eccentrics of this world but at least they have the courage to be themselves. Most of us lack the plain old intestinal fortitude to claim our own uniqueness. For fear of being ridiculed or shunned, we talk and dress and act just as everyone else does—often dwarfing our self-esteem in the process.

Yet all of us weren't born to dance to the same music. Each and every one of us is a one of a kind, an original. Unconventional ideas are the seedbed of innovation and progress. Offbeat humor is a wonderful way to share insight. The expression of imagination isn't the sole right of artists and performers, it's the right of everyone who wants to reach his or her full potential.

Frustration and self-pity are just two symptoms of the failure to express our true selves. Perhaps we have chosen colorlessness as camouflage against attack. Now that we're gaining more self-confidence, however, perhaps it's time to step out of the crowd, wave our own flag, and shout, "This is the real me!"

I am entitled to my own uniqueness.

Addictions medicate pain.
—Chuck Holton

Many of us are heroically trying to shake one or more addictions. Addictions and self-esteem, of course, are incompatible. But many of us find, even after we have broken a primary addiction, that our self-esteem doesn't soar as we had expected it would.

The fact is that the addiction itself is not the whole picture of the addictive life. After the addiction has been broken, we have to face our feelings. Now we must deal with reality without our crutch. Now we come to grips with all the character defects that were hidden behind the addiction. The battle is not merely to arrest our addiction, but to arrest our fear of all the repressed truths and hurts that were always there.

The ongoing journey seems especially tough when all the old "shoulds" crowd around. "I *should* be happier," "I *should* be making faster progress," "I *should* feel better about myself." But the only thing we really need to do is accept that once the addiction stops, the feelings start. Then the long walk begins—but so does the reward.

To run from my pain is to create more pain. The only solution for me is to stand fast and fight it out.

August 25

Forgive yourself for dreaming larger than you have lived.   —Carol Ann Morrow

Forgiveness can be the atomic power of personal growth. Sometimes it's the only force that can blast away the boulders of resentment, insecurity, and bitterness from the door to self-esteem. If such boulders are there, they obviously must be moved if our goal lies beyond them.

Often we most need to forgive ourselves. But oh, the pressure we put on ourselves with unrealistic expectations! How harshly we judge ourselves when we don't measure up! Sometimes self-forgiveness is as necessary as an electric shock to get our spirits going again.

We may be disappointed and ashamed at failing the mighty dreams of youth. But the young have faulty vision. They have no idea of the obstacles that lay ahead. In overestimating the cooperation of the world, all things seemed possible then. But it didn't work out that way. Reality turned out to be something other than a sugar mountain.

Forgiveness lies in accepting reality. What is, is. We are what we are—and that isn't half-bad. We are fighting the good fight. Let that be enough.

Youthful dreams can't be the measure of adult accomplishment.

Let him who gives without a care
Gather rubies from the air.
—James Stephens

Some kinds of giving are really ways of getting. We may give gifts to avoid taxes, salve a guilty conscience, obtain favors, or just to make ourselves look good. Because there is no love behind these actions, we can't expect them to enhance our sense of self.

Giving from the heart, however, is a sure path to spiritual and emotional richness. The loving hearts who give of their substance, not what they have left over, make many lives livable besides their own. Honestly generous spirits are at peace with themselves.

Let the red flag go up if we find ourselves worrying about what we are getting back. A gift isn't an investment. If what we give has strings on it instead of ribbons, it isn't a gift at all but probably a bribe of some kind. We'll never "gather rubies from the air" if a good rate of return is what we're after.

Because good flows from good, self-esteem flows from unselfishness.

August 27

A bitter heart that bides its time and bites.
—Robert Browning

Unresolved anger, especially of the long-lasting kind, can breed terrible bitterness. And bitterness always worsens self-esteem because it feeds on the wrongs, either real or imagined, that were done to us. Bitter resentments fixate on negatives. Frequently, the journey toward self-esteem brings us to mile-high "resentment roadblocks" that test the sincerity of our quest.

One truth of dealing with anger is that no one can get over or past repressed anger if something in us wants to hang onto it. A wound cannot heal if every day we pick the scab. This is where it gets hard. It is one thing to intellectually decide we will not be angry any more. It is altogether a different thing to directly confront an old grudge honestly in the here and now. If it were easy to address these issues, we would have done so long ago.

Are we deeply angry about a situation at work? A relationship? An issue with parenting? Perhaps we have a sore spot from an insult perceived many years ago? What is it that needs to be said, done, communicated? *Not* to act only creates more bitterness, and less self-respect.

Living with bitterness is like eating the peel and throwing away the orange.

When you have shut your doors and darkened your room, remember, never to say that you are alone; for you are not alone, but God is within, and your genius is within. —Epictetus

When we decide to work on self-esteem, we tend to approach it as we do any other new endeavor—first we call in the experts. Our Western perspective tells us that getting anything done means getting first-rate advice and then taking aggressive action. We've all heard that snoozers are losers so we try to get the job done as quickly as we can.

Yet often, in our unending search for more and better knowledge, the role of quiet reflection is never even considered. It never occurs to us to look for our answers within. So we consult impersonal, outside sources rather than the counsel of our own hearts. That's why some of our early starts are false starts; the information we gather doesn't quite fit.

Making a friend of solitude is a primary task for many. For it is in inner consultation, fearful as that may be, that the frightening voices of negativity are most clearly heard. But it is also when we are looking within that the beautiful, unmasked face of our true self is most clearly revealed. And our sincere admiration of that inner beauty is the very definition of self-esteem. Strange as it may seem at first—relying on reflection rather than research—there are great rewards in learning to seek the truth in solitude.

Achieving self-esteem is a discovery process as much as anything.

August 29

It is a sad weakness in us, after all, that the
thought of a man's death hallows him anew to us;
as if life were not sacred, too. —George Eliot

Why do we find it so much easier to compliment the
dead than the living? At funerals, the friends and family members gathered cannot say enough about the
deceased. During life, however, all those qualities that
now draw praise usually went unnoticed.

Life is as sacred as death. It's certainly appropriate to
remember a departed one fondly, but it's even better to
say what we have to say while the person can still hear
it. People don't become better or more deserving in
death than they were in life. Living, not dying, is what
makes us praiseworthy. It is no small thing to fall in
love, to raise a family, to strive to assist others, to live
each day with all its sameness, all its vexations, and all
its tedium, as well as we can.

We need to say all those loving words and express all
those loving thoughts on this side of death. The dead
are beyond the daily struggle, and thus beyond any
need for encouragement. It is we, the living, who must
depend on each other for mutual comfort and support.
If we have a word of appreciation to offer, let us say it
now.

**I will give credit where credit is due before it's
too late.**

Tough Counts.
—Dorothy Reznichek

There is an obvious connection between depression and self-esteem. The more depression we experience, the more difficulty we usually have in retaining a positive sense of self. Depression is flattening. It could actually be called a spiritual steamroller.

Many excellent books have been written on the causes and cures of depression in all of its many faces and degrees. In spite of their various approaches, all of them agree that courage is necessary in dealing with depression. It takes toughness to win. When all the strategizing is done, all the information gained, what is left is simply the call for stamina and grit. Even when "going on" is the last thing in the world we may want or feel able to do.

It takes enormous courage to make a simple affirmation when we feel the world is coming down around our ears. To get out to a meeting when all we want to do is sleep or cry is sheer bravery, and nothing less. To reach out when all we want to do is isolate may take the heroism of a medal-of-honor winner.

When all is said and done, toughness may be my best weapon.

August 31

*Who are "they" that hold so much power over
our lives?*   —Orville Thompson

Grace was facing a major decision. She didn't want to
go on living with her alcoholic husband. Grace knew
that alcoholism is a disease, that her husband was a
sick man who needed help, yet she now found it impossible to remain in the marriage. She wanted to be a
wife, not a nurse. For years she had remained in this
dead, toxic relationship because of "them." What
would "they" say? How would she ever face "them"?
"They" would never respect her again if she got a divorce.

Gradually, Grace's support group maneuvered her
into confronting the power of the nebulous "they."
Who exactly were "they"? Why were "they" so important? Was everyone she knew to be lumped into one
generalized "they"? If not, would the reaction to her
impending decision be the same for all of these people?

In time, Grace came to understand there is no universal "they." Those who would criticize her decision
were only one segment of "they." And not an important one at that. As she became strong enough to think
for herself, her fears about what "they" might think
began to weaken. By reclaiming her own power, she
also reclaimed her self-esteem—as well as the genuine
prospect of a happy new life.

**I am always at grave risk when I give my self-
esteem over to the care of a generalized, negative
"they."**

September 1

Honesty, without compassion and understanding, is not honesty, but subtle hostility.
— Dr. Rose N. Franzblau

In their attempts to rebuild self, recovering people can sometimes be cruel. Those who identify themselves as recovering Adult Children may be the worst offenders. This is because so much of our program requires that we get in touch with old messages and old feelings. As we look back, we often see that there was abuse in our past. We come to realize that some people have done us serious wrongs.

In the name of recovery, we can be tempted to honestly unload on those who hurt us long ago. With the cleanest of consciences, we can force them to share some reality whether they want to or not. But if our honesty is not tempered with sensitivity, we can say things that, although true, may be terribly hurtful. We can be as abusive to them as they were to us—and all in the name of recovery!

Self-esteem can never be gained at someone else's expense. There well may be truths that have to be shared. But it's the *sharing* that heals, not the person who listens. If what we must say will make it difficult, if not impossible, to improve the relationship, we need to check out our motives. Cruelty doesn't redress cruelty. Wreaking revenge and recovering are opposite processes. If sharing means violating the law of love, we need to talk to someone else.

If the collection process does more harm than good, the debt is better canceled.

September 2

*He who cannot rest, cannot work; He who cannot
let go, cannot hold on; He who cannot find footing,
cannot go forward.*

—Harry Emerson Fosdick

There is a part of the human psyche that wants to get
right along to the last step, to wrap things up. Sometimes before we barely get started, we want to jump to
the conclusion. Happy endings are our favorite part of
any project.

Yet behind every successful conclusion is a productive plan. Conclusions are consequences, and all consequences are *caused*—they're the result of something
that went before. We are wise when we take the time
to see and understand what it takes to make a happy
ending really happen.

There can be no productive work without rest, no
holding on without letting go, no going forward without firm footing—even if finding that footing costs us
some time and a few tumbles. Every step of the way is
made possible by the step that preceded it. Satisfying
conclusions come to be when we take *all* of the steps,
one at a time, and stop sabotaging the project with
shortcuts.

**Self-esteem thrives on the satisfaction of a job
well done.**

September 3

Self-pity is easily the most destructive of the non-pharmaceutical narcotics: It is addictive, gives momentary pleasure, and separates the victim from reality.
                                    —John Gardner

Fostering self-esteem means taking care of ourselves. Often we need to treat ourselves easy, give ourselves the benefit of the doubt, remind ourselves of how far we have come rather than how far we have to go. Yet there is a fine line between sympathizing with our own struggles and wallowing in self-pity.

Self-pity works against self-esteem because it blinds us to reality. Self-pity wears a black veil over its downcast head. Because it never looks up, it sees only part of the picture. And it is only on the anvil of reality that we are able to hammer out something of value. We can't work with what we can't see.

We need to stay on duty, hammering away, making the sparks fly. As we do, we not only see what is tragic in our lives but what we can do about it. The difference between bad luck and bad judgment will become clearer. What is beyond our power to change will be separated from what we can very well change if we so choose. Self-pity, in its dark glasses, can't see any of that.

My prospects are as real as my wounds.

September 4

It is by tiny steps that we ascend to the stars.
—Jack Leedstrom

Two years after a painful divorce, Jan decided it was time to pick up the pieces of her life. The first thing she did to renew her self-esteem was to start a modest savings program. Since childhood, Jan had an ongoing problem with financial irresponsibility. Not that she didn't work hard and make a fair wage. But for some reason, probably buried deeply in family-of-origin issues, she could not and would not save a nickel.

Because she *literally* couldn't save a nickel, she started by saving pennies. In an old peanut butter jar on a closet shelf, her program started. Over weeks, pennies led to nickels, nickels to dollars, and dollars to a brand new habit of fiscal stability.

Easy to look at a pathetic little jar and say, "Big deal! Pennies!" Yet it was a big deal because it was a first step, and any first step, no matter how small, is a legitimate cause for celebration.

It's not the size of the step that counts, but the fact that I take it.

September 5

Worry is a time-waster and ulcer-maker.
—Gail Grenier Sweet

Recognizing that we have serious self-esteem issues to deal with may rock us back on our heels. It may take a bit of time to accept the situation and even a little longer to figure out what to do about it. Nothing wrong with that. At this point, the only wrong thing we can do is to *worry* about it.

Worry is a form of wheel spinning. It wastes energy that could better be used to solve the problem we're worrying about. It wastes the time that could have been invested in the future. It wastes life because worry blankets every spark and flicker of joy. And without joy, what is there to live for?

Certainly we have genuine reasons for concern when we get honest with ourselves. Some of the tasks we face are far from easy, and we realize now that the stakes are too high to avoid them. But concern and worry are very different things. Worry is nonproductive and obsessive. Long after concern has done all it can, worry is still grinding away, wheels spinning in the sand.

Worry focuses on the things that I *can't* change, rather than the things that I can do something about.

September 6

The example of good men is visible philosophy.
—English Proverb

Just as we do not live in a vacuum, untouched by others and touching no one, so too, our efforts to maintain positive self-esteem are not isolated or self-contained. No matter how common and ordinary we think we are, we influence others. In ways we never notice or intend, everything we do reaches out and touches someone. And as with all human contact, the effect can be positive or negative.

Just think of all the people who see us or hear us in the course of a day. As we try to think well of ourselves and act that way, as we commit to the behaviors that evaluate our self-esteem, we are constantly having an impact on the people around us. Who knows the battles going on within the walled-up hearts of a brother or sister next to us? Who knows what really lurks behind the happy facades our fellow human beings are willing to show us? Perhaps a world of hurt.

A smile, a word of encouragement, or a compliment may well be the spillover of our own efforts to help ourselves. Transformed, any good we do ourselves may become the golden key that opens a long-rusted door in someone else's heart. We are more powerful people than we realize we are. What we do or fail to do is important to other people as well as ourselves.

Ordinary people often wield extraordinary influence.

A man was starving in Capri.
He turned his eyes and looked at me.
　　—Edna Saint Vincent Millay

Some people are both blessed and burdened with extraordinary empathy and compassion. Because of early social training or perhaps even a bit of genetic code, they're far more sensitive than most to other people's distress. They're quick to identify, understand, and vicariously "feel" the hardships and heartaches that less-aware people don't even notice.

Nobody knows how many hearts have been lightened, how many tears dried, by these tender, caring souls. But this capacity, whether it's born or learned or both, is a lovely rose with thorns attached. The danger, of course, is in going too far, giving too much, developing a soft head to go along with the soft heart.

Self-esteem soars when we honor our values. But our expectations of self must be grounded in reality. It isn't possible to respond to *every* cry for help. To be effective over the long haul, compassionate works must be guided by discipline and wisdom. Even the best impulses don't have a limitless bank of energy to draw on. If we want to have something to give tomorrow, we must learn to pace ourselves today.

Managing compassion takes as much thoughtful planning as managing any other powerful resource.

September 8

During his lifetime, an individual should devote his efforts to creating happiness and enjoy it.
—Ch'en Tu-hsiu

Happiness is not constant for anyone, but our capacity for it is. There is never a time in our lives when we cannot strive for happiness. Yet striving for happiness is a different proposition than wishing to be happy. Many of us have slipped into a passive role. We wait for happiness, we hope for it, we complain if we go too long without it, but we stop actively striving to be happy.

Yet to strive is to try. It is to consciously make plans and consistently keep to those plans in the pursuit of the desired goal. People who achieve any worthwhile goal are strivers. There's no other way it could be. Excellence is but the polished face of practice.

So too, in the pursuit of self-esteem, we must learn to be steady strivers. We must get off the bench and do our daily readings, practice the positive word, avoid those people and places that would cast us down—all the step-by-step behaviors that ultimately result in our reaching the goal.

My happiness is a result, not a gift.

September 9

Courage is walking naked through a cannibal village.
—Sam Levenson

Nakedness before people eaters has to be the ultimate vulnerability, doesn't it? The idea is so awful it would almost be funny—if it weren't somehow *familiar*. Unfortunately, horror images of vulnerability are nothing new to many of us.

Our own "cannibal village" is any place we happen to be when we decide, for the sake of self-esteem, that it's time to put our defenses down. Perhaps to win our freedom, we face the prospect of breaking an addiction to some substance or person. We know we'll have to strip ourselves of delusion and denial, to let go of our protective covering, to get the job done. Maybe we have to stand up and sound off to an overbearing parent who has dogged our lives well into adulthood; talk about feeling vulnerable! Maybe the cannibals we fear are the real feelings we have to expose ourselves to for the first time; surely they'll pick our bones!

We all have an especially dangerous place we want to avoid. We'll go miles out of our way to walk around it, to make sure we're not anywhere near there without a whole lot of protection. "Anything but that!" we say, "Anywhere but there!" But if going in there naked is what it takes, then that is what it takes.

My dangers diminish as my self-confidence increases.

September 10

Courage is contagious. When a brave man takes a stand, the spines of others are stiffened.
—Billy Graham

Courage is personal. All of us hammer it out—or don't—in the privacy of our own souls. No one can be courageous *for* you anymore than you can be courageous for someone else. The buck stops with us.

Yet there is a communal element in all individual growth. When any of us takes a stand, a model has been created to inspire the rest of us. In ways we would never guess, our smallest brave efforts—which may not even be particularly successful—have results that reach beyond us. A single deed of ours may become the stone someone else uses to start building a new foundation.

All human words and deeds are something like radio transmitters. Vibrations and messages are going out from us constantly. We have no idea how many may be "tuned in," but most of us have a far wider audience than we realize. A word spoken against bigotry, a refusal to use drugs, a willingness to keep on plodding against the odds—these are just a few of the courageous personal behaviors that radiate light into the darkness. Even though our intention isn't, and shouldn't be, to "wow" other people—it's good to know that our personal sweat, as a side effect, might water somebody else's garden.

Don't look now—but someone is watching!

Habit is stronger than reason.
—George Santayana

Loving or despising ourselves becomes habitual. And habits, as all living things, are in the business of staying alive. When habits are attacked they put up immediate, heroic defenses. All habits do this—the healthy as well as the not so healthy. Thus a habitual self-despiser who attempts radical change can expect plenty of resistance. There's no other way it could be.

In the midst of our efforts to bolster self-image—if these efforts go against a long-held habit of self-defeat—all of a sudden we may find ourselves thinking, "I have a right to be any way I want to be," or "This self-renewal stuff is all fantasy. I am what I am and will always be that way."

Self-pity often rears its ugly head in defense of old habits. This ingrained spoiler may seductively tell us, "Poor me. I had it so bad growing up, I have an excuse for not trying," or "I just wasn't born with many gifts. Other people have a much easier time than I, so if I try to be better, I will only fail." Old habits die hard. Resistance is to be expected, seen for what it is—and counterresisted.

Self-pity and despair are the bodyguards of long-enthroned habits.

September 12

The worst sin toward our fellow creatures is not to hate them, but to be indifferent to them: that's the essence of inhumanity.

—George Bernard Shaw

All of us remember hurtful times when we were snubbed or overlooked. Indifference can wound us as badly as hatred. How we handle those wounds is an accurate indication of how we handle our lives. Will those sore spots heal or fester, inspire or demoralize? Self-esteem decides.

Some fifty years ago a poor boy sat fishing with his cane pole on the banks of a river. Once in a while, a big, fancy boat would go by filled with laughing, well-dressed people. But none ever stopped. No one ever asked that little boy if he'd like to take a ride. The boy couldn't understand this. With a child's logic, he wondered why. After all, they had plenty of room, and they clearly saw him sitting there on the muddy bank. Some of them even waved. Why didn't they ask him to come along?

Today that young fisherman of yesteryear has several large boats of his own. Every week he invites groups of people who don't have access to such finery to join him on a nice, long boat ride. The pleasure he was denied he can now provide to others. And he never passes a boy on the riverbank without asking him if he'd like a ride.

Giving is sweet; giving what I didn't get is even sweeter.

Beware no man more than thyself.
—Thomas Fuller

If we're serious about reconditioning our attitudes and thus our self-perception, we want to stack the odds in our favor as much as possible. For one thing, we should stay away from naysayers, fools, fast talkers, seducers—or any others who would nail our shoes to the floor when we want to move forward. It is a wise person indeed who knows who and what to avoid.

Yet it is also wise to remember that we ourselves are both our own best friend and worst enemy. Bad companions or not, no one can force us to do anything without our consent. Every day may bring dozens of invitations to cynicism, negativity, self-pity, stinking thinking—but we can turn them down. If we accept, however, we have only ourselves to blame. We opened the mail, after all; we picked up the phone.

Because of ignorance, jealousy, or fear, other people may throw rocks in our path. But in the final analysis, *we* are the ones with both the bad habits that need to be overcome and the power to overcome them. It is we, not anyone else, who hold the key to all that power.

I must be aware of the enemy within as well as the enemy without.

September 14

Beware of your expectations for they become your reality.
—Elita Darby

Safeguarding our valuables only makes sense. Our homes, our families, our reputations are precious beyond price. Perhaps no valuable, however, needs more careful safeguarding than the integrity of our thoughts. For our habitual thoughts become reality.

If we allow ourselves, no matter how subconsciously, to mindlessly assume that the world's ways are predictable, fair, or controllable, then every knock that jostles us will be interpreted as a startling personal attack. We can easily see ourselves as victims of life rather than as participants.

If, however, we make sure to keep a balanced grasp of reality, many of the inconveniences, slights, and absurdities of life will be seen as just that: life as it is. Many, perhaps most, of the things that happen are not necessarily personal. Not necessarily pointed directly at us. When we expect life to be anything but what it is, we set ourselves up for unnecessary disappointment.

My vision of life as it should be is rarely the same as life as it is.

A life spent in making mistakes is not only more honorable but more useful than a life spent doing nothing.
—George Bernard Shaw

The ability to admit our blunders and mistakes is not only gracious, it's absolutely *necessary* if we want to hoist our self-esteem out of a ditch. Self-esteem can't be rescued if false pride comes first. To defend a mistake only doubles its impact.

Yet low self-esteem impels us to hide behind walls of denial or delusion, to blame our mistakes on others, or to protest that they never happened at all. All of which doubles the delusion. The obvious fact, of course, is that no one is perfect. There is no one who never makes mistakes. The separation comes between people who profit from their mistakes and people who do not.

Most of what we learn comes from the mistakes we make. Wisdom, the deepest form of all knowledge, can only be gained by getting out there, getting knocked down, but then getting up and going on—stronger and smarter than we were before. If we are wrong, let us be quick to admit it and make a correction. The only really damaging error is the denial of error.

Honest admission takes the sting out of my mistakes.

September 16

It is sad not to be loved, but it is much sadder not to be able to love.   —Miguel de Unamuno

What could be more crushing than to be in love with someone who is either not in love with you, or who simply does not have the skills necessary for a healthy relationship? Either case is a self-esteem killer. No matter how you try to take care of yourself, or work your program, one-way love is a misery as long as it lasts.

It hurts to reach out to someone who won't or can't reach back. Even if we know the loved one's chemical use or other unattended emotional impairment is the real reason behind the rejection—it's still rejection and it still hurts. Even if we rightfully say, "It's his problem," it's still *our* pain that we have to deal with.

Depending on the situation, what can and must be done varies greatly. What doesn't vary is the sad fact that we can't *make* somebody else love us, no matter how hard we try. No matter how many extra miles we're willing to go, if the other won't move an inch, the relationship won't move an inch either. Until we can accept that and achieve some detachment, we'll be stuck right where we are.

Others have survived doomed love relationships, and so can I.

Praise is the best diet for us, after all.
—Reverend Sydney Smith

As much as we yearn for it and suffer when we don't get it, praise makes most of us uncomfortable. "Thanks," we say, "but I should have finished it yesterday." "Thanks, but I still have ten pounds to go." "Thanks, but the color is all wrong for me." We're almost as bad at accepting compliments as we are at accepting criticism!

It may be that we're embarrassed by our need for recognition. Perhaps what makes us squirm is not the compliment itself—which may be long overdue and less enthusiastic than it should have been—but our fear of exposure. We'd die rather than let anyone know how badly we need to be singled out and appreciated. So we minimize and deflect words of praise as quickly as they are spoken; that way, we keep our "stroke hunger" to ourselves.

What we don't realize is that everybody else is as hungry as we are. Inside each of us, although we be gray or bald, sits a shiny-faced first grader hoping to get a star pasted on his forehead. We all need applause—and we get far less of it than we deserve. As we learn to accept our own neediness, we'll become less self-conscious about accepting praise.

The ability to gracefully accept a compliment is a sign of emotional maturity.

September 18

Half measures availed us nothing.
—*Alcoholics Anonymous* (the Big Book)

In launching any adventure there is a great deal of wisdom in not trying to do the impossible. We only defeat our efforts by burdening ourselves with expectations of doing something that is beyond our power at the present time.

The caution from the "bible" of AA applies not just to action, but to intent. The words *half measures* are also addressed to attitudes like "maybe" or "wouldn't it be nice if" or "someday I'll have to try that." These halfway attitudes get halfway results, of course. When it comes to managing self-esteem or any other valuable asset, we can't afford to end up with nothing.

We might not yet be ready or able to find another career—but the attitude that the change will come is what counts. Today we might not have the strength to confront an abusive situation—but the commitment to build that strength matters more. We might not be able to take a giant step at the present time—but the daily practice that strengthens and stretches our abilities guarantees that the day will come when the ability will be there. When we're doing everything we *can* do, we're making a full effort.

All-or-nothing thinking can also avail me nothing.

Nothing is easier than self-deceit. For what each man wishes, that he also believes to be true.
—Demosthenes

People with great energy and enthusiasm can accomplish wonders. If they're also intelligent and focused, the odds are even better that they'll succeed at whatever they try. Unless they're also dishonest.

A man named Alex was desperately in search of freedom from guilt and the serenity of positive self-esteem. In putting together a program of growth, he decided to go all out. There was *nothing* Alex wouldn't try, no new behavior he wouldn't initiate and practice doggedly. He read all the self-help material he could get his hands on. He kept a journal. He attended meetings every day. Yet for all of his efforts, he remained stuck in a swamp of guilt.

Alex had a drinking problem. Because his drinking was the true source of his nagging guilt, he wasn't going to make any progress unless, *in addition* to his new program activities, he also stopped the addictive drinking. All the energetic "starts" in the world aren't going to help Alex until he summons the courage to make that one, crucial "stop." He's only fooling himself by working so hard at what, for him, is the wrong job.

If success is the goal, first things must be done first.

September 20

*When virtues are pointed out first, flaws seem
less insurmountable.* —Judith Martin

It only makes sense that we can't mow down anybody
else's self-esteem without damaging our own at the
same time. We need to remember that fact when it is
our legitimate task to correct a child, an employee, or
anybody else who falls under our authority. When the
power balance between two people is unequal, insensitivity is all too easy.

Before we call out somebody's shortcomings, it's
only decent to lead off the conversation with some acknowledgment of his or her good qualities. Any positive, sincere statement will do to cushion and make a
context for the criticism that is to follow. Our goal, after
all, is to help that person do better; no one does better
after a bludgeoning.

Sensitive, constructive criticism creates a win-win situation. By beginning with praise, the person in charge
helps the other person to maintain dignity and self-
worth. When we enable others to save face, we demonstrate not only kindness but intelligence, not only
generosity but maturity.

**Criticism of others must be handled carefully,
for my sake as well as theirs.**

Nothing is more difficult, and therefore more precious, than to be able to decide.

—Napoléon I

There are psychological as well as dollars-and-cents reasons for using experts to advise us before we enter new ground. Scouts who have been there before help us minimize our risk. Consultants can help us decide whether we should get involved in the first place.

Yet in personal endeavors, like the quest for self-esteem, outside input has limited value. Ultimately, the build-up or tear-down decisions are ours and ours alone. Suppose, for example, that someone puts us down and somebody else compliments us for the very same quality. Who do we believe? Or say that we have to make a decision that will have a considerable impact on our self-esteem. We consult several wise people and get different advice from each one. Again, who do we believe?

Of course we'd rather share the responsibility and have someone else bear part of the load. Perhaps we'd even like someone else to decide *for* us. But then we would never know the joyful confidence that comes from learning to trust our own judgment.

I can use outside input to validate my reasoning, but I must decide for myself.

September 22

The distance from nothing to a little is ten thousand times more than from a little to the highest degree in this life.
—John Donne

All the "think big!" talk we hear from motivational speakers may actually be deflating when we consider how far we have to go. "Big, indeed," we may mutter to ourselves as we try to muster the courage to take even one baby step in a chosen new direction.

But there's nothing contradictory about thinking big and starting small. The small, realistic start, as a matter of fact, is the best indicator that real progress is in the works. The successes that undergird self-esteem don't come all at once. Real progress is always achieved inch by inch, decision by decision, baby step by baby step. But, oh how important are those first few inches that take us from nowhere to somewhere!

It well may be that *right now* we don't have the strength to overthrow some hated cycle of dependency. But the bottom line isn't what's happening *right now*. If we are making the small decisions and taking the small steps, we *will* have the strength to make our move when the time comes. It all adds up.

True progress takes time and patience.

Speaking is a beautiful folly: with that man dances over all things. —Friedrich Nietzsche

Raising self-esteem is a matter of growth and all growth requires honesty. The opposite of honesty is delusion and denial; nothing real or helpful comes from those deceivers. A common method of tap-dancing around honesty is through intellectualization. When we throw up a smoke screen of words that few can understand or follow, or have enough interest to even care about, we create an escape route from accountability.

In all the readings, verbiage, and meetings associated with self-improvement, we who are inclined to intellectualization can find infinite places to hide. It's easy to create a complicated maze of all the right words and phrases that leads to nowhere. At no point does the meaning of those words connect with *life as we live it*. When we find the buzzwords, we can lose the truth.

Clive recently got called on that in his support group meeting. After his usual twenty-minute display of fancy talk, a fellow group member said, "I don't understand a thing you've said. You're spinning your web again. Talk straight. Who are you? What is really going on with you? What do you want to do about it?" Clive was lucky enough to meet a real friend that night. Greater self-esteem became possible because someone challenged him to step out of the smoke screen.

Fancy words are a poor substitute for the plain truth.

September 24

Each new season grows from the leftovers from the past. That is the essence of change, and change is the basic law —Hal Borland

Coming to terms with ourselves and the world we live in is an ongoing negotiation. It's not the kind of deal we can hammer out once and be done with. Circumstances change. *We* change. The tools and techniques that kept us humming ten years ago may be useless to the people we are today.

When the children were home, for example, we may have invested most of our prime interest and energy in them. Fixing their bikes, chaperoning their dances, sharing in their joys and sorrows, made us feel needed and useful. Now that they're on their own, we need to find a new sense of purpose if this new stage of life is to be as happy and fulfilling as the last one was. Retirement from work presents us with the same challenge; to keep going forward, we need to retool.

Life transitions aren't terrible unless we fight them. Once we may have based our self-esteem on being "last up" in a spelling bee; then we matured a little and moved on to something else. We renegotiated with reality. To stay healthy and happy, we must accept and work with that ongoing, lifelong process. Our task is as ever, to find new and deeper sources of satisfaction.

The building blocks of my self-esteem change as circumstances change.

If the Aborigine drafted an IQ test, all of Western Civilization would presumably flunk it.
—Stanley Garn

Being called "dumb" is hard on our self-esteem. But accepting that insult is even worse. Who has the right to lay such labels on anyone else? There are *many* kinds of "smarts" that don't show up in IQ tests or shine in the classroom. At best, the definition of intelligence is relative.

Many of us shore up our self-esteem by judging others according to our own specialized standards. The schoolteacher who snickers at her mechanic's grammar probably doesn't realize that her own mechanical ignorance makes the mechanic snicker. The artist who can't do his own taxes may well feel superior to the tax preparer who would prefer a snapshot of his own dog to any of the artist's works. The list goes on and on, around and around, all egos vying for an upper slot.

Obviously what shows us as less than brilliant on one scale of measurement may place us near the top of another. As the quote above suggests, how well would any of us fare if we were dropped in the Outback and had to come up with the insights and skills to excel there? We need to stop making phony, superficial comparisons to aggrandize ourselves. We need to stop putting down and writing off people as "dumb." And *never* should we believe anyone who applies that label to us.

Only dumb people call other people "dumb."

September 26

> *The optimist fell ten stories.*
> *At each window bar*
> *He shouted to his friends:*
> *"All right so far!"*
> —Anonymous

Easy to laugh at the plummeting "optimist," but how many times have we ourselves been blindly hopeful about obviously hopeless situations? Have we not refused to look ahead simply because we didn't want to see what was coming? Manufactured "reasons" by the dozens for a totally unreasonable course of action?

Most of us have had times in our lives when we let ourselves float along without thinking about where we were going. Perhaps we knew we were heading for a fall, but somehow we couldn't or wouldn't read the writing on the wall. Maybe we even congratulated ourselves, as the optimist did, for surviving second by second!

Then came the inevitable crash, the devastation, the brokenness. Only then did we realize we aren't "surviving" when we're hurtling downward. Instead, survival was the painful process of cleaning up the mess and mending our wounds. We learned the hard way that flying is a fantasy, floating is far from a free ride, and false optimism makes a poor parachute.

A positive attitude about a negative behavior makes for a negative result.

*There came a certain poor widow, and she threw
in two mites.* —Mark 12:42

The dictionary tell us that a mite is a small coin "worth
very little." The Bible says that two mites were the
equivalent of a penny. By any reckoning, an offering of
two mites is so close to nothing that it almost doesn't
count. What possible difference could it make whether
you give it or not? Why bother if that's the best you can
do?

Jerry showed up at his Saturday morning support
group meeting. Depressed as he was, out of work as he
was, down on himself as he was, he showed up. He
didn't even have a quarter to throw into the coffee
kitty, but he came anyway. "I'm so depressed I hardly
feel I have a right to be here," he told a friend who
greeted him at the door. Jerry didn't speak at that meeting and certainly didn't dance out on his tiptoes, raring
to go. But he did sit there and try to listen. It was the
best he could do.

Like the widow in the Bible story, Jerry contributed
more than all the others that day because he threw in
everything he had—his presence. By simply having
the courage to show up, he added immeasurably to the
"treasury" of his group. Who knows how many others
there, witnessing his refusal to quit, went away im-
pressed and inspired? Who knows that that single act
of dogged determination wasn't Jerry's own turning
point?

No positive action is too small to count.

September 28

Any man may be in good spirits and good temper when he's well dressed. There ain't much credit in that.
—Charles Dickens

Of course, we smile back when fortune smiles on us first. During those times in our lives when everything comes up roses, we have no problem feeling good about ourselves. Why should we? The sun shines every day, everybody loves us, and we love them. When the living is easy, self-esteem is easy, too. But what happens when fickle fortune finds another friend? What happens when it rains on our "glad rags"?

As much as we bewail the effects of negative outside influences, positive outside influences, when we give them too much power, can also set us up for self-esteem trouble. After all, we can't control either the sun *or* the rain. If we base our self-regard on happy coincidences or lucky breaks, how secure will we be when our luck runs out? No honeymoon lasts forever.

The roots of self-esteem have to be deep enough to carry us through the bad weather that plagues so many of our days. That means that our health must depend more on what's going on inside than what's going on outside. Self-esteem is a gift from us to us. Fortunate circumstances can give us a boost, but it's we ourselves who must make the climb.

The core of my self-esteem is not dependent on outside circumstances.

He played five aces. Now he plays the harp.
—Tombstone, Boot Hill, Arizona

Humor is a little-mentioned aspect of self-esteem. We have so many serious matters to consider, humor often falls in the "nice if you can get around to it" category.

Yet much self-esteem is lost by concentrating on the pathological aspects of our lives. We get so intent on what is wrong with self, the world, and everything in the world, that we get depressed. Humor is an effective antidote to all that toxic input.

Self-improvement implies self-knowledge that can only be gained by poking and prodding around tender sore spots. But life was not meant to be one long anatomy class. The whole purpose of self-improvement is to get to a better place—and that's not an operating room or a morgue. Tears and laughter are *both* expressions of reality. If we don't find much to laugh about, we're flying with one wing.

To "lighten up" doesn't mean to lapse into silliness; it means to see the light.

September 30

Industry is a better horse to ride than genius.
—Walter Lippmann

How wonderful it would be to have genius abilities! We could solve problems without effort, or paint masterpieces as easily as a child scribbles in a tablet. Maybe we could even find a cure for cancer. How our self-esteem would soar if we could do such marvelous things!

Perhaps. Genius is a gift. Like all true gifts it is neither earned nor deserved, but given randomly. Genius misused or not used at all profits the recipient little. Many a genius, in fact, has led a miserable life.

Prudence tells us we would do better to rely on industry and hard work. Even if the dues are calluses and mistakes, it is the learning and the doing that make something of value, that make *of us* something of value. What we acquire through industry we value in proportion to our effort in the accomplishment. And that value is what gives us respect for ourselves.

My ability to do skillful work is an important component of my self-esteem.

A guilty conscience needs no accuser.
—English Proverb

Sometimes low self-esteem is a direct consequence of low-down behavior. This is what happens when we persist in doing things that simply are not estimable—to us or anyone else. Because we're not psychopaths, we just don't feel right about doing wrong.

In these situations, our self-estimate is accurate and appropriate. It's the behavior, not our feelings, that have to change. Suppose we're using alcohol or another drug as a substitute for skill and courage. We can't continue to do that and hold onto our self-respect. Or perhaps we habitually lie and cheat our way through business deals. Although our pockets might bulge, our integrity is always part of the trade-off. Gross irresponsibility in any area of our lives has gross consequences—not the least of which is a burdened conscience.

In the short run, bad behavior may bring us fun, relief, or profit. But the cost runs up over time. The day will come when we can't look at ourselves in the mirror or spend any time at all in the company of our own thoughts. Maybe then we'll decide that the cost of willfulness was too high. Maybe we'll stop the offending behavior and start to win back our self-respect.

Inner peace can't be manipulated; if I don't deserve it, I won't have it.

October 2

*Tell me what you pay attention to and I will tell
you who you are.* —José Ortega y Gasset

Where the mind is, there will be the heart; we become
what we think about. If that idea doesn't halt you in
your tracks, it should. Why? Our sense of self is totally
reflective of our habitual thinking patterns.

What is our everyday mind-set? Is our attention always drawn to the flaws in people and things? Are we
quick to notice that the soup is salty and the chairs
uncomfortable? If that is our mental habit, the ugliness
and human failure all around us will also be apparent.
Our self-images will wear those same faces: ugly, sad,
failed.

We come up with a different picture, however, if we
learn to look for the good. Then we see other commut-
ers on the freeway as fellow workers rather than as
wheeled antagonists. Then we become aware of the
care and love that cooked our dinner or bought us a
birthday card. When we focus on the beauty in the
world, knowing well that the opposite also exists, our
self-images shine in the same golden light. Let us take
charge of our thinking habits lest they blind us to the
light.

**Self-esteem reflects whatever light the mind
shines on the world.**

To "know thyself" is to be known by another.
—Philip Rieff

Self-help is synonymous with self-revelation. There will always be about as much personal growth as there is personal sharing. This is also the case with self-esteem. We know and value ourselves about as much as we are willing to let ourselves be known.

Talking isn't necessarily sharing. There are those who seem never to stop talking—yet they say very little. Self-revelation has little to do with how much or how often we talk. It has to do with the content of what we say. Does anyone really know us? Do we allow anyone to actually set foot on the *inside* of the garden that we are?

Many among us have always lived behind a few or more closed doors. At some early, tragic time we learned it was not safe to share, not safe to reveal feelings, not safe to let ourselves be known. We became experts at camouflage, masters at hiding who we really were behind various, clever disguises. Some of us simply agree—all the time and with everything. Some keep too busy to have in-depth conversation. Some present such a surly forbidding face that none dare draw near. And some respond to all questions with the word "fine" and let it go at that. Yet if self-esteem means we value who we are, hiding from others can only preclude that value.

Today, I can afford to take risks that I couldn't afford yesterday.

October 4

The greatest success is successful self-acceptance.
—Ben Sweet

Self-love is impossible without self-acceptance. As obvious as this may seem, as easy as it may be to run these words through our minds and out of our mouths, it is quite another thing to live as if we believed it. Hearing and repeating a truth are not the same as acting on it.

There's more to accepting ourselves than just saying, "I do." When we bad mouth ourselves over every mistake or overreact to every fault and foible we find in our character, our actions are saying, "I don't," much louder that our words are saying the opposite. And our capacity for growth must be accepted, too. Until we come to deeply believe that improvement is not only possible but well within our grasp, we're out of touch with our own potential. And how can we accept what we don't know?

Finally, to accept ourselves is to accept that we are never "finished," but always in process, always on the way, always becoming. It is to accept life itself as a journey and ourselves as travelers who, in spite of all our handicaps and limitations, are each and every one of us on the road to glory.

I can't love what I can't accept.

He who has once burnt his mouth always blows his soup.
    —German Proverb

Just as past experiences set up our expectations of what is to come, our expectations actually give form and shape to future events. Some people call this phenomenon *self-fulfilling prophecy*. Others just say, "I *knew* that was going to happen!" and never discover a pattern. But the fact is that expectations are the tracks our train runs on. As the tracks go, so goes the train.

That's why, when we're seeking to support our self-esteem, we need to find out just what our expectations really are. Do we *truly* expect to be happy? Do we really think that progress is possible? Do we honestly believe that we are capable of taking part in a loyal, committed relationship? Do we expect ever to have fun again?

It may be that we *don't*. Perhaps the truth is an ingrained certainty that "this will hurt," the worst will inevitably happen, failure and disappointment are right around the corner. If that's the case, we need to know it so we can do something about it. If self-esteem is a train running on the tracks of our expectations, we may need to lay down some new track.

Past experiences only foretell the future if I permit it.

October 6

It is only too easy to compel a sensitive human being to feel guilty about anything.
—Morton Irving Seiden

When our self-esteem account runs short, guilt is often the culprit. Not guilt in the sense of, "I took the money," but "I am responsible for everything—so this must be my fault, too." There's no surer way of depleting self-esteem than to take on the responsibility for everyone's feelings, happiness, or need to be accepted. Nobody's pockets are *that* deep!

Sooner or later our resources run out. Somebody's feelings are hurt, somebody else feels rejected, and yet another person and another and another are lining up, waiting for a "happiness handout," an ear to bend, a shoulder to lean on. Exhausted as we are, we may immediately blame ourselves for not having more to give. We may not see at all that our sense of obligation is seriously out of whack.

Managing self-esteem means trading in unhealthy guilt for healthy concern. Each of these responses to other people's miseries is very different from the other. Unjustified guilt springs from a false idea about our role in other people's lives. It implies that we not only can but should do for others what they should be doing for themselves. Concern is the loving, caring interest that helps other people find their own answers.

Knee-jerk guilt is a setup for low self-esteem.

Ask a toad what is beauty? . . . A female with two great round eyes coming out of her little head, a large flat mouth, a yellow belly and a brown back. —Voltaire

What is estimable to one person may be insignificant to someone else. Everybody doesn't aspire to the same ideals. It's a good idea to remember that when we're trying to build self-esteem by understanding ourselves and others. It is surprising how often we tend to assume that everyone of good sense and goodwill shares our predispositions and tastes. Then when they don't meet our expectations, we fault them for missing the mark. The truth is that they may have been aiming in a completely different direction.

Several years ago a young recovering alcoholic, an ex-convict, was about to address a high school audience on the dangers of drugs and alcohol. The occasion was important to him, and he had slicked back his black hair and dressed in a brown silk shirt with ruffled cuffs, tight brown pants of some shiny material, and spike-heeled Italian boots. As he watched the affluent, sweat-shirted, blue-jeaned students file in, his disbelieving comment was "My oh my, these guys sure dress funny!"

I do not see the world the way it is. I see it the way I am. Other people have their own legitimate viewpoints.

October 8

Enjoy the present day, trusting very little to the morrow.   —Horace

"Good days" are like pearls. One or two are lovely, but a long string is even better. What do we have to do to put together enough wonderful days to have a wonderful life?

No doubt the first thing is to be wise enough to *want* good days. Most of the time, in our habitual fatigue and stress and superficiality, what we yearn for is a "good forever." Thoughtlessly, we brush off individual days as insignificant little crumbs of time that are too small to think about. Carelessly, we may let dozens or even hundreds of such perfectly fine days roll by without even recognizing that each is a gift that will never come again. We let them run through our fingers almost without touching them, as if there were a limitless supply.

Yet our days *are* our lives. If we're "saving" our interest and attention for something more important—what could that something be? It's nothing but a mistake to think in terms of "when we go on vacation," "after I get promoted," or "when we retire." What are we waiting for? If we're not enjoying the good days we have *right now*, we may be turning our backs on the only pearls we're ever going to get. Like all living things, our days are numbered. What we can *do* with our days is the only unlimited dimension.

Every one of my days is too precious to waste.

Where is there dignity unless there is also honesty?
—Cicero

Reconstructing self-esteem can seem very complicated and confusing at first. After admitting our need of help, we can easily be overwhelmed by the number of issues involved—physical, emotional, spiritual, relational, and behavioral. Where to begin? How to get started?

A good beginning is just to sit still and think about it for a while. No vigorous action is nearly so important as truly and deeply understanding that self-esteem is first and foremost a matter of integrity. Actions that reinforce a positive sense of self reinforce integrity and thus self-esteem. Actions that barter away even a small piece of integrity also barter self-esteem—no matter what the justification.

Carefully considering the integrity question is always the first step. What actions, grounded in thoughts and feelings, diminish our integrity? Are we stuffing feelings or acting out some compulsion? Are we not standing up for ourselves at work or at home? Spotting these self-limiting behaviors has to come before stopping them—or at least getting ready to. If we're blind to the ways we sacrifice our integrity, we won't see much improvement in our self-esteem, either.

I take responsibility for my own integrity.

October 10

*Our remedies oft in ourselves do lie, which we
ascribe to heaven.*   —William Shakespeare

Darin is a huge, hearty, outgoing fellow. From the outside you'd think he had never had a doubt about himself or where he was going in his whole life. But the
truth of it is that he is often racked with self-doubt and
shaky self-confidence.

But he doesn't just sit there and suffer. Darin has
made an audiotape of positive affirmations, pep talks,
and just plain no-nonsense "get your mind on the right
track" kind of thoughts. The tape holding this mental
gold runs on a very small cassette player that fits neatly
into a hand, pocket, or lunch box.

One of Darin's jobs after he lost his career of thirty
years is driving a cab. "Anytime I don't have a fare,"
he says, "that recorder is on. People who see me driving around think I'm doing just that—cruising, looking
for a fare. But what I'm really doing is getting my head
screwed on straight. It works for me. It really works."
You just never know when you are going to meet a
giant busy with slaying dragons. And you probably
won't recognize him when you see him.

God helps those who help themselves.

I believe that it is harder still to be just toward oneself than toward others. —André Gide

Why oh why is it so much easier to find fault with ourselves than to acknowledge a virtue? Why do we focus so intently on our failures and give scant nod to our successes? Why are we more inclined to give the benefit of the doubt to our neighbors than ever to ourselves? Self-esteem slips a notch with every harsh self-judgment.

Courage could have no better arena in which to practice its strength. We need to stop being so hard on ourselves. We need to start giving ourselves the fair shake we give to strangers. So what if we make a mistake? Where is it written that we should be perfect? So what if others can do something that we can't do? Need everything be a contest? If we have done our best, what else matters?

Learning to be fair, let alone gentle, with ourselves may take more grit and determination than learning to climb a mountain. The negative messages from the past may howl in protest as we dare to challenge them. The urge to discredit our efforts may be very great. But how sweet the day we first rise up and demand a fair shake from the naysayers within.

It takes courage to lay just claim to my own merits.

October 12

Better never trouble Trouble
Until Trouble troubles you;
For you only make your trouble
Double-trouble when you do.
　　　　　　—David Keppel

Living in the present, as some Twelve Steppers say, is "simple, but it ain't easy." How often our fearful imaginings have borrowed trouble from the future, giving us headaches, stomachaches, keeping us awake at night. And all because we were living in some phantom tomorrow instead of today!

Some of us continue to have occasional "failure fantasies" when we're well into recovery. Perhaps we've set ourselves up by getting too tired or cutting down on our support group meetings. Whatever the cause, we lose our grip on the present and project our anxiety into the future. "What if I get fired? Oh Lord, if I lose my job, my family will be out on the street. And these days there isn't even a poorhouse to go to!"

Of course, most of the worst things we conjure up never come to be. When we lose sleep or serenity over "what ifs" we need to remind ourselves that today is all we have. We can't know what troubles will come tomorrow. We don't even know if we'll *be here* tomorrow. What we know for sure is that today is too precious to waste.

When I look for trouble, I often invent trouble.

The battle, sir, is not to the strong alone; it is to the vigilant, the active, the brave.
—Patrick Henry

Replacing something that we've lost usually involves a lot of effort and aggravation. The loss of self-esteem is no different As in any other area of life, catching up and patching up are poor substitutes for keeping up in the first place. What do we have to do to avoid self-esteem trouble? Are there maintenance techniques? Is there such a thing as a self-esteem tune up?

Vigilance is the heart and soul of loss prevention. Paying attention. Minding the details. Trouble-spotting. These are the habits and skills that consistently confident people use to maintain and increase the gains they've already made. They don't wait for a tiny leak to become a gusher. They don't allow a speck of rust to grow into a creeping plague. They avoid the need for a major overhaul by repairing as they go.

Maintaining self-esteem means taking action on a daily basis. It means that we find the company of interesting, upbeat people who are as forward looking as we are trying to be. It means talking out small problems while they're still small, promptly apologizing if an apology is due, and following through on our commitments whether we feel like it or not. It means reading inspiring literature *before* we're desperately demoralized. In short, it means staying on duty.

Unless I allow a major breakdown, I won't have to make major repairs.

October 14

*Know that you are the temple of God and that the
spirit of God dwells in you.*   —1 Cor. 3:16

Is "dwelling" possible in this hustle and bustle world?
To *dwell* doesn't mean to visit once in a while. Where
we dwell is where we *are*. The Scripture belief given
above—and all major religions have similar beliefs—
clearly states that God dwells within as an ongoing,
accessible, approachable presence.

The enormity of that belief and its incredible implications are awesome for any of us. But for those of us
who started out life under spirit-starved conditions,
the very idea seems about as real as a moon made of
green cheese. It's not hard to understand why we automatically feel we must go it alone, that no help can
ever *really* be counted on, that it's safer to hope for
nothing. There are real and well-remembered reasons
why we put up those impenetrable walls of distrust
and isolation in the first place.

Yet thousands and thousands of people throughout
the ages have accepted the belief/truth that the "God
within" is always there, available, and waiting. When
they learned to hush themselves from overburdening
worries, cares, fears, and vanities, they found that
presence within. They felt themselves lifted with
strength beyond their own. Because they were open,
they were able to receive. Why not us?

Faith must be sought.

Lives of great men all remind us
We can make our lives sublime,
And, departing, leave behind us
Footprints on the sands of time.
—Henry Wadsworth Longfellow

Greatness is certainly a relative term. When applied to people, it usually describes those whose achievements are unique, bigger than life even. Abraham Lincoln, Mother Teresa, and Christopher Columbus, for example, did great things that no one had ever done before. When the call to greatness came, they were there to answer it.

We are all called to greatness. Anonymous and ordinary as we are, that may seem absurd. But greatness has to do with doing great things, not with being famous. A well-publicized act of courage is no more courageous than an act done in private. Applause and recognition didn't make our heroes heroic, their *deeds* did.

It is a great thing to challenge the status quo and demand more from life. And it takes real heroism to confront the personal demons that chain us to the failures of the past. Every time we make a move in this direction, we are rising to the call of greatness and marching with the giants.

Private heroism is heroism nonetheless.

October 16

A good Example is the best Sermon.
—Benjamin Franklin

Caring people who get into recovery are often very quick to see how much their loved ones could be helped by getting into recovery, too. "Boy, could old Charlie profit from these principles," we think to ourselves. "If only my mother would come to these meetings, listen to the speakers, follow the steps. It could sure make a difference in her life!"

As we grow in self-esteem, we want the people we love to grow, too. We may become holy terrors of recovery. In our zeal to share the enlightenment, we may actually attack other people with our well-meant enthusiasm. "Just read this!" we may badger. "Just come along to this one meeting!" we may insist, as we hand them their coats and push them out the door. Because it's all for their own good, we feel completely justified in begging, shoving, pleading, moralizing, and scolding.

But what our loved ones may really need is for us to back off. Not for us to stop caring, not to tolerate untolerable behavior, not to pretend that it doesn't matter. Just to back off. Give them some breathing room. Lighten up. As much as we would like to share our new insights, manipulation and force are pretty unappealing recruitment techniques. Good example and attraction are far more powerful.

I defeat my best intentions when I try to force others to follow my path.

Loving and making relationships work are not the same thing.   —Earnie Larsen

Many people's self-esteem is shaken if a promising relationship begins to deteriorate. This is true especially if that relationship was entered into with a heart full of love and "forever" expectations. When we find that somehow, some way it is not working, we simply can't believe it. We always believed that if we loved enough, all other problems would solve themselves.

The truth is that loving and making a relationship work can easily be two different things. Successful relationships endure because of skills—not feelings. All the loving in the world does not necessarily translate into the ability to communicate, for example. To assume that these essential skills are present, when they are not, is to take a long walk on a short pier. Especially if our self-esteem rides on the back of that relationship.

The saving fact about skills, however, is that they can be learned. Lack of skill is no cause for loss of self-esteem. It can be the motivation we need to start learning how to make a relationship work over the long haul. No doubt when *we* are more reliable, honest, and realistic, our relationships will have a better chance of survival.

Making relationships work takes more than love.

October 18

A loving person lives in a loving world. A hostile person lives in a hostile world: Everyone you meet is your mirror. —Ken Keyes, Jr.

It's as easy to get lost in a forest of labels as it is in a forest of trees. Adult Children, co-dependents, recovering addicts by the hundreds of thousands seem to be moving in the same direction—but they're all marching under different banners! Figuring it all out can be very confusing. Do the differences really matter that much?

It's good to remember that all people who are striving to improve their lives are on fundamentally the same journey. By any name, the core effort of all these groups is the same: to embrace life from a positive self-definition. Because we view the world much as we view ourselves, the common task of all self-help groups is to help us grow out of the negative self-definitions that create negative results in our lives.

Those who have learned to define themselves as losers will lose. Those who define themselves as unlovable will not allow themselves to be loved. People who see themselves as victims will be at high risk for the abandonment they most fear. The goal of all groups is to support positive redefinition. No matter what our starting point, we are all on the same path. Growth is not a dozen journeys—it is one journey with a dozen names.

Labels point out differences that fellowship doesn't notice.

*Agreement is made more precious by disagree-
ment.*   —Publilius Syrus

In our longing for harmonious relationships, we can
sometimes get very stubborn, very insistent, very hard-
headed about how much agreement is possible—or
even desirable—between two people. Somehow it becomes our very mission to inform, persuade, and convince the other that our way of thinking is better than
theirs.

But real agreement can't be forced anymore than love
can. People have a right to their own opinions. They
aren't "wrong" if they disagree with our political or
religious beliefs, our tastes in humor or leisure time
activities. Different is just different. When we try to
convert people against their will, the best we can hope
for is sort of an arm-twisted conformity. They may go
along with us on the outside, just to stop the argument, but true conversion is an inside job.

As we grow in self-esteem, we'll have less need to
impose our own views on other people. As we become
more aware of and comfortable with the incredible di-
versity in ourselves, we'll find it easier to allow diver-
sity in others. Perhaps we'll even come to appreciate
and enjoy our areas of disagreement as the spice of life
that they are.

**Perfect agreement with others is an unrealistic
goal.**

October 20

When I finally realized there was no such thing as enough money, sex, or things to make me happy, I was finally on my way.

—George S.

Low self-esteem often reveals itself as a hollowness in the pit of the stomach and an emptiness in the heart. That hole hurts. Many have attempted to fill that void with "goodies" that don't do anything but make a bad situation worse.

George certainly was one of those. He had all the usual qualifications for low self-esteem—a long training session as a youth that taught him he had no rights and that he would never amount to anything. He heard the message loud and clear. He was totally unworthy of love. So he set out in a frantic search for something—anything—to heal the hurt within. His method was a nonstop scramble for more money, more sex, and more toys. He got plenty of everything he was after. Yet he found that none of them helped. When he finally discovered that the "Give Me More" trail always dead-ends, he began looking somewhere else. Eventually his journey took him into his own heart, where he found what he had been looking for.

Today, George has a different view. His face glows when he says, "I didn't need *to have more*, I needed *to be more*. Now I have value and worth because of who I am. My happiness doesn't depend on any outside condition or acquisition." Nearly bursting with pride, he says, "I am me, I am okay, and that's enough."

Today I recognize my greediness as spiritual hunger.

There is always an enormous temptation in life to diddle around making itsy bitsy friends and meals and journeys for itsy bitsy years on end.

—Annie Dillard

Habits of extreme caution can lead us to have small lives. If we only have trivial, lightweight interests, after all, we don't risk much disappointment. Especially if we pursue those interests with a trivial, featherweight of passion. Risk little, lose little; that's the way our thinking goes.

But passion is what makes life worth living. Passion is the big base drum that sets the beat and anchors the parade of life. Without good, sweaty, wholehearted involvement, our lives lack rhythm and bounce. It's hard even to stay interested in, let alone feel good about, a life that is lived in mincing little half-steps.

To be fully alive, we must find an interest that we truly care about. Maybe it's a hobby like bird watching or a cause like clean air. The only thing that matters is that we stop hedging our bets and go all out. The more excited and involved we get, the less itsy-bitsy will be our sense of self.

The measure of my passions is the measure of my life.

October 22

It is an easy thing for one whose foot is on the outside of calamity to give advice and to rebuke the sufferer. —Aeschylus

"I'd *never* put up with that!" we say to ourselves as we hear a friend's story of domestic violence. "I'd leave immediately! I'd hit him right back! I'd rat poison the dirty rat!" When neither the pain nor the decision is ours, we know *exactly* what should be done—and when and how as well. But that kind of righteous carrying on only doubles the hurt of our hurting friend. She's already taking on more fault than she deserves. The last thing she needs is to hear us say how much better *we* would do in her shoes. *Our* self-esteem is not raised by lowering hers.

Better by far that we shut up and listen. Just allowing her to tell her own story at her own pace will give her some relief. No raised eyebrows, no dropped jaws; belief and acceptance are what we want to communicate. Then, when the story is told, we can offer whatever facts we have about protection under the law, crisis hot lines, and the availability of shelters.

Battered women have the right to make their own decisions—even wrong ones. Our sympathy doesn't entitle us to step in and call the shots. Her mixed bag of fear, helplessness, and denial may still prevent her from accepting our advice. The most helpful thing we can do is to offer continuing availability and support. Accepting our own limitations is necessary to our own self-esteem.

Even in a good cause, I am wiser to be patient rather than pushy.

*The sorrow which has no vent in tears may make
other organs weep.*   —Dr. Francis Braceland

More than a few of us base our self-esteem on being
tough! We pride ourselves on our strength and judge
ourselves by an incredible standard of self-sufficiency.
Never will we let anyone know that we're in need. Just
as likely, we'll never admit it to ourselves, either.

Yet self-esteem, as true humility, is not the denial of
truth but the admission of reality. To be a whining
crybaby is one thing. But to acknowledge our own
pain, need, or hurt is quite another. "I must never
show weakness" is a mandate that leads to disaster. It
betrays an immature attitude that must be outgrown if
our self-esteem is to grow.

Denial of pain only drives the pain deeper. Commonly, repressed emotional hurt reveals itself in headaches, backaches, and stomach disorders. Perhaps the
toughest people are those who have the courage to
reach out for help when they need it—*before* their bodies cry out against the emotional turmoil that we were
too "tough" to deal with.

**Weakness parading under a banner of strength
can cost me my health.**

October 24

A man cannot be comfortable without his own approval. —Mark Twain

We have often heard that no one can make us miserable without our permission. A corollary of that idea is also true: No one or nothing can make us comfortable without our own approval.

Suppose every one of our wishes and dreams came true. Suddenly we have everything we always thought it would take to make us happy. Would that do it? Would our itch finally be scratched? Perhaps not. The fact is that it is something within, not treasures from without, that grants or withholds satisfaction. In other words, we usually need to "grow into" serenity.

If the lottery winner hasn't grown enough to handle new wealth, that prize may turn out to be a curse. If a golden opportunity arrives before we are prepared for it, it's just another reason to get down on ourselves. And our dreams of love and romance can easily be short-term if we don't have the personal stability to hold up our end of a relationship. Readiness can't be faked or wished into being. More inner growth may be necessary before we're capable of receiving what we most want.

Working my daily program prepares me for whatever comes.

What is a cynic? A man who knows the price of everything, and the value of nothing.

—Oscar Wilde

Some people defend themselves, and thus their self-esteem, by wearing an armored suit of cynicism. The worst thing they can imagine is being "taken" in any way. The shame and humiliation of being set up and then let down would be nothing short of unbearable. So every morning they strap on their armor plates and go clunking through another day, stifling, sweating, but puncture-proof, by golly! Nobody's ever going to get the better of *them*.

But the armor wearers aren't going to get the best of themselves, either. Too much is locked *inside*—good, human stuff like hope and tenderness and sincerity. It isn't possible to be so distrustful and defensive about other people without looking at ourselves in the same dim light. It isn't healthy to think of ourselves as so vulnerable that we couldn't survive even a pinprick of disappointment or deceit.

We can't use pessimism and suspicion to protect ourselves without becoming mummified. We can't learn to believe in ourselves and *also* have a sneering disbelief in the motives and integrity of every person we meet. And we certainly can't ever *dance* under all that armor. No. Until we rid ourselves of cynicism, the only step we know goes clunk, clunk, clunk.

As I gain confidence, my defensiveness fades.

October 26

The first duty of love is to listen.
—Paul Tillich

Dan and his daughter Sissy had been clashing for years. He found her unconventional lifestyle just as outrageous and unacceptable as she found his righteous criticism. Round after round of angry insults, like buckshot, had riddled the self-esteem of both father and daughter.

Then they went in to counseling. In the presence of a third person, each of them had a chance to talk without interruption. In that safe environment, swords were sheathed, shields were lowered, wounds were allowed to get some healing air. Amazingly, they began to talk *to each other* without shouting or accusing. By listening, each began to see, if not agree with, the other's point of view.

Dan had sincerely believed that Sissy's manner and dress were simply defiance of his authority. He learned that her style had nothing to do with him. It was merely her way to fit in, to be part of the group. Sissy learned that Dan didn't really want his own way so much as he wanted her safety from harm. He saw her far-out clothing and haircut as abnormal and dangerous. Slowly, as each came to understand the other a little better, they came to accept each other as human beings with different opinions, rather than as enemies locked in fatal combat. By listening and learning, they were able to call off the war and both be winners.

Understanding is a healing balm.

*This is what is hardest: to close the open hand
because one loves.*   —Friedrich Nietzsche

To protect our own integrity and peace of mind, we may have to redefine the word *love*. Sometimes *no* is the kindest word we can say to a family member or close friend who's in serious trouble with alcohol, drugs, food, sex, or any other ravaging obsession. Their suffering pushes all our "rescue" buttons. What we *feel* like doing is straightening out their messes and protecting them from further harm. If we could, we would banish all their miseries with the touch of a magic wand! But we can't. Often the only thing we *can* do to help our self-destructive loved ones is to stop helping completely. As hard as it is, as unnatural as it feels, we may have to make some or all of the following declarations of love if we want to shorten our loved one's path to the recovery turnoff.

- I love you, so I won't buy your groceries or pay your rent.
- I love you, so I won't loan you money or the use of my credit.
- I love you, so I won't call in sick for you at work.
- I love you, so I won't cover your bounced check.
- I love you, so I won't let you move in with me.
- I love you, so I won't listen to your excuses or accept your lies.
- I love you, so I won't make your bail.

If we know down deep that these words need to be spoken, we need to practice them until we can get them out. Many recovering people only got turned around become someone loved them enough to give them a cold shoulder instead of a helping hand.

Whoever said that love was easy?

October 28

Most ignorance is vincible ignorance. We don't know because we don't want to know.
—Irving Howe

Some very smart people choose to "dumb out" when they can't bear to face what's going on. They simply refuse to read the writing on the wall. Then, when absolutely predictable consequences erupt, they cry out, "I had no idea! Someone should have told me! How could I have known?" Their self-esteem is undercut because they wouldn't look at the writing on the wall.

Of course, there are plenty of ways they could have known. Early warning signs are hard to miss unless we want to miss them. Marriages don't crumble in an instant. Our children don't develop full-fledged drug problems in a single night out. There were signs and symptoms all along.

Some situations genuinely take us by surprise. They couldn't have been anticipated or avoided. But other situations might have been nipped in the bud; they became disasters because we weren't willing to open our eyes and see the truth that was staring us in the face all along. We didn't know because it seemed to us that knowing would be too hard. But at least when we know, we can do something about it.

Deliberate ignorance is a cowardly way of avoiding responsibility.

We do not know one millionth of one percent about anything. —Thomas Alva Edison

Like anything else we think we know, self-concept is a product of information. Because self-esteem is built on self-concept, it's important to check out our data from time to time. How much of the information we've acquired about ourselves is *mis*information? How much of it is opinion rather than fact? How much is out-dated?

Many of the key "facts" we use to define ourselves come to us from others, of course. It is their reactions, impressions, and judgments that at least initially dispose us to believe certain "truths" about who we are and *how* we are. Who were our most important sources of information when we were children? Who are they now? As we look back, can we say that those early information givers were reliable and accurate? How about the sources who give us input today?

On a daily basis, self-esteem is either supported or weakened by our processing of outside information. That's why we need to be very selective about our sources and even then to be very careful about accepting counterfeit "facts" for the real thing. As self-confidence grows, so does our ability to reject flawed information *before* we take it in.

Much of what I "know" about myself might be fallacy rather than fact.

October 30

When I'm not thanked at all, I'm thanked enough,
I've done my duty, and I've done no more.
                                        —Henry Fielding

Allen had just spent all evening sharing years of hard-won wisdom with a man who had asked for his help. Allen suggested a plan of action and then promised that he would help the new man every step of the way, if that was the man's wish. He gave the man his phone number and encouraged him to call at any time.

The next day Allen's teenage daughter congratulated him on his generosity. "I know you wanted to watch the play-offs on TV last night," she said, "but you spent all that time with somebody you don't even know! What a good deed, Dad!" Surprised, Allen responded, "Oh, that wasn't generosity. I was paying back my debt to the universe for all the help others have given me."

Allen is right. As far as he has yet to go on his own path, he only got this far because he had help. Unlike some, he has not forgotten all the hands that reached out to him, patting, prodding, lifting him up. He knows it's his turn. In Allen's economy, fair is no less and no more than fair. Integrity demands that debts must be paid.

No one goes alone. Either I take others with me or I don't go myself.

Getting people to like you is only the other side of liking them. —Normal Vincent Peale

Oh, to be popular! Although we don't usually talk about it beyond our teenage years, there's not a one of us who doesn't want to be sought out, liked, and admired. In no small way, our perceived popularity makes or breaks us. That's how crucial the love and acceptance of others is to our self-esteem. It's the wind beneath our wings.

Authors have made fortunes by telling us how to achieve popularity. But it doesn't cost a fortune to take a look at the evidence all around us. Courteous people, especially when they're courteous to those they don't need, earn respect and friendship wherever they go. Good listeners are always thought to be wise as well as likable. People who remember our names and ask about our families are welcomed warmly. And we have a special place in our hearts for people who have lent us a hand before we had to ask.

Making friends is not a technique; it's the natural activity of being a friend. If you want to be liked, first like other people. Wisdom doesn't get any simpler than that.

Prescription for popularity: Like other people and let them know it.

November 1

The only people for me are the mad ones . . . the ones who never yawn and say a commonplace thing, but burn, burn, burn, like fabulous yellow roman candles exploding like spiders across the stars.
—Jack Kerouac

The enormous success of the first *Rocky* movie surprised the experts. They saw it as just another low-budget boxing story. Little did they guess it would win so many awards and capture the imagination of millions all over the world.

The experts didn't foresee that the story was really about *us.* They didn't recognize that the magic of the Rocky character was in his very ordinariness. Rocky was "just a guy," after all, an unlikely, unpromising unknown who didn't look one bit different than any other young punk on the street. But viewers saw that immediately and they identified with it. When Rocky dared to buck the odds, to come roaring out of nowhere, and to shoot for the top, they identified with that, too. Rocky's success was *ours*; if Rocky can do it, maybe I can, too.

Real life is not lived on the silver screen, of course. But even movie messages may deliver important truths that can inspire our real lives. The central truth of the *Rocky* phenomenon is that passion and dedication can move mountains. However humble our beginnings, if we have "fire in the belly," those who bet against us will have a big surprise coming.

Desire and discipline can overcome impossible odds.

*One cannot be deeply responsive to the world
without being saddened very often.*
—Eric Fromm

One way to avoid hurt in this world is to kill all feelings. Another is to see nothing: withdraw, close up like a deep-water clam does when it senses a threat. Then everything that swims by is put off by that impenetrable shell.

Unlike clams, however, we cannot hide in a defensive shell without damaging ourselves. There's no way around it. If we take a good look at what's going on in the world, and try to be responsive to it, there will be sadness. At this stage of human evolution there is much to be sad about.

Compassion has a price. If we choose to care, we must first choose to grow in maturity. We must learn to acknowledge all that is painful in this world, all the human failing—*without being consumed by it.* As real and distressing as all the sad things are, they are not the totality of human experience. Just as our compassion is not the totality of who we are. We need always to recognize the existence of what is good as well as what is not.

As I seek truth, I will find enough good to keep me going.

November 3

Self-help must precede help from others. Even for making certain of help from heaven, one has to help oneself.
—Morarji Desai

When all is said and done, we are responsible for what happens to our lives. Not that we can control circumstances, but the ultimate decisions as to attitude, acceptance, and behavior are in our hands. Other people may give us our start, but our finish is up to us.

Sonny's self-esteem was taking a beating because of his many failed relationships with women. Again and again, this sweet, good-looking man had been certain that "this was it." Then, mysteriously to him, the woman always backed out, called it off. Until he got professional help, Sonny didn't realize that he was subconsciously restaging the drama of his mother's rejection. At forty-one, he was still looking to the woman in his life for the unconditional acceptance and approval that he had been denied so many years ago. Not so mysteriously, his women friends decided to look for partners who were perhaps less sweet, but certainly less needy.

Over time, Sonny learned that he had been unrealistic and unfair in his relationships. By letting go of the past, he reclaimed his power to function in the present—as a man rather than a boy. At last he took his self-esteem out of his mother's hands. As must we.

Until I leave "what was" behind me, I will keep reliving it.

To cope effectively with problems or to rise tri-
umphantly to challenges may require courage,
patience, sustained energy, and imagination, but
it also requires something even more basic: real-
ism.
— Joan Bel Geddes

Self-esteem is based on truth. Before it is the *cause* of good, it is the *result* of our ability to accept the truth about ourselves. Knowledge of our *real* selves is what we're after—not the puffed-up or shrunken images that come and go with good days and bad days. The core self standing naked before a mirror is the one we must come to terms with.

Lack of realism is a powerful enemy of positive self-esteem. If the truth is that we always hated school, it isn't likely that we're going to become college professors. If we're 100 pounds overweight, prospects are not great for a modeling career. Realistically, we need to focus on what *can* be, not what is impossible. We need to work with what we've got, not what we wish we had.

To live without realism is to live in a deluded world where self-esteem is impossible. We need to be honest with ourselves about our limits. Circumstances such as age or health may impose limits that weren't there yes-terday. So be it. It's today and who we are today that counts. When we match our dreams to our nakedness, we're on our way.

Bucking reality is a fool's game that always ends in defeat.

November 5

Fare thee well for I must leave thee,
Do not let this parting grieve thee.
Just remember that the best of friends must part.
—Anonymous

By far the most difficult decisions are of the "letting-go" variety. That's no surprise when we consider how hard it is to get rid of a trusty old car or a ragged, but favorite, old sweater. They've been around for a long time, they're comfortable, and we remember them as they once were. How much more we dread the loss of a sour relationship that once was sweet!

But there are times when we can't go forward until we say good-bye to what's behind us. When our best efforts can't make a relationship work, that relationship is over. We owe it to ourselves and to the other person to make a clean break. Painful as parting is, self-esteem demands that we find the honesty and courage to get on with our lives.

No matter what we tell ourselves, we're not doing the other person a favor when we stall and postpone a necessary farewell. It's *our own* pain and guilt that makes us drag our feet. Cowardice isn't kindness. Kindness is giving the other person the same chance for happiness that we want for ourselves.

Procrastination doubles the pain of parting.

The world is sown with good: but unless I turn my glad thoughts into practical living and till my own field, I cannot reap a kernel of the good.
—Helen Keller

Sometimes, when we're trudging the road of self-renewal, we get a free ride when we least expect it. It may be a dazzling insight, a rocketlike boost of emotion, or a profoundly deep faith experience. Maybe it comes while we're reading or walking down the street or just falling asleep. But whenever or wherever they happen, these unexpected peak experiences are marvels that we should treasure.

But we should also recognize that no moment of bliss, no lightning bolt of absolute certainty, can last forever. A peak experience is more of an indication of what *can* be than a stable state of being. Even the brightest flash of awareness is not in itself either change or growth, although it may be a powerful incentive to keep going.

As it was and always will be, after the experience comes the work. The freebies that come to us are meant to be appreciated, remembered, and then used as a shining star by which we plot our course. Trudging isn't thrilling, but it's the only known road to lasting change.

No one gets a steady diet of peak experiences.

November 7

> Responsibility (*n*): *A detachable burden easily shifted to the shoulders of God, Fate, Fortune, Luck, or one's neighbor.* —Ambrose Bierce

Blaming never healed a wound. Making excuses never made an improvement. It is one thing to recognize that there are reasons we may find ourselves in a self-esteem slump. But it is another thing entirely to take responsibility for pulling ourselves out of it.

After the fact, what difference do the whos and whys really make? If our toes have been run over, it's our flat toes we have to worry about—not what kind of vehicle it was or whether the driver had a license. Why were we standing in the street? That's the worthwhile kind of question that can do us some good: What's the "me factor" in the problem?

Much of my difficulty is created by something in *me*—a thought pattern, an ingrained habit, a perception of myself. *I* am my biggest burden and most difficult problem. "They" are not responsible for what happens to me. I am responsible. I have the power.

Hope and power abound when I take responsibility for myself in the here and now.

Happiness: I have earned it. I am taking it.
—Marva Collins

Most of us would say we want happiness more than anything in life. Strange, then, isn't it, that we have so many ways to postpone it, block it, even break its grip if it reaches out to hug us. Why do we do that?

The low self-esteem that prohibits happiness is often caused by shame. For very deep, subjective reasons, we have decided, or accepted someone else's decision, that we don't deserve happiness or success. "People like us" somehow shouldn't expect to be happy. The self-image that ties into "people like us" may have to do with our nationality or religion or race. It may have to do with the neighborhood we came from, or the fact that we never had much money. Whatever the negative, limiting identity, the fact is that it hobbles our pursuit of happiness just as surely as if our feet were roped together.

"People like us," who are sincerely learning and growing, have every right to be happy. We don't need the guilt and shame that have woven themselves into such a heavy, leaden overcoat. No one can make us wear it if we decide we're not going to anymore. And no one but ourselves can keep us from satisfying the deepest desire of the human heart.

"People like us" deserve all the happiness we can get.

November 9

*An agreeable companion on a journey is as good
as a carriage.* —Publilius Syrus

Everywhere we go we find good apples and bad apples. There are negative people who for many reasons walk a low road themselves and invite us to travel the same path. Because they don't expect clear weather or good road conditions, they never find them. Chuckholes are what they know and chuckholes are what they get. As long as we walk with them, we travel under the same conditions.

There are also positive people, who for equally varied reasons, have chosen to walk the high road. They, too, find pretty much what they expect to find as they mosey along. Mostly they get sunny days, straight routes, and interesting experiences along the way. They don't expect to run into problems they can't handle, so for the most part they don't. Walking in their company gives us the same kind of trip.

We can join either caravan we want to. As long as we're alive we're traveling one road or the other. Shall we define the journey in terms of sprained ankles and lost luggage, or in terms of progress and adventure? The choice would seem not too hard to make.

**The quality of my journey is largely defined by
the quality of my companions.**

November 10

Of all the passions, fear weakens judgment most.
—Cardinal de Retz

Fear is a terrible obstacle to healthy self-esteem. Our fear of everything from failure to success to rejection leads us first to a mental shutdown and then to paralysis. Stagnation results. And in that dead pool of stagnation, self-esteem drowns.

Fear has been explained as F-alse E-vidence A-ppearing R-eal. Although there certainly are many legitimate things to be afraid of, much of the fear that handicaps self-esteem is false. False in the sense that what once was real, no longer is. In the past, it may have been true that others abused us, or denied us our rights, or coldly ignored us. But that happened in childhood, when we had no choice.

What's true in the here and now may be that those old feelings, perceptions and boundaries are no longer relevant. Today, they are false in the sense that we have outgrown their power. As we make our own choices about how we want to live and who we want to believe, a whole new world opens up to us. Fear is slavery. Overcoming fear is freedom—and the very wings of the sweet bird of self-esteem.

Yesterday's threats can't touch us today.

November 11

All seems infected to the infected spy,
As all looks yellow to the jaundiced eye.
—Alexander Pope

It can be infuriating to hear someone say that a very obvious, concrete issue we're struggling with is an "attitude problem." When we're pounding away at some unyielding difficulty, the last thing we want to hear is, "It's all in your head." Such comments make us feel that our intelligence, not to mention our sanity, is being discounted. We resent the oversimplification of what seems to us a very complex dilemma.

The truth may well be that our problem is as real and as hard to crack as a slab of marble. Yet it may also be true that some attitude we're bringing to the problem is wearing us out more than the problem is! After all, our attitudes define our problems in the first place. Attitudes are the tinted glass through which we *see* our problems. So, of course, our attitudes always precede our actions; they get there first.

A creative attitude transforms many setbacks and disappointments into learning experiences. A receptive, sensitive attitude lifts the cloak of everydayness off many beautiful sights and amusing events. An independent attitude can spin the straw of loneliness into golden solitude. A roll-up-the-sleeves, can-do attitude is the best problem solver there is.

The power of my attitudes is greater than the power of my problems.

To the man whose senses are alive and alert, there is not even the need to stir from his threshold.
— Henry Miller

Low self-esteem is often associated with boredom. When nothing seems interesting or worth doing, we can lose interest in our own lives. Thus our hunger for excitement and entertainment. Often, when we feel empty inside, we direct our search for meaning outward. We look outside ourselves to find something to distract us from the monotony of the everyday.

Maybe it takes us a while, maybe it even happens by accident, but sooner or later we discover that our own minds can be a veritable entertainment factory! When we learn to tap in to our own creativity, our own ideas and musings can give us endless enjoyment. Who can be bored when there are so many interesting things to think about?

Who is the greatest person who ever lived? Why? What would be the best possible vacation? Why? What is the highest possible goal that I could realistically reach in the next year? What would it take to get started? What is my best quality? How can I showcase that quality? If I had three wishes, what would they be? What one thing would I change about the world if I could? What most needs to be done? There's no limit to the things I can think about.

My ability to wonder and think is a reliable source of pleasure.

November 13

Nothing is more fatal to health than an over *care*
of it.   —Benjamin Franklin

Modern health care has come a long way. Rather than focusing exclusively on illness, many enlightened practitioners now encourage their patients to focus on *wellness*, instead. By emphasizing the health of the whole, they are better able to deal with the dysfunctional part. The switch in emphasis makes a profound difference; much like the difference between studying peace and studying war.

Mental and emotional health can be approached in the same way. When we're only interested in what's wrong, that's all we'll find when we go searching for self-knowledge. And what is self-esteem but a positive picture of ourselves? We can actually *cause* ourselves self-esteem problems by dwelling on the various scars and bruises that life has given us. As if we're nothing more than the sum total of our injuries!

We are far more whole and healthy than we are sick. Of course, it's important to know what's wrong and get busy fixing it. But we should never, never define ourselves by our wounds. To do so is to discount our true value and to disclaim the many benefits of health and happiness.

By focusing on wellness, I give self-esteem a chance to heal.

There is nothing either good or bad but thinking
makes it so. —William Shakespeare

Assumptions are risky in every area of life. Because self-image so heavily depends on what other people reflect back to us, our assumptions in this area can be especially dangerous.

We may be hurt because someone snubbed us—but a whole different story often emerges when we check it out. Perhaps the person was preoccupied with a concern of his own, or may just have been tired. Or suppose we assume that someone doesn't approve of what we are doing. It isn't unusual to find out later that she didn't even *know* what we were doing. Or didn't care.

Wearing our self-esteem on our sleeve makes us very vulnerable. If we take other people's mistakes or honest disagreements as a personal affront, we turn our spiritual path into a mine field. We need to think twice before we assume once. We need to stop creating misunderstanding and start taking responsibility for our own thin skin.

Assumptions are not facts.

November 15

The really heroic people are not those who travel 10,000 miles by dog sled, but those who stay 10,000 days in one place. —William Gordon

When we hear someone shout, "Fire!" we'd better run. When we hear someone yell, "Twister!" we quickly look for cover. One of the first things we learn is to *get out of the way* when we see trouble or danger bearing down on us.

Many times running is perfectly appropriate. A quick response has often saved lives and limbs. But at other times, running away is the worst possible thing we can do. There are situations, in fact, when self-respect goes out the window if we go out the door. Unless we stand fast and face these situations, we leave too much of us behind.

Those who fear intimacy get itchy feet when a loving someone gets too close. Those who fear success can think of a thousand reasons to close down a promising operation and move on to something else. Those who fear failure hop from one idea to another without making a commitment to any. In all of these situations, our feelings of fear are telling us to quit before we're hurt. But reason tells us that quitting *is* hurting and that self-esteem means hanging tough.

Sometimes, devastation can only be avoided by staying put.

Sometimes I think, the things we see
Are shadows of the things to be;
That what we plan, we build.
—Phoebe Cary

Oh, the delight in making plans! Indeed, high-flying plans that never come to fruition can become exercises in frustration. They can knock down our self-esteem instead of building it up. But legitimate plan making is a victory in itself. Just honestly sitting down and starting to set out goals that translate into concrete, doable steps does much to convince us that we can accomplish something. And realizing what we can do is what positive self-esteem is all about. Making realistic plans is an achievement in itself.

We, and our self-esteem along with us, get bogged down when we don't see the light at the end of some tunnel or another. Perhaps we are stuck in a bad job, or a bad relationship or a negative state of mind. Plans are what get us unstuck. We can't make a plan without thinking out the steps we must take to get moving in a more positive direction.

What are the steps? Maybe the first step is just to encourage ourselves to *think* about it. When we tell ourselves that we have options, that we most certainly can do something about our lives, we are not victims.

When I make a plan, I put management back in my life.

November 17

Discern of the coming on of years, and think not to do the same things still; for age will not be defied. —Francis Bacon

As we reach our middle years, denial and delusion roll out a red carpet leading us back toward youth. "Turn around now!" these great pretenders tell us, "Reverse the aging process and you can outwit old Father Time!" To pull off this trick we're advised to try everything from starvation to surgery. Sometimes we cripple ourselves with near-violent exercise and vigorous nightlife—all in the hope of thinking and looking and feeling like the young people we no longer are!

Why do we allow ourselves to be hustled into such a vain pursuit? Was the first half of life such a series of delights that anything beyond it must be less? What are we trying to prove by trying to stop, or even turn back, nature's clock? Are we trying to fool other people or ourselves? And why are we trying to fool anybody?

Of course, we should do everything we can to maintain our health and a positive, upbeat outlook. But all the artful manipulation in the world doesn't slow the aging process. At best, it keeps it from *showing* quite so quickly. The important question isn't whether or not we should get a hairpiece or a tummy tuck. It's much more important to know *why* we want to go to so much trouble to be what we aren't.

At midlife, I have many more interesting things to do than fight wrinkles.

Names are but noise and smoke,
Obscuring heavenly light.
—Goethe

To ask, "Who am I?" is much like asking, "What is reality?" The answer can be a complex exercise in mental gymnastics. On the other hand, because so much of our self-esteem depends on how we define ourselves, the question is an important one that can lead to major growth.

Often an off-the-top-of-the-head answer reveals that we tend to base our identity on what we *do*. "I've always said I was 'Loren the truck driver,' " a man told his support group. "Now I'm learning to say, 'I'm Loren and I happen to drive a truck.' " Loren is on his way because he knows that he is other than, more than, what he does for a living.

What we do can be taken away. It can change as a result of age, accident, or just plain fate. If our identity is based on that, we are building the castle of our self-esteem on sand. Who we are is a deeper and broader reality than where we go to work or what we do when we get there. Doing contributes to being—but being is the point of the exercise.

My identity doesn't begin and end with my occupation.

November 19

The wise man does at once what the fool does finally. —Baltasar Gracián y Morales

As embarrassing as it may be to have to line up with the "fools," most of us have more than a little expertise at procrastinating. Of course, we know better. We know that avoiding something that we have to do makes us die a thousand times before we finally act and get relief. And we also know how ashamed we feel when we repeatedly cut and run.

Now that we're working on our self-esteem, we need to take a serious look at behaviors that shame us. The next time a major decision comes up—should I leave or stay? Speak up or stuff it again? Start a recovery program or put it off one more time?—we need to remember what *not* deciding does to our self-esteem.

The issue that demands decision will not let us rest in peace until we act on it. The shame that squashes our self-esteem will keep building up, layer upon layer, until we finally do what we have to do. How much better to summon the courage we need *today*, not six months from now, and simply *get it over with*. We've surely spent enough time hanging out with the fools.

The sooner the better is the only way for recovering procrastinators.

A decision is a risk rooted in the courage of being free.
—Paul Tillich

When faced with a difficult decision, we have an unfortunate tendency to focus on the "before" rather than the "after." The prize the decision will win for us seems shadowy and vague, while the pain of *making* the decision is just as real and immediate as a screaming toothache!

New life has never come into this world without labor. We need to remember this the next time a painful decision must be made. Certainly it will be wrenching to give up an addiction of one kind or another—but think of the freedom we're gaining! If we decide to go back to church or school, we'll probably feel awkward and out of place for a while, but soon we'll be full-fledged members of a new community.

Deciding to try anything new may conjure up feelings of fear and self-pity. But self-confidence waits on just the other side of the door. Sometimes we have to take a mighty leap just to keep going forward.

The labor of birth is soon forgotten in the joy of new life.

November 21

History is the record of an encounter between character and circumstance.
—Donald Creighton

The history of the world is a terrible and wonderful story of the contest between people and their circumstances. From the invention of the wheel to the splitting of the atom, the human race has struggled to do, to be, to leave its mark from one generation to the next. Through revolutions and wars, inventions and discoveries, the choices that people made told the story. Dishonorable, cowardly decisions invariably have led us to corruption and destruction. Honorable, visionary decisions have led us to creation and advancement.

The course of our own, personal histories is much the same. Each life is a struggle between the opposing forces of deterioration and creativity, hope and despair, vision or blindness. Chapter by chapter, we make the choices. Because this is our own story, we are both the bad guys and the good guys. So what will it be—Attila the Hun or Charlemagne the Wise? Hitler? Gandhi? The death dealer or the peacemaker? We decide.

Everyday circumstances await the content of character to determine if this moment will be a golden renaissance or a dark age. Choosing is our privilege as well as our responsibility. Whether we want it or not, the pen is in our hand.

My self-esteem rides on the roles I assign myself.

God made the world round so we would never be able to see too far down the road.

—Isak Dinesen

If we could see into the future, we'd save ourselves from more than a few dead ends and stubbed toes, wouldn't we? Just a quick peek is all we'd need. Then we could make mistake-proof judgments about what's worth working at and worrying about. We wouldn't have to stretch and strain so much because we'd *already know* what was going to work out and what wasn't.

Ah, but there's the rub. Nothing of value comes to be without stretching and straining. It is *not* knowing that keeps us going and growing. It's the very uncertainty of the search, the challenge flung in the face of doubt, that builds character and integrity. The patience we bring to the process is what builds self-esteem.

An easier life is not always a better life. Fat cats have little muscle—and muscle is what gets us down the road. The fact that we're left to our own devices, our own path finding, means that we're free to create our own fortress.

A thoroughly mapped-out, predictable life wouldn't be very lively.

November 23

The fundamental defect of fathers is that they want their children to be a credit to them.
—Bertrand Russell

At first glance, the statement above seems absurd. What could be wrong with a father wanting his children to be a credit to him? The point, however, is the difference of emphasis. Is it more important for a child to be a credit to his parents—or to himself? How much deference does a child owe his parents? How much credit can a parent realistically expect?

Repairing our self-esteem often includes disentangling from our sense of guilt or failure over not measuring up to what we thought our parents wanted us to be. Even if that was not what *we* wanted to be—we may feel we let them down, that we weren't a credit to them.

But what a child wants to do, within the boundaries of the good and healthy of course, may differ considerably from what the parents see as suitable. Even such minor considerations as hairstyles, choice of music, or church attendance can become major issues that deeply affect the self-esteem of both parent and child. Twice blessed is the parent who can say, "I love you, of course—but what really makes me happy is that *you* love you."

The best parents know they succeed when they put themselves out of the job.

Holidays
Have no pity.
—Eugenio Montale

Some of us would rather face a month of Mondays than a single holiday. The worst are those, like Thanksgiving, that are supposed to deliver enough family warmth to carry us through the rest of the year. How shamed and resentful we feel when it seems that everyone else is going "over the river and through the woods to Grandmother's house" while we're eating a baloney sandwich in front of the TV.

The fact is that many of us do not have loving, welcoming families. We don't want to go home for Thanksgiving. But that doesn't mean there's anything wrong with *us*. We aren't less worthy than people who come from healthier families. And it doesn't mean that we have no reason to give thanks, either. The baloney is of our own choosing; we could pop a little turkey into the oven if we wanted to. Invite a friend. Talk and laugh.

Depression over holidays is understandable but not inevitable. Those who have the heart to celebrate *will* celebrate. They'll bow their heads in prayerful gratitude, mindful of the blessings they *have* received, rather than those they haven't. At the end of the day, they'll feel good because they chose to have a good day. We'll get what we choose, too.

How I handle holidays is a test of emotional maturity.

November 25

He who would be superior to external influences
must first become superior to his own passions.
—Samuel Johnson

Building self-esteem is terribly difficult for hotheads,
fanatics, and crybabies. It's precision work. Artistic
work. The object is to develop control over our self-
talk, inner judgments, and the outlandish expectations
we so readily place on ourselves. The art of maintaining one's own respect and friendship requires a certain
independence from outside influences. But this is impossible if we can't control our own passions.

Of course, we shouldn't grip our control levers so
tightly that we can't tolerate spontaneity or some mistakes. But we musn't be "owned" by anger, jealousy,
or fear either. Passion and reason can't *both* sit in the
driver's seat.

Dedication to building a reasoned, balanced life takes
a cool head. Positive self-esteem cannot abide in the
same house with raging, out-of-control anger, or the
neurotic fear that others are getting ahead at our expense, or the frantic greediness that passes for "being
good to ourselves." The inner balance between thinking and feeling has to be the first goal, the first step.

My passions are good servants but bad masters.

Practice is nine-tenths.
—Ralph Waldo Emerson

When we expect too much too fast even a good result will seem like too little too late. Because the something we achieved wasn't everything, we got frustrated. And then we quit. Not because our effort wasn't working, but because we badly underestimated how much effort the job was going to take.

Frustration is always relative to expectation. We don't expect to play professional-level golf after a few months of lessons. Nor do we imagine that our early tries at oil painting will produce perfect portraits. But somehow we *do* think that self-improvement should be a whole lot easier and quicker than it is. Thus the frustration.

Years ago, a memorable piece of film was aired on TV. It showed Nadia Comaneci practicing gymnastics. She fell off the balance beam. Then the same thing happened again and again and again. At first it looked like one fall was being endlessly replayed. But then it became apparent that this film was a chronicle of many failed attempts, one after the other. Later that year she won a gold medal in the Olympics, scoring a perfect ten. That couldn't have happened if she hadn't persistently practiced. Achievement takes what it takes.

Breaking old habits may well be harder work than breaking athletic records.

November 27

The first of earthly blessings, independence.
—Edward Gibbon

Cutting the cord between parent and adult child used to be a natural, painless, and taken-for-granted process. Now, however, it is commonplace for grown children to be emotionally and economically dependent far into their twenties or even their thirties. Some bounce in and out of the family home as casually as if they were coming and going from student holidays. Some never leave the nest at all.

Whatever the reasons for these drawn-out dependencies, the result can be a terrible toll on self-esteem. Because self-respect is largely built on self-sufficiency, both the supporters and the supported lose face with themselves as independence is delayed. In their heart of hearts, most parents know that too much help can handicap grown children just as surely as too little help can stunt the growth of young children. And grown children know, down deep, that they would feel better about themselves if they stood on their own two feet, no matter how shakily.

Self-reliance is the widest plank in the platform of self-esteem. Those of us who cushion our adult children's every fall need to recognize that our "helpfulness" is actually fostering helplessness. Those of us who "go home" when the going gets tough need to think about the crippling consequences of prolonging the dependencies of childhood.

My self-sufficiency is the backbone of self-respect.

Hatred is a feeling which leads to the extinction of values. —José Ortega y Gasset

Hatred is taboo to most moral people. That's why we consciously try to keep our distance from whatever or whoever it is we hate. But unconsciously, it's impossible to avoid what we truly hate. The very act of hating is too riveting.

Hate is a hook. What we hate we tend on some level to obsess about, ruminate over, and plot against. Worst of all, and perhaps most mysteriously, hate has the power of metamorphosis; it can actually transform us into the object of our hatred. People who hate the deprivations of their childhood, for example, very often *become* the depriving parents they despised. Hatred of some prejudice creates its own prejudice. Vigilantes become violent, teetotalers become drunk with power.

Campaigners against any evil need to guard against becoming evildoers themselves. It is too easy to become what we hate. Healing self-esteem often means bringing runaway hatred under control.

The trouble with hatred is that it doesn't recognize boundaries.

November 29

To say the right thing at the right time,
Keep still most of the time. —John W. Roper

Some truths are more difficult to communicate than others. We may know very well that we badly need to take a stand, clarify a long-term misunderstanding, or share a vital new insight with someone close to us. Perhaps our very self-esteem hinges on communicating this difficult-to-express truth. But precisely *because* the message is so difficult, we may not be able to deliver it *right now*. We may simply not be ready.

Working on readiness is not the same thing as backing off or caving in. Rather than garble the message and thereby ensure misunderstanding, isn't it better to be still until we can be clear? Isn't it wiser to take smaller, intermediate steps before we take a giant leap? If a task is too big for us today, there is great wisdom in setting out on a course of action that will get us ready to do it tomorrow.

Communicating a difficult truth to a certain someone must often be prepared for by talking to someone else. If we need to take a stand with our mate, we can practice on a trusted friend. If we need to raise the awareness of an Adult Child, we can say the sentences we need to say to our mate. We can rehearse our lines in the shower or in the car. With enough practice, we can be confident that we *will* have the wisdom, words, and courage to say what needs to be said to the person who needs to hear it.

Like all other skills, assertiveness is developed by practice, practice, and practice.

*Truth telling is not compatible with the defence of
the realm.* —George Bernard Shaw

Healthy self-esteem grows from self-acceptance based
on self-knowledge. That's why it's so important to tell
ourselves the truth and get our facts straight. If our
self-knowledge is spotty or inaccurate, the very basis of
our self-esteem is threatened.

Self-knowledge is gained by degrees. Many of us
worked hard, for example, to own up to the hurt in our
lives. For years we said, "It's fine," "It doesn't matter," or "I'm okay, let's talk about you." We had to
struggle to say, "That bothered me a lot," "My feelings
were hurt," or "I decided not to put myself into that
situation again." That's progress!

But even then we may be "defending the realm" of
the fearful ego. Acknowledging pain and acknowledging the *depth* of the pain are not the same. It is one
thing to admit hurt and another to admit a broken
heart. It is one thing to say, "I don't like this," and
another to say, "I feel like dying." Minimizing our pain
is better than denying it. But self-knowledge constructed of half-truths will always be spotty.

**To be honest about the depth of the hurt is the
only real honesty.**

December 1

Action should culminate in wisdom.
— *The Bhagavad-Gita*

If anything, we of the Western world are a people of action. We are frantic to be doing, whether or not we quite understand the game plan or our role in it. Just watch us kick up the dust!

This same "Do It Now and Evaluate It Later" attitude can mock our best efforts to raise self-esteem. Without understanding the goal, we may well plunge with reckless abandon into an exhausting program of action. Walking, reading, dieting, going to meetings and speaking up may all be part of such a program.

Wisdom may dictate moderation, however. The results of past frantic action may often have been disappointing. Perhaps this time we should accept that less can be more, that motion and forward movement aren't the same thing, that peaceful self-acceptance is the goal—not a self-improvement list with a hundred items on it.

Most of my progress does require action. But action not guided by wisdom can be wearing and wasteful.

December 2

I mustn't go on singling out names. One must not be a name-dropper, as Her Majesty remarked to me yesterday. —Norman St. John Stevas

Nobody wants to be a nobody. That's why we sometimes teeter around on the slender stilts of pretense. We want to rise up from the crowd and look like more than we are. Because we haven't yet learned to admire our real selves, we try to trick the rest of the world into admiring the selves we pretend to be.

One tactic we use to hike up our social status is to seek approval by association. Perhaps we don't name-drop as obviously as the man quoted above, but we all have our methods—especially if we're feeling insecure—of telling others that they're not dealing with just anybody. Perhaps we say we heard something "at the club." Perhaps we affect the language and dress of a group that excludes us. Maybe we even lie about where we live or went to school.

Borrowing status may lend us short-term security and get us by in a pinch. But if we want to get in touch with our *true* selves, we're going to have to learn to walk out in the world on our own two feet and leave the stilts behind. Until we stop implying that we're "with them," we devalue our personal worth.

As my self-acceptance grows, my need for pretense diminishes.

December 3

Rule Number 1 is don't sweat the small stuff.
Rule Number 2 is it's all small stuff.
—Dr. Robert S. Eliot

"How important is it?" is one of the slogans used by people in the Twelve Step programs. The suggestion is that newcomers to the program ask this simple question to catch themselves before going off in a tizzy about something that doesn't matter that much. Like all the slogans, this one is a tool to make a quick correction before a small problem becomes a big one.

Until we learn to discipline our priorities, every item on a long list of things to do or think about can somehow move up to number one or two. Especially when we're in turmoil, we forget the simple fact that we can only do one thing at a time! And all tasks, of course, don't have anything like equal importance. Picking up the dry cleaning, for example, hardly ranks up there with showing up for a long-postponed doctor's appointment. Yet in the habitual haste and hurry that marks modern life, many of us don't stop to reevaluate our tasks in the light of our goals.

Far and away the majority of our daily activities fall into the "small-stuff" category. Much self-esteem is gained by recognizing that and by learning to make wiser, more efficient use of our time and energy.

It's a good idea for me to take a daily "think break" to reassess priorities.

*Our major obligation is not to mistake slogans for
solutions.* —Edward R. Murrow

People who become involved in any of the self-help
movements can become mighty glib. Especially today
when there is such an abundance of books, speakers,
seminars, and courses, each sporting its own jargon
and pet phrases. Slogans come easy.

Without even realizing it, we can become quite good
at pasting these pet phrases on others, judging our
own or others' motives with labels, or substituting
some little nugget of packaged truth for a hard-won
insight of our own. How satisfying finally to have some
smooth, pat answers to questions that bedeviled us!

But slogans and jargon are nothing more than
streetlights shining in the darkness. Each casts only an
isolated cone of light, creating a little island of knowledge. Our task is not to cling to the streetlights, but to
keep trudging off into the darkness.

Insight isn't change and words are not behavior. The
goal of our self-help programs is not to make us smug
and superficial. The goal is to motivate life-changing
behavior. To do that we have to move beyond the labels, stop talking the talk and start walking the walk.

My actions speak louder than my words.

December 5

Cursed be the social lies that warp us from the living truth.   —Alfred, Lord Tennyson

Our status-hinged society places well-educated professionals high above the rest of us. If people are doctors or lawyers or professors, they are automatically honored and respected for the prestige of their position. But as human beings, highly placed people—even presidents and kings—are not one bit better than anyone else.

The story is told of a famous physician who telephoned AA in a moment of alcoholic despair. The AA member who was sent to make the call found the intoxicated doctor in a pitiable but belligerent state. "What kind of work do you do?" he slurred. "I'm a housepainter," answered the visitor. "I can't believe they sent a workingman!" the doctor shouted. "Don't you know the difference between you and me?" "Yes," the AA member replied, "You're a drunk doctor and I'm a sober painter."

All human beings are subject to defeat and despair. Behind titles, people are just people—brave and afraid, lazy and vigorous, compassionate and indifferent. Much of the distance we perceive between ourselves and others is just social smoke.

Society's way of ranking people doesn't have to be mine.

*Any work looks wonderful to me except that
which I can do.* —Ralph Waldo Emerson

Much of self-esteem is based on a positive regard for
what we can do. Not what somebody else can do, not
what our idealized selves *may* do some distant day in
the future, but what we can do and are doing right
now.

False modesty and "politeness" have conditioned
many of us to make little of our skills, abilities, or contributions. Heaven forbid that anyone think we were
showing off! Yet modesty is carried too far when we so
quickly and automatically dismiss praise that the value
of our work doesn't even register with *us!* Raving about
other people is fine and generous, but discounting ourselves can become a self-defeating habit.

You alone are you. Your comments in group are not
like any others. A letter from you will mean something
that nobody else's letter could. Your insights, your
frame of reference, the particular experiences you've
had—are all unique to you. If you don't share what
you alone have to share, then that special something
will never be shared. Modesty isn't becoming or
healthy or appropriate if it convinces us that much is
little.

**Avoiding grandiosity doesn't mean denying my
own gifts.**

December 7

Everything that has been gained can be lost.
—Everett T.

Whether we're thinking of a fortune in stocks and bonds or the gold of self-esteem, the above quote makes us feel nervous and insecure. Even though it is no doubt true, the possibility of loss seems terribly negative. But there is more to it than that. Implicit in this note of caution is the very real caution that to slack off on the daily disciplines that create growth is to run the risk of relapse. As sure as "pride goeth before a fall," so does carelessness in sticking to the course precede the possible slipping back to what was.

If daily reading has been helpful in turning the lights on an otherwise dark situation, then we'd better keep reading. If affirmations have gotten us moving down the right road, why would we stop doing them? If meeting with sponsors and going to group have been the handholds pulling us up and out of some despairing pit or other, let us beware of becoming lackadaisical in keeping up these contacts.

The programs we have set up for ourselves work if *we* work. Lest the night return, let us be very careful to tend the fire.

It's simply common sense to protect what I value

Part with self-conceit. For it is impossible for anyone to begin to learn what he thinks he already knows.
                                        —Epictetus

In World War II, the Germans boasted that their panzers would easily rout the Russians. They knew that their tanks, built to perfection and tight specifications, were better engineered than the much more loosely constructed Russian tanks. In the Russian winter, however, the tightness of the German tanks became a disadvantage as the oil froze. The greater tolerance of the Russian tanks allowed far more flexibility and function under subzero conditions. And so the Germans were routed time after time.

Sometimes we make the same kind of mistake when we compare ourselves and our abilities with others. We may assume that we are far more able, far more advanced, than they are. If we have an unbroken record of accomplishment, we may find it hard to imagine that, in some areas, we may be clumsy and slow while others are competent and quick.

There is a mighty lesson in the tank story. What works *for* us in one situation may very well work *against* us in another. The superaggressive, "Get it done now" mentality that serves us so well in the outside world may grind us to a halt in the inside world. Conceit and self-esteem are not the same. We may have to walk a little more slowly, a little more humbly, when we're dealing with frozen areas in the human heart.

Whatever makes me smug also makes me vulnerable.

December 9

When we do what works, why are we so surprised that it works?   —Reverend David Stier

Locking horns with low self-esteem can be a fierce, exhausting contest. Only the value of the prize makes it worth the continuing effort required. Yet it is a common experience for people in the midst of the fray to be *surprised* when consistent, committed effort actually gains ground. But why should it not?

If we do our affirmations regularly, even when we don't feel like it, we *will* learn to think healthier thoughts. Day by disciplined day, the positive will force out the negative. If we consistently act in a confident, loving manner, we will come to expect such actions from ourselves. By repetition, these new behaviors feel natural. If we persistently refrain from thought patterns that erode our self-image, these mental chains will be broken, link by link.

We who are so accustomed to failure are often amazed and even shocked by success. Yet what is so unusual about a fair day's pay for a hard day's work? We deserve success.

I'm not only making progress, but I'm becoming more aware of it.

We are more than what we have.
—Don Wilson

Preachers and teachers have forever advised us that we are more than what we own. Being is not the same as having. This precious piece of wisdom almost always is associated with the possession of material things. And rightly so.

But we have more than things to distract us. We also have feelings. And the same thought is true here—we are more than the feelings we have. We are not our feelings anymore than we are our possessions. Feelings of shame, guilt, unworthiness, insecurity, and alienation—and a raft of others—often seem to define us. In our interpretation of those feelings, we must realize that just because we *feel* a certain way doesn't mean we *are* that way. To lose this distinction is to lose our way on the road to self-realization.

Much of what we feel about ourselves has been learned. Shame-based people may have been told that they were unworthy for such a long time that the feeling wrapped around that tragic message became the truth. But the real truth is that we have choices about how we feel. Our feelings can be, and often need to be, challenged. Perhaps we can't change our feelings as easily as we change a pair of shoes, but they *can* be changed if we decide they don't fit anymore.

My feelings are a part of me—not all of me.

December 11

Judgment comes from experience and great judgment comes from bad experience.
—Senator Bob Packwood

Low self-esteem plays out like a movie made up, frame by frame and scene by scene, of all our misjudgments and misdeeds. It's our own horror story. The plot never changes, so we come to know it well: Life is just one bad experience after another, and we shouldn't expect anything else.

How we shortchange ourselves when we pay so much attention to the cost and so little to the wisdom we have purchased! Surely it's just as realistic to think of our mistakes as lessons rather than permanent black marks on our record. If our bad experiences taught us something we didn't know before, are they wholly bad? The fact is that failure is a better teacher than success.

Of course, it's sad when relationships crumble, time is wasted, money is lost. But for all the anguish of these bad experiences, didn't they give us some clues as to how to avoid the same pitfalls in the future? If we learned, we didn't lose everything. We're not wiped out or doomed to live out the future as we have lived out the past. We need to think of our "movie" as a training film, not a horror story.

Good judgment is built, brick by brick, from painful lessons learned.

A man consists of the faith that is in him.
Whatever his faith is, he is.
—*The Bhagavad-Gita*

Most of us find great security in guarantees. If "it" doesn't work—whatever it is—we want to know we can get our money back. In some areas of our lives, this demand for assurance not only works but is just plain common sense. But in many areas there are no guarantees.

Maintaining or building a healthy self-esteem, for example, is largely a proposition of faith. Of course, we'd like to be promised that if we do this difficult thing—like talking straight in a relationship, standing up for our rights, or going back to school for career enhancement—the results will be there immediately. We want to be assured that our efforts at reeducation by way of new readings or listening to speakers will make a real difference *soon.* We want a warranty such as we would get on a car or refrigerator. We want to *know,* not hope, that our self-improvement programs will perform as advertised.

But there are no guarantees. We are all different. We grow at our own pace. Spiritual experiences of breakthrough happen at different times for different people. Often it is faith alone that keeps beckoning us on into new waters. To keep on going, we have to keep on believing.

Self-trust is self-granted.

December 13

A definition encloses the wilderness of an idea
within a wall of words. —Samuel Butler

Of all the specialized rhetoric surrounding recovery, the term *dysfunctional family* seems most in danger of losing its original meaning and thus its value and validity. First used to define families in which there was incest, child beating, or criminal neglect, the term is now used as a catchall description for nearly *all* families. Some experts claim that 90 percent of families are seriously dysfunctional in one way or another.

But like all buzzwords that kick up a lot of interest, the *dysfunctional family* label becomes inaccurate and misleading when it's too widely applied to too many different situations. A child who was regularly whipped or molested carries a much more grievous burden than a child whose Dad wouldn't go to ball games or a Mom who wouldn't carpool. We need to be careful about claiming and blaming root causes that scarcely exist.

All families are flawed because all people are flawed. All of us came from, and most of us *are*, incomplete and inexpert parents. Considering the difficulties, most families deserve credit for simply hanging together as bravely and hopefully as they can. We best promote our growth when we stop short of indicting our families and instead look back only for information and insight.

I am responsible for what I make of my life.

Follow your bliss.
—Joseph Campbell

Fortunate are those who have a clear vision of what is important to them and how they wish to live their lives. So many of us flounder like rudderless ships, steered only by the vagaries of chance. But we can't get there unless we know where "there" is.

Years ago, during the Depression, a young man was hitchhiking around the country. He struck up a conversation with an older man who had offered him a ride. The older man asked him what his goal in life was. The young man replied that his greatest desire was to be a millionaire. "Oh, no it isn't," said the older man. "If that were true, you would not be wasting your time right now floating around the country. You would be hard at work trying to make your dream come true." And, of course, he was right.

Over time, we become what we do. If we want our dreams to come true, we need to give them muscle. We need to know ourselves, to set goals, and then to put all our effort into achieving what we have set out to accomplish. Just wishing won't do it.

I have the determination to achieve my goals.

December 15

To the mean all becomes mean.
—Friedrich Nietzsche

It's an embarrassing truth that what we clearly recognize as good in other people can make us feel bad and behave even worse. When we're struck by someone's youthful beauty, we may quickly remark on their inexperience and naïveté. If we see someone showing a kindness that wouldn't have occurred to us, we may neutralize our admiration—and thus our grudging envy—by calling that person a "soft touch" or a "bleeding heart." Somehow it's hard for us to simply give credit where credit is due.

Insecurity is the problem. When other people's good qualities alarm us into petty mean-mindedness, it's a sure sign that we're on the defensive. For some reason we feel threatened or diminished when we become aware of strength or character or beauty that is greater than our own. As if those other people don't have shortcomings to go along with their gifts! As if we have anything to lose by acknowledging that all beauty and goodness doesn't begin and end with us! What an absurd and indefensible position *that* is!

If we're so insistent on finding flaws in the beautiful, let us begin with ourselves. Integrity and pettiness don't go together.

As I feel better about myself, I feel better about other people.

Men are not against you; they are merely for themselves. —Gene Fowler

Some decisions made by bosses, bureaucrats, other powerful higher-ups can wreak havoc on our personal lives. As carefully as we planned, some things we counted on just aren't going to be. And some things we thought would never happen are laid squarely in our laps. Perhaps a freeway is going to come through our neighborhood; the house we were going to retire in will have to be torn down. Or perhaps the company we work for is being relocated and we weren't invited to come along.

When such things happen, we feel betrayed and devalued. Our self-esteem takes a nosedive along with our plans. In our resentment and fear, we may turn on the "culprits" with a personal vengeance that hurts us a lot more than it can ever hurt them.

After we reflect on it a while, we can usually see that these decisions were not really *against* us, but *for* the decision makers. Their actions were taken to protect or advance themselves. As distasteful as this realization may be, it does us far less damage than taking impersonal events personally. We can't do anything about the fact that power structures can be greedy and insensitive. But we needn't let a decision made by people we don't know, perhaps thousands of miles away, have access to our self-esteem.

My value as a person is separate, distinct, and independent of impersonal events.

December 17

Do not put your faith in what statistics say until you have carefully considered what they do not say.
— William W. Watt

Way back in kindergarten we started learning to sort out same from different. When we could separate the red buttons from the blue, the short sticks from the long, we got a pat on the head. Categorizing is a thinking skill that helps us organize facts so we can deal with them better. If we couldn't sort things out, our world would be an unmanageable mess.

But human beings are neither facts nor things. When we categorize ourselves or other people, we deceive ourselves. Such categorization dehumanizes and makes self-esteem impossible. People are too complex to fit into our pigeon holes. Labels like *unemployed* and *welfare recipient*, for example, only mean what they mean. They tell us only a little piece of an individual's rich story. Such labels describe, but they do not define. They turn people into statistics.

In our pursuit of right thinking, we begin to see that other people, just like ourselves, are not nearly so neatly classifiable as we thought they were. In discovering our own rich mix of pluses and minuses, we realize that tidying up people into neat compartments has been a way of discounting them. Instead of categorizing to think better, we have categorized to slap down a label so we don't have to think at all.

I can only be as appreciative of myself as I am of other people.

Jealousy: that dragon which slays love under the pretense of keeping it alive. —Havelock Ellis

Adolescent girls are flattered and thrilled when their adolescent boyfriends get jealous. Sometimes they even deliberately try to provoke jealousy—"to see if he really loves me." But jealousy is not and never was a sign of love; it's a sign of immature insecurity.

Now that we've grown up, we need to get our facts straight about what does and does not signify a loving relationship. As adults, both men and women may confuse possessiveness with love. But in truth no one can "belong" to anyone else. Chronic suspiciousness is a character flaw, not a compliment. Obsession with someone else's coming and goings is a poor substitute for devotion. And accusing your blameless partner of having an affair says more about you than it does about your partner.

If we are the jealous ones, we need to get help with the fear of loss that generates those feelings. If we are the ones who feel reassured and validated that our mates "care enough to be jealous," we need to work on growing up.

Love promotes the freedom of the other; jealousy limits freedom.

December 19

If a man insisted always on being serious, and never allowed himself a bit of fun and relaxation, he would go mad or become unstable without knowing it. —Herodotus

Contradictory forces often pull us up and push us down at the same time. Who needs enemies when we've got ourselves! While one hand is busy building self-esteem, the other may be just as busily slapping down those efforts.

This can happen when we try to enrich our lives by taking up a new interest or hobby. Suppose we join a bowling team or enroll in a ceramics class. The first time we go we feel enthusiastic and excited—this is going to be *fun!* We congratulate ourselves for making the effort and wonder why we waited so long. The second or third time, though, we start to notice how far we have to go to get really good at what we're doing. Compared to us, the others seem so skillful! Then we suddenly remember that our favorite TV show is on that same night, so we stop showing up and let our new interest fizzle.

It isn't easy to let go enough to have fun for fun's sake. Strange as it may seem, many duty-driven adults have to retrain themselves, patiently but persistently, just as they might retrain some lost faculty after a brain injury. But the payoff is marvelous; reclaiming fun is as close as we can get to reclaiming childhood.

The ability to have fun is not a luxury.

Knowledge is the process of piling up facts. Wisdom lies in their simplification.

—Martin H. Fischer

A new product on the market is described as "so advanced, it's simple." What an interesting point to make—and how wise! At the core of many complex things is a simple thought, a single idea that is altogether clear and understandable. Self-esteem is a case in point. In spite of all the complicated analysis of causes and cures, it all comes down to learning to like ourselves. Simple!

Not surprisingly, we like ourselves when we behave in likable ways; we respect ourselves when our behavior is respectable; we honor our own honorable deeds. There's nothing confusing or complicated about it. Nor is there anything mysterious about feeling bad when we behave badly or feeling abused when we walk in the company of abusers.

We learn to like ourselves when we do the things that boost our integrity and refrain from doing what damages it. The truth couldn't be plainer and neither could the implication. Any action we take, no matter how small, either adds to or diminishes our treasure. If we forget everything else we know about self-esteem, let us not forget that.

I make more progress when I keep it simple.

December 21

This is a world of compensation.
—Abraham Lincoln

Some of us decide early in life that the only way we'll ever get to the winner's circle is by riding on someone else's shoulders. Others of us only give up on ourselves after years of setbacks and disappointments. But in either case there comes the point, usually on a deep, subconscious level, where we turn to someone else to do it for us. If we can't have personal glory, we decide we'll go for the reflected kind. That's when the status of other people—our parents, our spouses, even our children—becomes more important to us than our own.

It isn't at all unusual to see "stage parents" abandon or slight their own affairs on behalf of Johnny's future in sports or Jennifer's dancing prospects. Or to see a grown man define himself in terms of his more successful father. Or a wife hide out in her husband's shadow. But putting all our hopes and dreams in someone else's hands only does further damage to our self-esteem, of course. Not only does it put an unfair burden on the people we're expecting to carry us, but any rewards we get for doing that will always be secondhand.

Using a relationship to make us *look* good usually makes us *feel* bad. Beyond carrying in bags of groceries, we don't have the right to use our children at all. Nor are we being mature, responsible adults when we hang onto the coattails of our parents or spouses. *Our* self-esteem will always be a matter of standing in our own spotlight.

No one can achieve my potential for me. I am capable of doing that myself.

*Watch how a man takes praise and there you have
the measure of him.*   —Thomas Burke

Criticism is hard to take, but accepting compliments
gracefully isn't easy either. In fact, most of us find it
takes a good deal of poise and practice. We seem to feel
that we are lacking in modesty unless we quickly disclaim the praise.

We must not rob ourselves of the support our egos
need by thinking we must be falsely humble. How
many times have we seen people respond to a compliment by making disparaging remarks about themselves? Such self-effacing behavior takes much of the
joy out of well-earned praise.

In those dark days when the fog of failure is especially thick, remembered compliments bolster our ego
and help us count our blessings. A simple and gracious
"thank you" is all that need be said when someone is
kind enough to give us a verbal pat on the back. True
humility accepts both kinds of truths about ourselves—
both the flattering and the unflattering.

**I can accept compliments with graceful appreci-
ation.**

December 23

*Denial is the act of pulling down the shades in the
search for light.*   —Dr. James Rogel

Many varied elements come to play in our decision
making. Reason, emotion, spirit, experience, fear, and
love all have something valid to contribute. The best
decision always comes from collaboration.

As with the deliberations of government, personal
deliberations can only be based on the data available. If
any element is left out, a truth is withheld, and the
validity of the decision is diminished, if not destroyed.
To deny any part of ourselves a voice is to hear only
part of the story, and thus to blanket the whole truth.

Self-esteem is enhanced by sound decision making.
We cannot be other than the result of our own delib-
erations, especially on issues that concern ourselves.
Yet it is quite possible, even within the confines of our
own person, to silence valid input, to keep secrets.
And self-esteem is always the victim.

**I usually have my own answers if I take the time
to listen.**

A rich child often sits in a poor mother's lap.
—Danish Proverb

In the self-esteem department, many parents rise or fall according to how they provide for their children. If Mom and Dad give their kids "the things they never had," whether it be tap-dancing lessons, fancy clothes, or expensive bikes, they feel good about themselves. If they come up short, they lose stature in their own eyes. Perhaps our parents felt diminished by what they couldn't give us.

Yet many of the advantages that parents lavish on their children may not be advantages at all. Living as we do in a grossly materialistic society, parents may get confused about what children really need. The truth is that it's not designer tennis shoes or elaborate parties—no matter how loudly kids wail that "everybody else" has twice as many. Upon reflection, we know in our hearts that the best gifts we have to give are time, attention, interest, and love.

Self-esteem must not hinge on whether or not parents have a Santa Claus suit. Kids may think they want it, but "happiness by acquisition" only sets up a lifetime of wanting. Beyond shelter, food, and health care, money can't buy what kids really need—someone to listen to them, share with them, and respect their struggles. If they have that, they are truly blessed. And so are their parents.

Children learn to honor the values their parents honor.

December 25

It's Christmas Day! Thank God I haven't missed it! —Charles Dickens

As we grow older, it's entirely possible to lose a lot more than the dimples in our knees and elbows. Through busy-ness, laziness, or just inattention, we can actually forget how to have fun. Whole summers go by without a single picnic, a swim, or a ball game. Birthdays become nothing more than restaurant dinners. What a far cry from our youth when looking forward to a good time and then wringing every drop of pleasure out of it was what we knew best!

Christmas is one of the occasions that many of us forget how to celebrate. "Christmas is too commercial," we say as an excuse for our crankiness. "Christmas is for children." Yet for all the greed and phoniness that surround the holidays, there is also much that is lovely and inviting of spiritual growth. The warmth on so many faces, the increased sense of caring and giving, the gathering of families, the beauty of the music—all are invitations to turn away from worry and lift up our hearts.

We don't have to become like Scrooge just because we're not children anymore. The wonder of Christmas is available to all comers. Let us not miss it.

Deepening my capacity for enjoyment deepens my self-esteem.

Parents have rights, too.
—Dr. Denise Cook

No one would argue the point that children need all the love they can get. Child abuse, in its many forms, is among the world's greatest crimes. All parents know that raising children requires sacrifice, and often it is necessary to put the children's needs first. True, true, true.

But it is also true that when parents sublimate their needs and wishes so totally under the demands of parenthood that they themselves nearly disappear, they can find themselves in trouble. Any sacrifice of integrity always translates into a loss of self-esteem. Granted that kids have rights, but it is also true that parents have rights.

Positive self-esteem requires individuals—children included—to accept that, though they are important indeed, they are not the center of the universe. To be parents who serve the needs of their children to such an extent that they deny their basic right to sane living is to do their children a disservice. Such parents foolishly sacrifice their own self-esteem, and also give their children an unrealistic model of healthy adult behavior.

I can only be a successful parent if I have a strong identity of my own.

December 27

Jealousy is no more than feeling alone against smiling enemies. —Elizabeth Bowen

Jealousy is the mortal enemy of self-esteem and, obviously, our esteem of anyone else. Born of fear, jealousy is never about what "they" have or are, but always about us. People who are often jealous are people who habitually make comparisons—and always come out on the short end of the deal.

The antidote to jealousy is to become convinced that we are just fine the way we are. It is to know that whatever we have—more than some, less than others—means next to nothing in the final accounting. After all, if we are on good terms with ourselves, how much difference can it make if we add more things to our catalog of possessions? It's nice but not necessary. On the other hand, if we aren't convinced of our own substance, even boatloads of new things will never be enough. And the losing comparisons between ourselves and others will never end.

Jealousy makes it impossible to have friends, and because friendship is essential in self-esteem building, the two cannot coexist. We can't be much of a friend if our friend's happiness or success is threatening to us. Who wants a friend like that? When I am okay with me, I can only celebrate whatever good befalls those around me. If I am not—all the world is a threat.

I sincerely wish all success and happiness for my friends.

If we wanted to be happy it would be easy; but we want to be happier than other people, which is always difficult, since we think them happier than they are.

—Baron de La Brède et de Montesquieu

How am I doing? We automatically ask ourselves that question many times a day. Always, of course, in relation to other people. How else could we make a judgment? Am I smarter? Younger? More successful? Richer? Better looking? And how about *them*? Are they more self-confident than I am? Luckier? Happier?

Yet the only way we can draw a conclusion is to imagine that we *know* about "them." Usually, we do not. Oftentimes we tend to overrate and exaggerate the quality of other people's lives. Because we're keenly aware of our own inadequacies, we may accord "them" most of the advantages we think we lack. (No doubt it would bowl them over to realize how happy they didn't know they were!)

What a relief it is when we arrive at the state where our self-esteem depends not at all on "them"—either what they think of us or what we think of them. Sure, the comparison questions are intriguing and fun to wonder about. Just as long as the answers don't count for anything but idle entertainment.

Comparing my insides with other people's outsides makes for some wrong conclusions.

December 29

What is this self inside us, this silent observer, severe and speechless critic, who can terrorize us? —T. S. Eliot

Shame is a powerful barrier to positive self-esteem. However undeserved, it is shame that constantly scolds that we are not doing enough or well enough. It is shame that says we are not as far along as we should be. And when our hearts and souls are harassed by shame, we find it difficult to make any progress on the spiritual walk that building self-esteem is. Or at least we have a hard time *recognizing* that we are making any progress.

This negative inner talk is all subjective, of course. That's why it helps to set absolute, objective measuring points against which we can measure success. There is no arguing with objective goals; they're either met or they're not met. Are we having more positive days than before? Have we given our significant other more hugs, of both the verbal and physical kind? Are we in fact trying new things? Have we in fact resisted some compulsion or said that word we found so hard to say? If so, we are on our way.

All of these and dozens of similar behaviors are objective measuring points against which progress can be verified. Acknowledging progress points not only feels good but it's good *for* us. In the face of documented success, shame tends to back off.

Undeserved shame flies from the light of objectivity.

December 30

I must govern the clock, not be governed by it.
—Golda Meir

Sometimes we feel let down and somehow sad as the year draws to a close. Partly, we may simply have let ourselves get too tired with all the hustle and bustle of the holidays. And partly, we may be feeling some regret about the wonderful progress, the amazing turnaround, that we *didn't* make this past year. Perhaps we had promised ourselves that we would be much slimmer, healthier, wealthier, or happier by now. Last January, when we made all those brave new resolutions, we felt so strong, so dedicated, so undefeatable!

But the clock and the calendar aren't the only ways to tell time. They're not even the best way—especially in these days of slush, bare trees, and little sunshine. Even if we're tired, we're still alive and kicking, aren't we? Even if we're disappointed in our rate of progress, we still *believe* in progress, don't we? The fact is that we're demonstrating our continuous commitment to growth simply by reading this meditation.

As long as we keep moving forward, we *are* getting ahead. If we've kept our heads high and our feet in motion, we're still in the race. We needn't worry about our pace as long as we're headed in the right direction.

These days may be dark and gloomy, but my prospects are still bright.

December 31

Easy does it.
—Twelve Step Program Slogan

For everyone of us who can't get down to business, there is another who is *too* dutiful. We are the hard-at-it souls who make such grinding, intense work of improving our self-esteem that we miss the point of the whole effort. Which is to live happier, more joyous lives. We can't do that and work double shifts, too.

In a sense, positive self-esteem is like a beautiful butterfly. If we don't try to grab it, it often comes softly to our shoulder. Of course, self-esteem building does require effort, but we can focus so fiercely on this task that we're too tired and tense to enjoy the benefits.

Self-esteem is for the sake of laughing more, of relaxing more, of taking more time off. We know we're esteeming ourselves more when we're gradually making progress in those areas that are important, like communicating with the people we care about. Self-esteem is about creating and enjoying beauty wherever we can. That doesn't happen *after* the work gets done—it *is* the work. Self-esteem is a process, not a payoff. We get to enjoy it *while* we're earning it.

Relax. There is such a thing as trying too hard.

Chronological Index

Topic Index